Unions and
Public Policy

Recent Titles in
Contributions in Political Science

UNIONS and PUBLIC POLICY

The New Economy, Law, and Democratic Politics

Edited by
LAWRENCE G. FLOOD

Contributions in Political Science, Number 364
Prepared under the auspices of the Policy Studies Organization
Stuart Nagel, Publications Coordinator

GREENWOOD PRESS
Westport, Connecticut • London

Library of Congress Cataloging-in-Publication Data

Unions and public policy : the new economy, law, and democratic
    politics / edited by Lawrence G. Flood.
        p. cm.—(Contributions in political science, ISSN 0147–1066
    ; 364)
    Includes bibliographical references and index.
    ISBN 0-313-29800-9 (alk. paper)
    1. Trade-unions—United States. 2. Industrial relations—United
States. 3. Labor market—United States. 4. United States—Economic
policy—1993– 5. Democracy—United States. I. Flood, Lawrence G.
II. Series: Contributions in political science ; no. 364.
HD6508.U445 1995
331.88′0973—dc20   95–22976

British Library Cataloguing in Publication Data is available.

Library of Congress Catalog Card Number: 95–22976
ISBN: 0-313-29800-9
ISSN: 0147–1066

First published in 1995

Greenwood Press, 88 Post Road West, Westport, CT 06881
An imprint of Greenwood Publishing Group, Inc.

Printed in the United States of America

The paper used in this book complies with the
Permanent Paper Standard issued by the National
Information Standards Organization (Z39.48–1984).

10 9 8 7 6 5 4 3 2 1

To Professor Robert G. Smith
Professor Emeritus, Drew University
and
To the memory of Professor James Prothro,
University of North Carolina at Chapel Hill

Contents

Preface

The 1990s are a difficult decade for American workers, with declining incomes, increasing wage gaps, more poverty, and fewer good jobs. Workers look to government for assistance, but the government struggles with debt, fractious politics, and its attempts to "reinvent" itself. Who can represent them to their government?

Labor unions remain a prime voice for workers. Weakened in many respects, they struggle to speak at the workplace and in government, in a policy environment that has been hostile to their very existence.

Policy shapes unions as they attempt to shape policy. This was clear in the failed 1994 attempt to pass national legislation prohibiting the permanent replacement of strikers. Unions were not strong enough to force passage of the legislation, and part of their weakness is accounted for by the absence of such legislation.

Unions will continue to be important targets of public policy, as they attempt to influence that policy—and that is the general subject of this book. We look closely at a series of policy areas, asking what worker/union interest may be and how that interest might be achieved. We hope this book will contribute to debate about these critical issues.

My first debt as editor is to the contributors who make this book possible. They have written challenging, insightful, and consistently useful chapters for those concerned with work and public policy. They have shown remarkable patience with a long editing process. I have enjoyed working with them and hope they will find some satisfaction as this book reaches print.

Gratitude also to Stuart Nagel of the Policy Studies Association. His responsiveness to the first idea for this book and his attention throughout its preparation reflect the best traditions of the policy studies field. My

Greenwood editor, Jim Dunton, also deserves thanks for taking this project on in midstream and seeing it to its final conclusion.

United University Professions (UUP) (AFT 2190), the union that represents academic and professional staff in the State University of New York, supported this project (and a preceding special journal issue on unions) from the beginning. Past president Tim Reilly and his Executive Board made publication of the journal possible, and current president William Scheuerman, a political scientist, is a contributor to the book. I am proud to be an active UUP member.

The book is dedicated to my political science mentors. Professor Robert Smith was my first inspiration for this discipline and for teaching as well. Professor James Prothro guided me through graduate school and a dissertation with a gentle but quite discernible hand. As I look back on my own twenty-five plus years of teaching, I can see how much I owe those two fine scholars.

Finally, thanks, Carolyn.

I

Introduction

I

Unions and Policy Problems

Lawrence G. Flood

Each February the Bureau of Labor Statistics releases a report on union membership in the United States. From a union perspective, the news is never very good. The 1995 report (with data not directly comparable to previous years) showed a slight increase in total number of members (to 16.7 million) but a decline in percent representation (to 15.5 percent) (Bureau of Labor Statistics, 1995b). Most of the growth in total membership was in the public sector, and the proportion of represented workers in the private sector continued its sixteen-year slide. This, of course, is just one point in a long-term decline, which Richard Edwards has described as "qualitative and moral, as well as numerical." This analysis of unions led him to subtitle his book on workplace rights "employment relations in the *post-union era*" (Edwards, 1993; emphasis added).

There was other bad news for unions in early 1995 as well. They had suffered major defeats on North American Free Trade Agreement (NAFTA) and General Agreement on Tariffs and Trade (GATT), health care reform had failed, and layoffs and downsizing continued. The worst political news was the Republican capture of Congress and many state governments in the fall 1994 elections. The "contract with America" promised no strengthening of government support for unions.

Yet, in the words of two leading analysts of labor relations, "we must also be careful not to write off the labor movement in this country" (Juravich and Bronfenbrenner, 1995). Unions continue to be supported by nearly half of American workers, and public workers (under less attack from employers) continue to add numbers. Unions, local to international, are experimenting with new tactics and new programs (Shostak, 1991). Mergers are strengthening the base of previously weakened organizations.

New populations are being organized. There is even renewed discussion of a Labor Party (Bernard, 1993). Union militance, as measured by strikes, rebounded somewhat in 1994 from its record low of 1993 (Bureau of Labor Statistics, 1995a). Several key policy struggles, perhaps especially the NAFTA fight, have led to energized national and international coalitions among unions and community groups.

In key respects unions in the United States are the product of public policy. Public and private sector labor law and practice determine eligibility for membership, union responsibilities, and restrictions on their actions. Indeed, "[g]overnment is the dominant actor in industrial relations systems" (Adams, 1992, 517). This message was sent clearly to the public sector by the experience of the Professional Air Traffic Controllers' Organization (PATCO), but it is equally well understood in the private sector. The largest strike of 1992, by machinists in rail freight carriers, was stopped by act of Congress in its second day; President Clinton halted the summer 1994 Soo Line strike because of fears it would spread. Labor law is not the only policy of concern to unions: all major social and economic legislation and its implementation affect workers and their unions. Trade and industrial policy, health care, taxation, social services—all these and more are a concern to unions. So, unions, the targets of policy, also attempt to influence it. This book is about major policy concerns of unions, the choices they face, and what difference it all makes for the practice of democracy in the United States.

A CHANGING POLICY ENVIRONMENT

The Reagan–Bush years took a "blame the government" approach to public policy. Tax reductions, elimination or weakening of government regulations, support for the "market," and attacks on unions were the order of the day. The Clinton–Gore victory promised a new approach.

The new administration was more activist and interventionist. Clinton eliminated the Competitiveness Council, which had been a backdoor way for businesses to avoid regulations. He established a National Economic Council. That council, comprising top administration officials, had coordination and monitoring functions reminiscent of late 1970s proposals for industrial policy. Clinton also proposed a "comprehensive new technology initiative," which went well beyond a market approach suggesting pilot programs, targeted investments, and national coordination.

Other signals were promising to organized labor. Clinton selected Robert Reich as his nominee for secretary of labor. While Reich was not known for labor connections, Lane Kirkland described him as "exceptionally well qualified," and Gerald McEntee, president of the American Federation of State, County and Municipal Employees (AFSCME), called him "the foremost innovative thinker in America on building a new workforce"

(Bureau of National Affairs, 1992, 4). In his confirmation hearings Reich expressed concern about the long decline in union membership and called his agency the Department of the American Workforce (Salwen and McGinley, 1993).

The selection process for Clinton's appointee to head the National Labor Relations Board was very slow, but William Gould IV was known through his writings as a supporter of the unions' workplace role. At his confirmation he promised respect for workers and their unions, and in office he took action to improve access to collective bargaining (Noble, 1994). This was quite a change from Donald Dotson and his solicitor Hugh Reilly of the National Right to Work Legal Defense Fund.

Another Clinton action viewed favorably by labor was his early revocation of three of his predecessor's antiunion orders. One order had banned all-union federal project agreements (thus assisting nonunion contractors), and another required federal contractors to notify workers of their right to receive rebates of part of their agency fees (but not of their right to organize and bargain). Perhaps most important symbolically was his lifting of the ban on federal hiring of former PATCO strikers.

Clinton also supported positive Hatch Act reform, established an Office of the American Workplace, created the Dunlop Commission on the Future of Worker–Management Relations, and created a national partnership with leaders of federal employee unions. The Family and Medical Leave Act was strongly endorsed by unions.

Of course, this new environment was not without threats, difficulties, and defeats. The federal deficit loomed as the largest Clinton political problem, and he was forced to make quick compromises in his economic approach. His promised $16 billion economic stimulus package was dropped in the face of a Republican filibuster. Vice President Gore's "reinventing government" proposal suggested elimination of a number of union jobs. Most of the Clinton appointees were better known for ties to business than for ties to labor: Lloyd Benson, Roger Altman, Robert Rubin, Leon Panetta, Alice Rivlin, Micky Kantor, Ron Brown, Hazel O'Leary, Les Aspin—and the list goes on. Union or labor appointees were hard to find.

The greatest union defeat came on NAFTA. President Clinton backed off his promise for clear worker protection in the agreement, attacked organized labor for its failure to support him, and used every pressure or promise available to the presidency to get NAFTA through Congress. Labor fought hard against it but lost. In the process, the president's ties to business and his views of organized labor were clarified as well.

Internal union disagreements also suggested limits on union power in the policy arena. The union movement was unable to produce a strong consensus position on national health care or to lobby effectively for it. Not all unions were happy with the economic program: the National Treasury Union organized "antifreeze" campaigns against Clinton's plan to freeze federal pay at the same time other union leaders were praising the president. The Clinton years would be a better environment for the policy concerns of unions, but there were no guarantees.

Then came the fall 1994 elections.

CONTINUING POLICY PROBLEMS

Regardless of the Washington outlook, most of labor's old problems continue. The vast majority of the workforce remains unorganized, and old organizing strategies work poorly. Corporate union-busting campaigns continue to be effective (Levitt, 1993). Labor law, especially as interpreted in the Bush–Reagan years, made winning votes, strikes, and contracts extremely difficult. Congress was unable to act on a bill outlawing the permanent replacement of strikers. As Paul Weiler makes clear, deep changes in the social and economic environment of the workplace—in product and capital markets, technology, and the heterogeneity of the workforce—make old labor relations and related labor law less relevant. Collective bargaining has been in a "long and inexorable downhill slide" (Weiler, 1990, 9). Most commentators agree it is time for changes in labor law, but the questions remain, What changes, and how to achieve them?

Labor's social agenda has been on hold for many years. A national health care plan, improved safety and health on the job, better opportunities for the new workforce of part-time and temporary employees, and enforcement of civil rights for women and minorities are only some of the issues of concern. All of these items require public policy response.

The Dunlop Commission on the Future of Worker Management Relations was the administration's major promise for labor law reform. But after more than a year of hearings and analysis, its "Fact-Finding Report" and "Final Report" were not encouraging to many unionists (Commission on the Future of Worker–Management Relations, 1994, 1995). The main thrust was promotion of "cooperative" labor management relations, despite considerable evidence the commission received of management unwillingness to cooperate. It did recognize the failure of current practice to protect collective bargaining rights, and the commission also resisted proposals to weaken the Wagner Act Section 8(2)(a), which prohibits management-dominated worker organizations. But it proposed only very modest changes and did not address such issues as a widening wage gap (Boal, 1994; Bacon, 1994). In any case, the Republican majority in Congress was unlikely to support labor law change favorable to unions. The newsletter *Labor Trends* described labor law reform as "dead on arrival" (Business Research Publications, 1994, 1).

Perhaps the major general concern of unions is the state of the economy. Economic transformation—capital flow, new trade patterns, and the shift from manufacturing to service jobs—is associated with major problems for workers and their unions and communities. Deindustrialization took many good union jobs and left behind unemployment and low-pay service positions. Unions struggled to understand the new economy and to mold it to serve their members' interests. A wide range of issues, including worker ownership, plant closings, and trade rules, tested the unions' ability to respond.

Behind all of the particulars of policy choices lies the political question: unions deciding what they want and then organizing politically to get it. The old-style politics—work with Democratic candidates and lobby—failed. The new style is being invented. This new approach involves reinvigorated memberships, labor–community coalition building, corporate campaigns, and even bolder initiatives. In the absence of an effective politics, union policy preferences will be ignored.

SCOPE OF THIS VOLUME

Editing this collection was a challenge. With all of the policy issues confronting unions (and all issues can be viewed from a "labor" perspective), the temptation was to go for coverage, to produce a large number of short articles on all of the concerns of unions. But reflection and discussion with colleagues suggested the limited value of such brief pieces. Instead, the decision was made to focus on three key questions—economy, law, and politics—and to encourage depth rather than breadth in the chapters.

Investigation of union policy questions yields one unstartling conclusion: there are no simple policy solutions. Indeed, even the questions are not simple, as this text demonstrates.

We begin with consideration of workers in the new economy, with focus on two key contemporary questions: the contingent worker and the "new" labor–management relations.

Françoise Carré, Virginia duRivage, and Chris Tilly draw on the most recent data and analysis to develop a policy perspective on the new "fragmented" workplace. This new work setting—including part-time, temporary, contracted, and other forms of work—poses problems for unions and workers alike. Many workers desire this flexibility, but many others do not. As the authors note, whether desired or not, these forms offer, at best, "truncated" possibilities. Unions face a contradictory pressure: to defend against the growth of this workforce while also advocating for their members who desire flexible work. Carre and her colleagues present a careful analysis of the several dimensions of this question and identify a series of significant difficulties associated with it, including problems with wages, benefits, security, and productivity. They conclude with an investigation of current approaches to the new workforce and suggest those most promising for both unions and policymakers. They investigate a new model of unionism that may be appropriate to new circumstances.

As the workforce has been changing, so has the character of the relationship between workers and managers. New labor–management relations—especially the move toward "cooperation"—is one of the most controversial labor policy questions today. Different segments of labor, management, government, and academe take different positions on the question. No single union or business position has appeared, for the good reasons that different versions of cooperation have different results, past practice has been mixed, and the future is not predictable. But leading business and union interests have developed clear positions, and the courts and the National Labor Relations Board (NLRB) are deeply engaged. The Clinton Dunlop Commission is studying the question closely.

Professor Stan Luger steps back from the current debate to place it in the context of changes in the world economy and their impacts on the shop floor. He recognizes the clear risks of employee involvement for unions but also sees it as an "opening wedge" for true worker participation in corporate decision making; it may even be a "precursor" to workplace democracy. But these positive results can occur only with an awareness of the threats, as well as the opportunities, that the end of Taylorism may provide. And a variety of government policies, including much more thorough protection of unionization, will be necessary. Luger concludes that it is simply too late to go back to the old forms of labor–management relations and thus proposes deep union involvement in the new forms.

One major cause and reflector of economic change in the last decades is corporate restructuring: conglomeration, takeover, expansion, and contraction. This restructuring, essentially a change in the financial and organizational assets of corporations, has clear and often negative implications for workers, unions, and communities. John Russo provides a description and analysis of the restructuring of the past twenty years, highlighting the practices, their defense, and union reactions. He concludes that, on balance, restructuring has been costly both to the economy and to unions, and he presents a set of policy alternatives supported by unions. Concluding that even they are "inadequate," he presents more "radical" proposals for confronting corporate restructuring in the future.

With the changing economy have come new forays by unions in areas traditionally reserved for capital: banking, insurance, pension fund investment, worker ownership. While these forms are not new, they take on new significance in this era as labor struggles for survival and new directions. Peter Pitegoff's extended discussion of unions and their role in capital is of both theoretical and practical significance for policy practitioners. The theoretical issue: What happens when a "labor" institution becomes a "capital" institution? The intersection of labor and capital may lead to hybrid forms not currently anticipated by public policy. The practical questions: What capital policies make most sense from a union perspective, and how can unions become more effectively involved in capital strategies?

Pitegoff presents a set of highly technical issues in quite readable form and goes on to analyze the political complexities that arise. Capital strategies promise much for labor, but the risks are great as well.

Trade policy in the era of a globalized or integrated world economy is a central concern of unions and workers in the United States. "Free trade" encourages capital mobility but does not deal with working conditions or environmental threats. In the words of one group of analysts, a free trade "atmosphere becomes little more than a license for U.S.-based firms to bring down wages and working conditions, and to 'downsize' by slashing workforces" (Cavanagh, Broad, and Weiss, 1994, 33–34). Gerald Glyde discusses the labor and employment implications of expanded international trade. His chapter documents the growth of trade and identifies labor's concerns. Next he describes the rather different motivations of the Canadian, U.S., and Mexican governments as they negotiated trade agreements. He presents a set of four alternative policy positions on trade and concludes by raising and answering several key questions suggested by a more formal approach to trade policy. The chapter demonstrates the risks for unions of the current ad hoc U.S. trade policy and promotes a more explicit and interconnected set of policies.

While external factors have significant impact on unions, their own internal characteristics are also important for the future. Strategic use of resources, organizing efforts, and the quality of internal democracy—all occurring within a public policy context—are each important.

One key for the future of labor organization is union democracy. Unions are among the very few American institutions expected to practice democracy. In Susan Jennik's terms, "most union officers are decent, honest advocates for workers." But failures in democracy, whether in the form of antidemocratic practices or corruption, have weakened the movement.

Jennik draws on her experience as executive director of the Association for Union Democracy to present a thorough analysis of problems of union democracy and policy responses to them. She outlines the National Labor Relations Act, the Labor–Management Reporting and Disclosure Act (Landrum–Griffin), and the Racketeer Influenced and Corrupt Organizations (RICO) act. For each she describes relevant provisions, analyzes its effectiveness, and proposes additions and changes. While encouraging "self-regulation" by unions, she concludes that government protection for members will be necessary until such internal discipline becomes a more dominant norm.

Bruce Nissen's study of local plant-closing coalitions brings together several themes of this text, with a clear focus on the importance of local policy decisions in an international context. He presents case studies of local plant-closing coalitions and sets his cases in the context of a changing international political economy. He highlights the various policy options chosen by those who resist capital mobility, including use of public funds for research, court battles, threats of liens or the use of eminent domain, and public subsidies. He also proposes national policy changes that would increase local political clout. His case studies provide evidence of a mix of local success and failure and support for union strategies that emphasize both grassroots coalition building and labor leadership.

Lawrence Flood, William Scheuerman, and Sid Plotkin investigate policy questions from the perspective of public sector unions. While public sector issues often mirror those in the private sector, significant differences appear. The chapter focuses on an ideological struggle over the role of the state. The public sector and public workers have been under direct attack since the late 1970s. After documenting the attack, the authors consider union responses (collective bargaining, program defense, and occasional strikes) and propose alternatives. Public unions must focus on improving quality and performance in government and must build both internal strength and external alliances. There are positive signs of change for the public sector, but fiscal crises and moves toward privatization pose deep threats.

As unions work for improved public policy, they must, of course, consider labor policy. James Atleson provides key insight into prospects and problems of improved labor law in the United States. Collective bargaining was called into question by the many defeats of the 1980s and by declining government enforcement of labor law. That led to calls for more law, but Atleson cautions that such calls may be misguided. He documents persistent judicial values that undermine unions regardless of the law. He also compares U.S. and Canadian unions, noting the greater strength of the movement in Canada. The laws are "better" there, but Atleson asks why they are better and answers that it is because of a stronger labor movement in the first place. His conclusion—that the current U.S. legal situation may well be the *result* rather than the cause of union weakness—is a reminder to unions of the importance of new organizing and political approaches.

II

Workers and the New Workplace

2

Piecing Together the Fragmented Workplace: Unions and Public Policy on Flexible Employment

Françoise J. Carré, Virginia L. duRivage, and Chris Tilly

The growth and sustained presence of part-time, temporary, and contingent employment in America's workplaces have generated a tension in the perspectives and practices of U.S. unions in recent years. In the face of a newly fragmented workplace, unions must move in two directions. They are the *defensive* front of action on part-time and contingent employment. They advocate for policies and contract provisions that slow down, or prevent, the conversion of full-time, permanent jobs into part-time, externalized, or casual jobs. But unions also have taken a *responsive* stance on part-time and contingent work. They see their role as responding to worker needs and desires for alternative work schedules, for shorter and more flexible work hours and careers, and for part-year work. To the extent that part-time and contingent employment fits these needs—and to the extent that workers choose these employment arrangements—unions must advocate for their increased availability to their current and potential membership and make sure that these job options offer the same protections as standard schedules.

This twofold purpose raises a dilemma for unions because it propels them in seemingly contradictory directions but also because it clearly calls into question their historical response to nonstandard work. Unions have long been committed to conversion of secondary jobs (low pay, little training and employment security, absence of due process rules) to primary jobs that entail higher pay, steadier employment, access to training and promotion, and due process protection in conflict, layoffs, and promotion. Over the post–World War II period, unions following this goal have sought to transform as many jobs as possible to full-time, year-round, long-term employment with a single employer.

Unions' ability to push for this agenda was predicated on the widespread adoption of the industrial union model as the most appropriate for worker protection and as most compatible with the organization of production. The existence and extension of the industrial model were dependent on forces specific to an historical era, such as explicit federal government support of unionization, weakened employer resistance to organization drives, and rapid economic growth, particularly in the unionized heavy manufacturing sector. These forces no longer operate in favor of unionization and preclude rebuilding the industrial union model. Support for this agenda also depended on widespread agreement that the "normal" family configuration featured a husband holding a long-term job earning a "family wage," with any paid work by the wife making only marginal contributions to the family's budget. Demographic, economic, and political changes have also undermined this consensus. Both collective bargaining and existing public policy lag behind these changes.

As unions address the specific conditions of workers in part-time and contingent employment, they must reinvent their world in a number of ways. They must shift their collective bargaining agenda to reflect new worker needs and wants. They must devise a model of worker representation better suited to the fragmented workplace. Most important, they must join efforts to formulate a new set of public policies that can control employer abuses of part-time and contingent work arrangements, extend the benefits of flexibility to as wide a group as possible, and supplement employer-provided fringe benefits with universal benefits—even though these policies may make unions appear less necessary.

In this chapter, we make the case for a new labor and public policy agenda to respond to the fragmented workplace. We discuss the growth trends in part-time, temporary, and other nonstandard forms of work; the problems posed by part-time and contingent work; existing bargaining and policy approaches to these forms of work and the approaches we expect to be most fruitful; and brief conclusions.

TRENDS TOWARD FRAGMENTATION

Part-Time Employment

Part-time employees make up almost one-fifth of the total U.S. workforce. Almost 23 million people in the economy's nonagricultural sector worked part-time in 1992, making up 18.9 percent of people at work. About two-thirds of part-time workers are women, and another one-tenth are teenage men.

Since the late 1950s, the fraction of part-timers has grown gradually from 13 percent in 1957 to its current 19 percent. In the short run, the rate of part-time employment has grown during economic recessions and dipped during expansions. But over the long run, increases have exceeded decreases, so that, on average, since the 1950s, the fraction of the workforce employed part-time has trended upward at roughly 0.19 percentage points per year. The long-run increase in the rate of part-time employment was most rapid during the 1970s.

Until about 1970, the growth trend was driven by expanding voluntary part-time employment, as women and young people desiring part-time hours streamed into the workforce. But since that time, the rate of voluntary part-time employment has stagnated, and the growing rate of *involuntary* part-time work has propelled the upward trend.[1] Of the 3.4 percent increase in the rate of part-time employment between 1969 and 1992, 3.1 percentage points are accounted for by growth in involuntary part-time employment. In other words, companies are creating part-time jobs, even though workers do not want them.

During the 1970s and 1980s, demographic trends cut *against* the rise in part-time employment. The proportion of teens in the workforce dropped, and even women of child-rearing age shifted from part-time to full-time work. What, then, caused the increase? First, industries that traditionally employed part-timers—especially retail trade and services—grew faster than the rest of the workforce during these decades. Second, the rate of part-time employment grew *within* every major industry, particularly during the 1970s.

Many companies have shifted toward part-time and contingent employment because they have decided that cutting labor costs and enhancing staffing flexibility are more important—at least in some areas of work—than maintaining the productivity and reliability of the labor force. The retail food industry offers a case in point. In retail trade as a whole, part-time employment climbed rapidly from 24 percent of the workforce in 1962 to 36 percent in 1987.[2] Among grocery stores, in particular, the rate of part-time employment soared from 35 percent in 1962 to 60 percent in 1985 ("The Changing Product Mix," 1986). According to *Progressive Grocer*, the supermarket industry's main trade publication, grocers expanded part-time employment in search of cheaper labor: "To cut labor costs by switching to lower-paid part-timers with fewer benefits, the industry's percentage of part-timers has continually grown" (Sansolo, 1987, 75).

The initial impetus for the use of part-time workers in retail food came from the extension of store hours. But then, as one retail union official recalled, "The retail industry woke up one day. The light bulb went on. They got the profit and loss picture, and started to create more part-time for that reason. This started in early to mid '50s. Since then, it has grown and grown. In the late '40s, early '50s, the key was flexibility. Since then, the key is cost" (Tilly, 1989).

The flip side of the rapid growth of part-time jobs in the retail sector has been falling productivity. Between 1967 and 1985, retail productivity fell by an average of 0.1 percent per year (Waldstein, 1989). In food stores, labor productivity plummeted by 12 percent between 1970 and 1982 (Haugen, 1986).

Part-time jobs in retail exemplify one particular type of part-time employment: what one of us (Tilly, 1992) has called *secondary* part-time employment, marked by low skill, low pay and few fringe benefits, low productivity, and high turnover. A second key category in service industries is *retention* part-time employment. Retention part-time jobs are created to retain (or, in some cases, attract) valued employees whose work circumstances prevent them from working full-time, for example, women with young children. Unlike secondary part-time employment, retention part-time work is characterized by high compensation, high productivity, and low turnover.

Secondary and retention part-time employment do not exhaust the repertoire of part-time jobs. For example, in some blue-collar occupations (particularly the building trades), part-time work results from temporary hours reductions during slack times; U.S. Postal Service employees hold part-time jobs at the entry level while they wait for full-time jobs to open up. But secondary and retention part-time work is particularly important in service jobs, which account for 86 percent of all part-time jobs. Secondary, or "bad," part-time jobs appear to be the largest category of all (Tilly, 1991a).

Temporary Employment

Unlike part-time employment, temporary employment does not have a statistical definition that matches its total size. It consists of employment in both the temporary help supply (THS, temp) industry and "direct hires." In THS employment, an intermediary service puts workers on assignment with user firms that supervise them.[3] "Direct hires" are workers hired directly by firms under conditions that spell out that their attachment to the firm is temporary and that the worker is not covered by company personnel policies or collective bargaining agreements that cover the regular workforce of the firm. These workers are on "on-call" or "short-term" assignments.

Data collection lags well behind the configuration of the workplace. We can infer from microstudies that the direct hiring of workers is on the rise, but a national count is still elusive. National data are available only on the temporary help supply industry; they are a reasonable indicator that temporary employment as a whole is on the rise.

During the 1980s, employment in the temporary help supply industry grew much faster than employment in other industries, even if the industry's relative size remains rather small.[4] Average annual employment in the industry grew particularly fast over the period, going from 406,700 in 1982 to 1,165,200 in 1989 and amounting to slightly over 1 percent of jobs in the

U.S. economy.[5] This growth represents a 187 percent increase over the period.

Average annual employment figures provide only a partial picture of the number of workers who cycle through the industry. According to an estimate from the industry association for 1988, while 1 million workers were employed by the industry at a given time during the year, actually about 6 million persons worked in the industry over the course of the year.[6]

Additionally, receipts reported by THS firms nearly doubled, from $11.2 billion in 1985 to $18.8 in 1989 (Callaghan and Hartmann, 1991). Moreover, workers in temp employment worked an average of 27.1 hours per week in 1982 and 30.8 hours in 1990.[7]

Onetime surveys indicate that, during the 1980s, the use of direct hires within firms has expanded along with that of temp industry workers. Abraham (1988) reports survey results that show an across-the-board growth in all short-term work arrangements from 1980 to 1985. Over 90 percent of the 442 firms surveyed reported using at least one of three categories of workers (THS workers, short-term hires, and on-call workers) during 1985. Abraham estimates that if these proportions hold true for all other firms in the economy, then the total use of *all* types of temporary workers is probably twice as large as the use of THS workers alone.[8]

Why did THS employment and the direct hiring of workers grow during the 1980s? Two opposing arguments have been proposed to account for this rapid growth. Some argue that the growth is "supply-led," determined by workers' needs for alternative schedules, careers, and work arrangements and, more broadly, by the changing patterns of labor market participation. Others contend that the growth is "demand-led," determined by the requirements of individual firms for labor flexibility, cost cutting, and social control of the workforce. Research on this issue has been hampered most by the lack of statistical coverage of temporary employment. Nevertheless, a growing body of research on growth trends in the THS industry has looked specifically at worker characteristics and patterns of demand.

If the growth of THS industry employment were supply-led, we would expect workers in the industry to differ markedly in terms of their labor market characteristics from those in the rest of the economy. THS industry workers are disproportionately female, young, and black. In May 1985, women accounted for 64.2 percent of THS workers as opposed to 45 percent of workers in all industries. Black workers constituted 20.2 percent of temp workers as opposed to 10.4 percent of workers in all industries.[9]

Women in THS employment differ little from women workers in the economy at large, however. In the same Current Population Survey (CPS) sample, Lapidus (1989) finds few, if any, statistically significant differences between female THS workers and the total female employed workforce in terms of marital status, number and age of children, educational level, and wage ($5.96 per hour for THS workers and $5.92 per hour for all women).

Lapidus also tested the impact of family responsibilities on the likelihood of being a THS employee. Her results do not support the hypothesis that the THS industry attracts women who are more likely to have family responsibilities. Her results suggest that either women's family responsibilities constrain their job options, whether in THS or other employment, and/or that the industry's growth is demand-led (Lapidus, 1988). Results presented by Golden and Appelbaum (1992) also indicate that, from 1982 to 1987, all other things held equal, an influx of women, youth, or older workers in the workforce does not generate growth in THS jobs.[10]

In support of arguments for a "demand-led" growth, Golden and Appelbaum find that demand-side variables and declining union presence have played a role in the accelerated growth of the THS industry from 1982 to 1987.[11] Temporary employment is particularly appealing because it can serve both as a cost-cutting tool and as a tool to restore management's prerogatives in controlling work schedules, assignments, and other aspects of the production process. They find that a decline in relative union bargaining power has increased the ability of employers to expand their temp workforce.[12]

Other Indicators of Flexibility

Increasingly, firms, in manufacturing in particular, have relied on *contracting out for business services*, for tasks outside their production activities. A 1986 Bureau of Labor Statistics special survey of establishments in four manufacturing industries that had increased output and decreased employment from 1969 to 1984 found that a majority of establishments did contract with another firm for some services such as payroll, data processing, trucking, and janitorial services.[13] Manufacturing firms, which often are restricted by union contracts from hiring temporary and part-time workers, are more likely to contract out peripheral activities rather than hire temp employees (Bureau of National Affairs [BNA], 1986).

In yet another indication of fragmentation, firms expanded their use of *independent contractors* during the 1980s, using them to perform specific tasks for a limited time period. These contractors work at home or on the premises of a company. They are treated as self-employed workers rather than regular wage and salary workers, which relieves employers of payroll taxes, unemployment insurance, and worker compensation taxes. Often, the self-employed work for only one employer rather than handling several clients, as the term "self-employed" has traditionally implied. National statistics do not separate out these independent contractors from entrepreneurs, making it difficult to assess the size of this phenomenon (Becker, 1984).[14] The U.S. General Accounting Office estimates that the number of workers reporting only nonemployee compensation in tax returns grew by 53.4 percent from 1985 to 1988 to reach 9,480,000 persons.[15]

In the public sector, financially strapped state and local governments have opted to contract out many social services and public works to cheaper private employers, a move that has disproportionately hurt women and minority workers (du Rivage, 1992). During the 1980s, the Federal Office of Personnel Management extended the length of time individuals could be hired to perform temporary work from one to four years. This policy has resulted in thousands of new public sector jobs that provide no benefits or seniority rights (Labor Research Association, 1990).

Dual job holding is also on the rise. In May 1991, 7.2 million people—6.2 percent of the workforce—held more than one job (Bureau of Labor Statistics, 1989, 1991a). This is the highest rate of multiple job holding recorded since the first survey on the subject was conducted in 1970 and marks a steady increase since 1978. Multiple job holding rose fastest for women. Presumably, the rise in multiple jobs represents families' response to the downward trend in real wages since 1973.

Schedule flexibility is becoming more common, as well. Fifteen percent of full-time workers reported that they worked flexible hours in 1991, up from 12 percent in 1985 (Bureau of Labor Statistics, 1992).

In addition to these relatively well measured changes in job holding, there is considerable anecdotal evidence that workers are moving more frequently from one employment arrangement to another. As a growing proportion of women remains in the workforce during child-rearing years, recourse to parental leave and movement back and forth between part-time and full-time hours have become more common patterns. Tilly (1989) found that in some companies, retention part-time arrangements were virtually invented during the 1970s and 1980s to meet the needs of new mothers.

In summary, every variety of workforce flexibility and fragmentation has grown in the last twenty years. Several forces have driven this trend. Most important, employers have sought ways to increase their own scheduling flexibility, cut costs, and reduce long-term commitments to the workforce. Union resistance has been limited, given the weakened state of the labor movement. Service industries, heavy users of flexible work arrangements, have grown most quickly, and at the same time firms in almost every industry have gravitated toward contingency-based staffing. But, in addition, workers—particularly women—have, in many cases, sought flexibility themselves in order to meet the competing demands of family and workplace. Given this movement from both the employer and the employee, the old patterns of stability are unlikely to return.

PROBLEMS OF THE FRAGMENTED WORKPLACE

Many workers participating in flexible work arrangements do so voluntarily. For example, only 30 percent of part-time workers report that they are working short hours due to involuntary hours reductions or an inability to find a full-time job (Bureau of Labor Statistics, *Employment and Earnings*, January 1993). Yet, for too many workers in the United States, this flexibility breeds social and economic insecurity, particularly as many workers remain in these arrangements for a substantial part of the year. Many part-time, temporary, or contracted jobs fail to provide employment security, fringe benefits, a living wage, any accommodation of family responsibilities, or opportunities for union representation. In some cases, the shift toward more flexible work forms relieves employers of federal obligations under such programs as the Occupational Safety and Health Act (OSHA),[16] Unemployment Insurance, Employee Retirement Income Security Act (ERISA), and Equal Employment Opportunity.

The expansion of contingent forms of work raises the potential for renewed growth of a secondary labor market. Employers are shifting more responsibility for health care insurance, an adequate wage, and in some cases even job creation itself (as in the case of the self-employed) onto workers. This unilateral employer abdication of responsibility has turned flexibility from a positive into a negative, in many cases. The resulting catalog of problems represents a mandate for intervention in the public policy and collective bargaining arenas.

Wages and Benefits

The most visible disadvantages faced by contingent workers are lower wages and diminished access to fringe benefits.

Part-time workers earn about 60 percent of the hourly wages of full-time workers ($4.83 in 1989, compared to $7.83 for full-time workers). In 1984, more than one part-timer in four earned the minimum wage; only one full-time worker in twenty fell at the minimum (Mellor and Haugen, 1986). Only a small part of the wage gap can be explained by differences in productive characteristics between part-time and full-time workers, such as education. In fact, some companies have paid part-time workers much lower hourly wages than full-timers performing the identical job. For example, the now-defunct People Express and Presidential Airlines paid part-time airline reservation workers half the hourly wage of full-timers (Nine to Five, 1986).

Temporary workers also earn less, averaging $7.73 per hour in 1990, compared to $10.03 for all wage and salary workers (Callaghan and Hartman, 1991). Business services, the sector that provides contract services for other companies, pays wages ranging from 15 to 30 percent below the wages of similar workers in manufacturing (Abraham, 1988).

Part-time and contingent workers are clustered at the lower end of the economic scale. One in six part-time workers has a family income below the poverty level, compared with one in 37 year-round, full-time workers (Levitan and Conway, 1988). Tilly, Bluestone, and Harrison (1986) discovered that 42 percent of the growth of inequality in annual wages and salaries between 1978 and 1984 could be accounted for by the growth of part-time employment and the widening gap between the earnings of part-time and full-time workers.

The crisis of health care coverage has affected all workers, but it has hurt contingent workers most acutely. Eighty percent of full-time, year-round workers receive health insurance from their employers, compared with only 25 percent of part-time, full-year workers and 12 percent of part-time, part-year workers (Congressional Research Service, 1988). Another quarter of part-time workers gain health care coverage from a spouse's employer (Employee Benefits Research Institute, 1988). Among temporary help supply workers, one-quarter work for companies with a health plan (Bureau of Labor Statistics, 1988).[17] Eligibility is severely restricted, however. The few temporary agencies that offer health coverage often extend benefits to employees only after they have worked a minimum of 1,000 hours with the agency (Nine to Five, 1986). For instance, only about 23 percent of Manpower's workers meet company eligibility requirements (Fromstein, 1988, 111). The self-employed are similarly unprotected, with only 46 percent holding private health insurance (U.S. Small Business Administration, 1988). Medicaid offers little help, since it was designed to cover poor nonworkers—not the working uninsured. The Clinton administration's universal health care proposal would have taken a major step forward, mandating prorated employer contributions to health coverage for part-timers working ten or more hours a week.

The public and private pension system in the United States is based on an outmoded profile of the American worker: a lifelong breadwinner with an at-home spouse and children—a definition fitting less than 10 percent of current households. Contingent workers are ill served by this system. Part-time workers are one-third as likely to be included in an employer pension plan as full-timers (Woodbury, 1989). Few temporary agencies provide pension coverage at all (Fromstein, 1988). The Employee Benefits Research Institute estimates that in 1985, 63 percent of THS workers had no pension plan. ERISA does not require companies to offer pensions, nor does it require that a company cover all of its workers. Social Security, a system designed to supplement, not supplant, retirement income, offers only limited relief to contingent workers because benefits are pegged to their low lifetime earnings.

Low wages and minimal benefits clearly pose a problem for contingent workers and their families, but they also impose costs on taxpayers and other full-time workers. In 1985, persons experiencing involuntary part-time employment were almost twice as likely to receive public assistance as the average person in the labor force. Full-time workers pay part of the price as well. According to research by Rebitzer (1987; see also Rebitzer and Taylor, 1991), the greater the number of part-time workers in a given industry, the lower the wages of full-timers, and the less likely full-time workers are to receive health insurance or pension benefits. For example, full-time workers employed in a sector where one-third of the workforce is part-time earn $1.21 less an hour, on average, than identical full-timers located in an industry with no part-timers.

Employment Security, Advancement, and Unemployment Insurance

Part-time and temporary workers enjoy little employment stability and face major obstacles to job advancement. Temporary and contract employment, by definition, is short-term and dead-end. For part-time workers, the average job tenure is 3.4 years, well below the average of 5.7 years for full-time working women and 8.1 years for full-time working men (Rebitzer and Taylor, 1991). Part-time workers are also more likely to be dead-ended in their jobs than are full-time employees. A group of managers surveyed in the late 1970s considered part-time workers "less promotable" than full-time workers (Nollen, Eddy, and Martin, 1978). According to Nine to Five (1986), company policies often discourage promotion of part-time workers. For example, Control Data Corporation, the University of Cincinnati, Los Angeles Community College, and CIGNA Corporation treat their part-time employees' applications for full-time work no differently than applications from outside.

When a contingent worker loses his or her job, the unemployment insurance system offers little protection. Thirty-three states exclude casual laborers from unemployment insurance, while self-employed workers are eligible for coverage only in California—and only on a case-by-case basis (U.S. Department of Labor, 1988). Thirty-eight states bar independent contractors from unemployment compensation. In addition, minimum earnings and work time requirements exclude still other part-time and temporary workers. For instance, a temporary worker earning the industry's hourly average of $6.42 for thirty hours of work a week would fail the minimum earnings test in at least nineteen states! Similarly, a part-time worker working thirty hours per week and earning the 1988 average part-time hourly rate of $4.42 would fail to meet minimum earnings tests in at least half the states. In addition, a number of states routinely deny benefits to workers who limit their job search to part-time employment (Pearce, 1985).

Choice

One of the most troubling aspects of the fragmentation of the workplace is the evidence that many workers hold part-time and temporary jobs solely because they have no other alternative. As noted before, Tilly (1991a) documents that growth in the rate of part-time employment since 1970 reflects an expansion of *involuntary* part-time jobs. The 6 million involuntary part-time workers counted in September 1991 (Bureau of Labor Statistics, 1991b) represent the (full-time) equivalent of 3 million unemployed.

Lapidus (1989) finds no evidence that women workers choose this arrangement to accommodate family responsibilities; she finds that women THS workers are no more likely to have family responsibilities than other women workers in the economy. In addition, manual work, performed disproportionately by minority men and women working as day laborers, assemblers, and freight handlers, makes up the second largest category of work in the THS industry. Most workers in this category—the fastest growing and poorest paying segment of the industry (Hartmann and Lapidus, 1989)—likely would prefer permanent employment (Williams, 1988). A laid-off General Electric assembly worker from Tennessee testified that the state unemployment office suggested that she and her coworkers contact temporary agencies for work. "When we went to the temporary agency, the jobs they had listed paid terrible wages. They were sending us in to work side by side with people who were making decent money and who had adequate fringe benefits, but we were entitled to none of these things. We began to hear more and more stories of this abuse" (Reinhardt, 1991). Even temp industry leaders recognize that many workers in THS employment are looking for permanent work. Dick Gorman, vice president of FLexi-Force in Milwaukee, was quoted as saying that 75 to 85 percent of the workers sent out by his agency were looking for permanent jobs (Bernstein, 1985).

Both black men and black women are overrepresented in the temp industry (Plewes, 1988). This overrepresentation reflects the concentration of low-paying occupations in the THS industry, in which black workers also cluster in the economy at large.

Workers are constrained not only by the limited availability of permanent and full-time jobs but also by inadequate child care. Nearly 35 percent of women who are working part-time or looking for part-time work say they would work more hours if good child care were available (Presser and Baldwin, 1980). The problem is most severe among the one-quarter of U.S. families with children that are headed by a mother only. Half of these women who worked part-time in 1983 said they would rather work full-time but were constrained by the high costs and unavailability of quality child care (U.S. Congress, House of Representatives, 1989).

Finally, while some workers hold part-time jobs involuntarily, others would *prefer* part-time work but are stuck in full-time schedules. Such involuntary full-timers, which include mothers, some fathers, and older workers, numbered 4 million in 1985 (Tilly, 1992). Although part-time jobs with low pay and low skill are plentiful, involuntary full-timers often cannot obtain a part-time schedule in their particular industry or profession.

Union Representation

Part-time and contingent workers are much less likely than full-timers to have union representation. In 1990, 6.7 percent of part-timers were union members, compared with 19 percent of full-time workers (U.S. Bureau of Labor Statistics, *Employment and Earnings*, January 1991). Even after controlling for gender, race, age, and education, over two-thirds of the gap in union membership rates between part-time and full-time members remains (Tilly, 1991b). Similarly, in 1988, only 7 percent of workers in the personnel supply service industry (which includes temp agencies) were unionized, compared to 17 percent of workers in other industries (Tilly, 1991b).

Such low rates of unionization result from the tremendous obstacles unions face in bargaining for part-time and contingent workers. Much of this difficulty stems from the complex employee classification schemes associated with the diversification of employee work schedules, as well as the failure of labor law to protect contract workers. The National Labor Relations Board has issued inconsistent rulings on whether part-time and contingent workers should vote along with full-time employees in representation elections (Bronfenbrenner, 1988b; SEIU, 1993) and often has inappropriately split full-time workers apart from other groups. In addition, of course, part-time and contingent workers may feel they have a limited stake in gaining benefits and representation in a particular workplace.

In some cases, employers have expanded flexible forms of employment to undercut union organizing drives or exact concessions during contract negotiations. For example, the Wisconsin Physicians Insurance Corporation, following bitter negotiations with the United Food and Commercial Workers, brought in hundreds of part-time, temporary, and home-based workers (Costello, 1989). During a recent organizing drive by the United Auto Workers, Hudson Department Stores in Detroit increased its hiring of part-time workers and began phasing out full-time workers (Colatosti, June 1990). In the construction industry, an increasingly common practice is hiring workers as self-employed contractors to avoid hiring through the union (Capece, 1991). In nearly every public sector case, contracting out has resulted in the loss of union protection for the new workforce (Dantico, 1987). No legislation prohibits the hiring of THS workers as strikebreakers. Numerous employers have resorted to this strategy, a practice outlawed in many Western European countries.

Productivity

When part-time and contingent employment undermines worker security, it also erodes productivity and efficiency.

The evidence is most substantial for part-time employment—specifically secondary part-time jobs. As noted before, the years of rapid expansion of part-time employment in the retail food industry were years of negative productivity growth. A supermarket manager told Tilly (1989) that the minuses of hiring part-time workers include "[t]he abilities, experience and work level they achieve. Their loyalty to the position and the company. . . . I'm talking about absenteeism, I'm talking about tardiness, shrinkage [theft], attitude. . . . [And] the part-time . . . turn over much faster than the full-time (98)."

Another store manager added, "In my produce department, one good full-timer can do as much work [per hour] as any three part-timers," due to greater experience and effort. By the late 1980s, grocery trade journal *Progressive Grocer* was reporting: "Some retailers are rethinking the pros and cons of part-timers vs. full-timers. The high turnover rate and the costs of training replacement employees may outweigh the advantages of part-timers. These operators point out that full-timers tend to be more loyal and add stability to a store's staff" ("The Changing Product Mix,", 1986, 63).

Even beyond retail, part-timers turn over rapidly. Rebitzer and Taylor (1991) find that 28.4 percent of part-time workers surveyed in a given month are out of the labor force twelve months later, compared with only 5.3 percent of full-time women and 2.9 percent of full-time men. Studies of specific industries and occupations reveal similar patterns; for example, the turnover rate for part-time letter carriers in the U.S. Postal Service is more than four times as great as for full-timers (Tilly, 1991b). High turnover and low commitment add up to low productivity. Appelbaum (1987) and Carré (1992) conclude that the growing use of temporary workers may likewise reduce worker productivity.

The particular form of productivity differences, of course, varies by industry. In retail, a part-time produce clerk may stock vegetables slowly or sloppily. In higher education, Flood (1987) points out that second-class status for part-time faculty can lead to poor education and the corrosion of academic freedom.

POLICY AND STRATEGY

Current Approaches

In meeting the challenges posed by part-time and contingent employment in the United States, public policy and collective bargaining have pursued four general approaches: to *limit* or prevent the growth of part-time and contingent work; to *control* compensation and working conditions; to *exploit* new possibilities for flexibility; or to *supplement* employer benefits with public or universal protections.[18]

Limiting or Preventing Growth

Historically, many unions have attempted to hold the line, through collective bargaining, on the growth of nonstandard forms of work. As a United Food and Commercial Workers (UFCW) official told Tilly (1989), the union has long been "trying to increase and enlarge the full-time work-force" in retail stores, through bargaining over the permissible proportions of full-time and part-time employment. "But," the official acknowledged, "the tide has been running the other way" (157). A wide variety of unions in manufacturing, food processing, transportation, and the public sector have negotiated full-time percentages. In some industries, unions have won "no subcontracting" clauses. For instance, the Hotel and Restaurant Employees' contract with Yale University bars the use of casual and temporary employees to replace permanent positions (Bronfenbrenner, 1988a).

To date, federal, state, and local governments have made few efforts to help unions contain the growth of casual employment. In fact, one of the few restrictions in place, the ban on industrial homework effective since 1942, was lifted by the U.S. Department of Labor in 1984, despite lobbying in support of the ban by the International Ladies Garment Workers Union (ILGWU), the Amalgamated Clothing and Textile Workers Union (AC-TWU), the Service Employees International Union (SEIU), and the American Federation of Labor and Congress of Industrial Organizations (AFL-CIO) itself (duRivage and Jacobs, 1989). Some innovative strategies have enabled unions to make headway toward prevention; for example, Connecticut recently enacted a law permitting competing contractors to sue a contractor who is awarded a contract after having misclassified employees as "independent contractors" in order to reduce labor costs—a common practice in construction.[19] Labor–community coalitions such as Citizens against Temporary Services (in Tennessee; Reinhardt, 1991, Yount, and Williams, 1990) and the Coalition to Stop Contracting Out (in Los Angeles; SEIU Local 660 Research Department, 1991) are currently pressing local and state governments to adopt more restrictive policies. The California labor federation has been monitoring the temp industry association attempts to get a bill passed in the state legislature that would limit temp workers' eligibility for unemployment insurance.[20]

Controlling Conditions of Employment

For unions representing a workforce with substantial numbers of part-timers or others with nonstandard work arrangements, regulating the use of these workers has become a central goal. The first step toward this goal is inclusion of part-time and contingent workers in the bargaining unit, with a separate status. Existing labor agreements typically include part-timers (at least above some minimum number of hours) but exclude THS workers, although some include other contingent categories such as casual or on-call workers (Bronfenbrenner, 1988a). The next step is to bargain for parity in wages and benefits. For example, since the UFCW has been unable to prevent growth of the part-time workforce in most retail settings, it has targeted equal wages and prorated benefits for part-time workers, with some success. According to John Reilly, then president of United University Professions (American Federation of Teachers Local 2190), "The best strategy is to fully integrate part-timers into the union and academic life with pro-rated benefits and equivalent participation" (United University Professions, 1992).

In addition, many contracts mandate upgrading of part-time and contingent workers. Part-time workers typically accumulate seniority and the right to bid for full-time jobs, although the formula for calculating seniority is sometimes controversial (Bronfenbrenner, 1988a). Some contracts automatically convert temporary or on-call workers to permanent, regular status once they have worked continuously for some specified duration.[21]

In some cases, workers providing public sector services under contracting-out arrangements have found ways to affect their conditions of employment, short of being able to stop contracting out altogether. In rare cases, where union locals have been powerful, they have obtained prevailing wage legislation (requiring that contract workers receive the same pay and benefits as equivalent public employees). More common, however, are cases where unions participate in the contract award process and thus gain some control over its outcome. For example, in 1990, the California Bay Area Local 250 of SEIU organized the emergency medical personnel, paramedics, and emergency technicians working for private sector providers to San Mateo County. After the existing contractor business announced it would not go out for bid at the end of the service contract, Local 250 used its political clout to ensure that the new contract issued by the county would require that the winning bidder give preference to the incumbent workforce, thus ensuring continuity of jobs and membership for the local. The local then participated actively in contractor selection, thus conveying union concerns about providing improved emergency services while maintaining worker benefits (Shostak, 1993).[22]

Interestingly, while most unions have opposed homework outright, the Newspaper Guild and the American Federation of State, County, and Municipal Employees (AFSCME) have sanctioned electronic homework under carefully controlled conditions. In a pilot project initiated by AFSCME District 24 and the University of Wisconsin Hospital, medical transcriptionists working at home received the same pay, benefits, and promotional opportunities as in-house workers. Working conditions were closely monitored by the union, which stayed in touch with the home

workers via an electronic switchboard and weekly meetings. AFSCME
judged the experiment a success (duRivage and Jacobs, 1989).

Existing government policies assist only in limited ways union attempts
to control the levels of compensation and benefits for part-time and contingent workers. Since the passage of the 1982 Tax Equity and Fiscal Responsibility Act (TEFRA), section 414 (n) of the Internal Revenue Code requires
employers to treat certain long-term contract employees as "leased employees" and to count them as part of their regular workforce when applying
Internal Revenue Service (IRS) "coverage" tests for retirement plans and
certain fringe benefits such as group life insurance and "cafeteria" plans.
This section does not apply to the coverage test for group health plans,
however. Both leased and temporary help service workers are subject to this
provision. Anyone working under a temping or "leasing" arrangement for
1,500 hours a year is counted as a regular employee for retirement plan
coverage.[23]

President Clinton's proposed health plan, building on a number of state
plans, would have mandated employer contributions to health coverage
costs for all employees working over ten hours a week. However, self-employed workers would have paid their own way (though eligible for a tax
deduction), and employer contributions to part-timers working thirty
hours per week or less would have been prorated, with employees responsible for paying the remainder unless they qualified for low-income subsidies. Since many employers currently provide *no* health benefits for
part-timers, it is not surprising that one restaurant chain told the *Wall Street
Journal* (1993) that if this mandate became law, "[W]e would definitely be
looking at moving those part-time positions into full-time positions." This
echoes retailers' response to earlier proposed legislation along the same
lines ("Health Care Reform," 1992, 1).

Exploiting the Opportunity for Flexibility

Though unions have typically opposed part-time and contingent employment, a growing group of unions has concluded that flexibility is a
benefit for part of their workforce and, accordingly, has bargained to make
that flexibility available. SEIU Locals 6 (representing private mental health
clinics in Seattle), 535 and 715 (representing Santa Clara County workers)
have bargained for a full-time employee's right to request job sharing or a
permanent part-time arrangement. Local 6's agreement protects part-timers from overtime demands by requiring that overtime be offset by compensatory time. The contract for Locals 535 and 715 even sets a *minimum* of
part-time positions in the bargaining unit (Nollen, 1982). The Boston Globe
Employees Association, an independent newspaper union, bargained for
employees' right to bid for reduced hours and then, subsequently, to bid
for increased hours—an arrangement particularly attractive to parents of
young children. Essentially, these unions are creating what we have called

retention part-time jobs. Similarly, the AFSCME Local 24/University of Wisconsin Hospital agreement on homework was designed, in part, to meet the needs of employees who preferred to work at home without sacrificing benefits or career mobility.

Policies to improve part-time employment also have been adopted by federal and state governments. The Federal Career Part-Time Employees Act of 1978 allowed the creation of permanent part-time positions at all levels, offering the same hourly wage as full-time jobs and prorated fringe benefits. Twenty-five states have similar programs to create better part-time employment options, often at the urging of public sector unions. Unfortunately, a 1984 evaluation of the federal program found that managers were dragging their feet in making high-level part-time positions available to federal workers (Kahne, 1985).

Supplementing Employer-Provided Benefits

Unions historically have sought to obtain benefits from the individual employer. They have begun, however, to explore benefits provided directly by the union itself, such as credit cards or special insurance rates (AFL–CIO Committee on the Evolution of Work, 1985). These benefits are particularly important for workers who move frequently from job to job, shift in and out of the labor force, and/or are employed in nonstandard work arrangements.

Federal and state governments have long supplemented employer-provided benefits through programs such as Social Security (technically, Old Age, Survivors, and Disability Insurance), Medicare, and Medicaid. President Carter's 1981 Commission on Pension Policy recommended that Congress establish an employer-funded minimum universal pension scheme to supplement Social Security, with a mandated minimum contribution and assured pension portability from one employer to another. Although other countries, including France, Finland, Denmark, Sweden, and Switzerland, have universal employer-funded pensions in parallel with publicly funded retirement benefits, the United States has yet to act on such a plan.

What Will Work?

Labor's position toward part-time and contingent work builds on two legacies. One is a long-standing commitment to converting secondary jobs into primary ones. The other is a deep ambivalence and even antagonism toward nonstandard forms of employment, based on the view that all such jobs constitute secondary employment.

The changing economy and a diversified labor force require that unions reevaluate both of these tenets and develop new strategies to protect today's workers. On one hand, the strategy of using collective bargaining to convert secondary jobs into primary ones is blocked by growing employer and government antagonism, concerted attacks by the political Right, and shifts in industry composition and competition that sap traditional union organizing efforts. On the other hand, part-time and contingent employment is here to stay—in part, because large numbers of workers have chosen nonstandard work arrangements to meet their own needs. Changes in the organization of production, in labor markets, and in family structure have fueled the growth of flexible employment—while simultaneously making these forms of employment untenable in their current form. For instance, part-time work without benefits may have been acceptable to the wave of white married women with children who entered the labor force beginning in the late 1960s, but it is not workable for the growing number of women workers who are single heads of households or whose husbands now lack access to employer-provided benefits. Similarly, part-time jobs without benefits have always been untenable for minority women with limited access to a spouse with high earnings and benefits or for the growing numbers of minority males forced into part-time and contingent employment as alternatives to unemployment.

How do these changes affect labor's choices among strategies of prevention, control, exploitation, or supplementation? First, the goal of preventing, or limiting through regulation, the number of part-time and other contingent jobs may be misplaced in the current era—given the number of workers who want these schedules—as well as unattainable. The French government's attempt to limit the creation of temporary and fixed-duration jobs is instructive. In 1982, early in Mitterand's socialist government, France directly restricted the creation of such jobs. By 1986, however, the government dropped these restrictions. French labor market inflexibility was widely believed responsible for the country's persistently high unemployment. In addition, the sharp distinctions between temporary and permanent positions had become blurred by the "flexibilization" of permanent jobs (Carré, 1994).

Nonetheless, outright prevention and/or strict regulation will still be required for those forms of employment that contain a significant potential for abuse or represent explicit employer attempts to undercut compensation and working conditions. The best example of this case is industrial (e.g., garment) and electronic homework. As duRivage and Jacobs note, homework can be a viable option only "if unions are involved in the decision to implement such a program, if homework is voluntary, if labor and management negotiate every feature of the program, and if strong contract language exists clearly stating the terms and conditions of such work" (1989, 267). In many situations, however, these features are absent, and only legal prohibitions can protect workers against abuse. Some forms of contracting out to the self-employed likely also fall into this category.

If prevention is limited to a small subset of nonstandard work arrangements, control becomes all the more important. The control strategy attempts to enhance the quality of part-time and contingent jobs, transforming them into primary labor market jobs without necessarily changing their scheduling attributes. Wage and benefit parity is particularly important, since it makes part-time and temporary work less attractive to employers using them primarily to cut labor costs or reduce union presence. Most European countries require equal pay for work of equal value, regardless of hours worked (International Labour Office, 1989).

Even if government regulations mandating wage and benefits parity are adopted, unions will play a crucial role in monitoring and enforcing these regulations—just as they do for current wage and hour laws that, in principle, apply to all (nonexempt) workers. The impact of unions on wage parity is best illustrated by the contrast between the United States and Canada. In Canada, unionization rates of both part-time and full-time workers are higher, and the ratio of part-time to full-time rates of unionization is greater. Eighteen percent of Canada's part-time workers and 40 percent of full-timers are unionized, compared with 7 percent and 19 percent, respectively, in the United States. This smaller differential benefits Canadian workers; part-timers, on average, received an hourly wage that was 79 percent of the full-time average in 1981, compared with 60 percent in the United States in the same year.[24] In the Canadian union sector, part-timers earned a full 98 percent as much per hour as their full-time counterparts (Commission of Inquiry into Part-Time Work, 1983).

Monitoring wage parity in nonunion settings is problematic at best. American policymakers probably are not ready for universal works councils of the type in place in Northern European countries but may support representative institutions with limited mandates. A recent example is the proposal, in the Occupational Safety and Health Reform Act of 1991, for the formation of labor–management safety committees in all workplaces of over ten employees, union and nonunion, with workers electing their own safety representatives. Kindred or overlapping structures might be established to oversee wages and benefits parity.

Measures to expand and exploit flexibility from the employee's side, such as parental leave, flextime, or the right to move between full-time and part-time status, are likely to become increasingly important as women of childbearing age become more entrenched in the workforce, and as men show a growing responsibility for child care and involvement with their families. Ensuring that a wide range of jobs allows flexibility, in response to changing worker preferences, is the other side of the coin from making sure that flexible jobs bring decent wages, benefits, and security.

In fact, a strong case can be made for reducing work time for all (Schor, 1992). In many European countries, both unions and governments have made work-time reductions a priority, in large part, as a job-creation measure.[25] Some Western European countries also allow older workers to reduce their hours of work and receive assistance from the public pension system. While this policy has sometimes been used to progressively phase out older workers in industries undergoing restructuring and as an alternative to a complete layoff, it has also constituted a welcome benefit for many workers. In the United States, however, public policy discourages mixing work and Social Security (International Labour Office, 1989).

Union support for universal benefits supplementing or replacing employer-provided fringe benefits offers a particularly important strategy for the labor movement, given the declining rate of unionization and unions' corresponding diminution of bargaining power. Advocating for universal benefits, such as health care, facilitates the formation of coalitions of union federations, employee associations, and public policy reform groups. Together, both types of organization can argue for the design of a mechanism of social protection more "rational" than the current one, which is better suited to a fading form of production organization. By "more rational" we mean a mechanism that prevents large segments of the workforce from falling outside the protection of either employer-provided benefits or the public welfare system.[26]

"Rationalizing" employer benefits extends beyond a universal health care plan. Public policy reforms are needed to allow for the conversion and portability of worker pensions, as well as to standardize eligibility for unemployment insurance and for workers' compensation (for details, see duRivage, 1992). One possible model for reform is the national collective bargaining agreement governing terms of employment in the French temporary help industry. The agreement includes rules for industry-wide seniority and pension portability that allow workers to build seniority and protection not only across temporary assignments but also as they shift across temp help service agencies over the course of their career.[27]

Toward a New Model of Worker Organization and Representation

Finally, while adjusting the current system to the fragmented workplace, unions can explore new models of worker organization particularly suited to workers who move in and out of part-time and temporary employment or simply do not stay with the same employer for the major part of their work career (see Carré, duRivage, and Tilly, 1994, for a longer discussion). As Cobble (1990) points out, the most natural place to look for these models is in the rich history of occupational unionism.

For example, unions could borrow aspects of the construction trades unions (laborers, carpenters), which developed to meet the needs of workers with fleeting attachments to contracting firms. In this model, the union, not the firm, provides stability and equity in terms of wages, health benefits, and pension. Training is actively controlled by the union, and, in many instances, unions control the hiring process. Construction unionism demonstrates the possibility of stable worker representation in a highly fluctuating sector.

Arts and entertainment unions, which also represent workers with short-term, project-based jobs, offer an alternative model (Kleingartner and Paul, 1992). These unions provide a variety of services to ease job transitions, including referral and placement, and transitional loan funds. They have bargained for pension portability and for health coverage that can be self-paid during spells of unemployment. As with the construction unions, the arts and entertainment unions are directly involved in a number of areas traditionally left to management, such as hiring and the administration of compensation. These unions also index dues to income, so that those who find little work owe little in dues, and accommodate worker membership in multiple unions.

Cobble (1990, 1991) cites examples in a variety of other trades, including waitress unions that successfully ran hiring halls in Butte, Montana, and Los Angeles for over half a century.

How readily can these models be extended more generally to part-time or contingent employment? The construction model clearly depends on the bargaining power of the skilled building trades, their control of apprenticeships, the threat of strikes, and government regulation of the construction industy. On the other hand, Kleingartner and Paul (1992, 3) note, "Unions in arts and entertainment are effective, relevant, and valued by workers in the industry without being powerful in the sense of being able to impose their will on employers through strikes." Unions can replicate parts of these models, even in the absence of traditional sources of bargaining power, if they take on a role in maintaining continuity and communication that makes them essential to management and workers alike. This role would include ensuring continuity of benefits (possibly through direct union sponsorship of health or pension plans, which is not a new idea). It could also encompass participation in recruiting and placement and in training and certification of skill within a particular occupation. Successful implementation would require modifications of union structures, such as expanded associate membership programs (available even to workers not currently working in a unionized shop), broadened bargaining units, and representation organized primarily along the lines of occupation and geographic area rather than work site and industry.

Some of these elements also resemble those that enter into the model for "associational unionism" put forth by Heckscher (1988) to enable unions as a whole to coordinate and effectively represent the growing diversity of claims and concerns in the workforce, be it in permanent or contingent employment. Heckscher advocates for unions to provide multiple forms of representation and services in addition to traditional collective bargaining.

Unions and worker associations, he argues, can perform other functions such as providing direct services and extra insurance and benefits to those within, as well as those outside, the collective bargaining unit. They can also help establish training funds for new jobs even if these fall outside the bargaining unit or the industry. In this way, "workers who cannot be protected by a contract nevertheless can get help from their representative organization"(189).[28]

CONCLUSION

Part-time, temporary, and other contingent forms of employment make up a lasting and growing portion of jobs. In some cases, nonstandard work offers desired flexibility to workers. At best, these job arrangements usually compel workers to give up security in order to enjoy flexibility; at worst, they often represent employer efforts to reduce compensation and union bargaining power. Either way, arrangements that provide temporary means to avoid unemployment may turn into long-term forms of participation in the labor market.

The labor movement will continue to be compelled to respond to these workplace changes in its bargaining and policy agendas. Unions will accomplish most if they move beyond a reflexive opposition to all nonstandard forms of work and instead focus on controlling, exploiting, and supplementing these employment forms. The union objective of transforming secondary jobs into primary ones remains salient. However, that transformation need not imply that the jobs cease to offer employees flexibility; indeed, a linked objective becomes introducing options of flexibility to primary labor market jobs.

The interests of part-time, contingent, and even other workers can be met best through a combination of collective bargaining and policy changes. On one hand, union presence in the workplace plays a critical role in enforcing new policy measures. On the other hand, new forms of worker representation oriented toward today's more fragmented workplace would work best given a set of "enabling" policies, just as the industrial union model was complemented by a set of government policies regulating employment. Piecing together the fragmented workplace requires that labor and government let go of outdated definitions of workplace and worker protection in favor of reforms that ensure that flexibility benefits workers as well as employers. Without this joint and concerted effort, arrangements accepted by workers as short-term solutions to scheduling and employment problems may yield truncated opportunities for their entire work career.

NOTES

1. The U.S. Bureau of Labor Statistics defines someone as an involuntary part-time worker if he or she works part-time because of inability to find a full-time job or because of temporary hours reductions due to slack work, materials shortages, or other economic reasons.

2. From unpublished Current Population Survey results provided by Thomas Nardone, Bureau of Labor Statistics.

3. This discussion of the THS industry relies heavily on Carey and Hazelbaker, 1986. The THS industry is often taken to represent most forms of temporary employment or of personnel services, but other industries provide personnel to user firms as well. They include janitorial services (SIC 7349), guard services (SIC 7393), and managerial services (SIC 7392). However, these other industries provide a specific service, the worker is supervised by the service-supplying firm, and it is unclear what proportion of these jobs is temporary (Carey and Hazelbaker, 1986). Employee leasing firms (SIC 7369 before 1990) is another form of personnel supply that may or may not entail temporary employment duration.

4. Carey and Hazelbaker (1986) note that between 1978 and 1985 employment growth in the THS industry was 104 percent and represented three times the growth rate of the services division as a whole and eight times the rate for all nonagricultural industries during the same period.

5. THS employment trends have been particularly hard to follow because of definitional changes in employment statistics over the years. From 1968 to 1982, the Bureau of Labor Statistics (BLS) Current Employment Statistics (CES) series reported statistics on SIC 736 (Personnel Supply Services) that included employ-ment/placement agencies as well as temp services. From 1982 to 1989, the CES series reported average yearly employment for SIC 7362, the Temporary Help Supply industry. Starting with 1990, however, SIC 7362 was folded into SIC 7363 Help Supply Services (HSS), which also includes the employee leasing industry (previously reported separately) and miscellaneous personnel supply services (not elsewhere classified.) However, it does not include employment agencies, which are in a separate SIC. Callaghan and Hartmann (1991, 6) report results of a data series especially commissioned from the BLS that applies the HHS definition back to 1982. By this recent definition, employment grew from 417,400 workers in 1982 to 1,295,900 workers in 1990, a 210 percent increase.

6. Current Employment Statistics and National Association of Temporary Services estimate based on data reported by membership and cited in Hartmann and Lapidus, 1989, 3.

7. Help Supply Services (supra 6).

8. Using an unofficial estimate of average THS employment (750,000 persons), Abraham estimates that the aggregate employment for all types of temporary workers would average over 1.5 million persons for that year (1988, 7).

9. For a review of available research on THS workers, see Carré, 1992.

10. A similar comparison has not been conducted for black workers. However, the group of occupations in which black workers concentrate in THS employment mirrors those in which black workers concentrate in the economy as a whole. The clustering of these occupations (service occupations, casual manual labor) in the

THS industry likely accounts for their overrepresentation in the industry relative to their share of the U.S. workforce.

11. These demand-side variables with positive effects on THS employment growth include a rise in output demand above its long-term trend; the intensification of international cost competition; the growth of fixed, nonwage, labor costs relative to wage costs; the availability of paid time off for the regular workforce; the need for workweek adjustment in the regular workforce and any expansion in skill requirements (temp worker used until a permanent worker is hired).

12. For details on models see Golden and Appelbaum, 1992.

13. Industries included industrial chemicals, shipbuilding, and wood household furniture. See Norwood, 1988.

14. The self-employed amounted to about 7.5 percent of nonagricultural employment in 1989 (Mishel and Frankel, 1992, 149).

15. (U.S. General Accounting Office [GAO], 1991, 20). Another 8,300,000 workers reported both 1099 MISC (nonemployee) income and wage income in 1988, a 21.3 percent increase from 1985.

16. Rebitzer and Kochan (1992) also note that contract workers in petrochemical plants experience significant higher accident rates than do permanent employees. They note that host employers are not held responsible for the workers' compensation costs of contract employees; in this way, the workers' compensation system encourages arm's-length relationships between host employers and contract employees. They conclude that although workers' compensation responsibility lies with the states, the Occupational Safety and Health Administration could foster change by holding host employers liable for safety violations relating to contract employees.

17. The Employee Benefits Research Institute estimates that, in 1985, 30 percent of THS workers had no health insurance, whether provided through a job or a spouse (cited in Dillon, 1987, 49).

18. For a useful review, see Appelbaum and Gregory, 1988.

19. Contractors have hesitated to use this law, however.

20. The bill proposed—at the time of writing—would disqualify laid off temps for unemployment insurance benefits if they fail to ask their service for an assignment within five working days of their layoff or fail to accept an assignment regardless of pay level or health risk (Cook, 1994).

21. Indeed, author Tilly benefited from such a provision while a hospital worker and member of Service Employees International Union Local 250, converting from on-call to regular status.

22. Local 250 participated by formulating and raising questions of each bidder at a membership meeting, communicating to local media the service deficiencies of the prior contractor, and formally conveying to county commissioners the local's preferential ranking of bidders. In three out of four such union attempts in the area, the union recommendations were seconded by the county commissioners. The union local was able to convey its concerns to the community and developed a working relationship with the contractor "to be" prior to the start of the contract (Shostak, 1993).

23. Passage of this law was in reaction to the widespread use of employee leasing arrangements by small business owners. The latter would "fire" their employees and could provide their executives and managers with generous pen-

sion plans without having to cover their lower-paid support staff, a practice common in doctor offices, for instance (National Association of Temporary Help Services [NATS], 1992).

24. The two figures are not fully comparable because the Canadian figure is based on weighted mean wages, whereas the U.S. figure is based on median wages. This discrepancy means that the difference between the two countries is probably *understated*.

25. One example is the 1987 agreement between German unions and manufacturing employers to reduce the workweek to thirty-seven hours in metalworking.

26. In a history of the development of internal labor markets in large firms, Jacoby (1987) argues that in the United States more than in other countries, the "social protection" tradition has become embodied in workplace benefits and personnel policies. If it can no longer be carried out in the workplace sphere, it must be so in other spheres.

27. This collective agreement was attained partly under government intimations of strict regulation of the industry in the absence of a national collective bargaining agreement.

28. In addition to multiple forms of representation, the author establishes other key elements of "associate unionism" to include (1) a focus on principles and general goals that are negotiated with the membership; (2) increased internal education and participation; (3) a wider choice of tactics other than the strike; and (4) the formation of extended alliances with interests within and outside the union movement.

3

The Team Concept and the New Global Economy

Stan Luger

During the past twenty years accelerating international economic competition has challenged a number of basic assumptions of American society. For many, the American dream of increasing economic growth and prosperity has become a hollow promise. Wages have stagnated, poverty has increased, and the middle class has shrunk. Meanwhile, *Business Week* reports that young people today may be the first generation in U.S. history whose economic prospects to attain, let alone surpass, the living standards of their parents are unlikely (Bernstein, 1991).

In the decades immediately following World War II, on the other hand, living standards increased as American companies profited handsomely from a system of administered prices, or what Baran and Sweezy characterized as monopoly capitalism (Baran and Sweezy, 1966). Alongside postwar monopoly, capitalism emerged as a stable pattern of labor accommodation. The postwar labor accords were predicated upon a depoliticized labor movement that eschewed social democracy and ceded control over the labor process to management for higher wages and better working conditions.

A fundamental realignment of labor relations is currently under way. American companies are increasingly turning to "cooperation," "teamwork," or "employee involvement" (EI) in order to respond to the challenges of competitive markets. Yet, these changes have not been embraced in some circles of the labor movement. This chapter argues that EI offers an opening wedge for workers to assert their rights to participate in corporate decision making and can be a precursor to a form of workplace democracy. In addition, it is the only way for American companies and workers to meet the challenge of international competition. For these reasons, attempts to cling to traditional postwar "business unionism" will doom unions to virtual extinction (Turner, 1991, 238), lead to the continued decline of U.S.-based corporations, and further undercut the standard of living of large segments of the public.

The importance of these changes and the significance of the opportunity that EI represents are stressed by labor relations expert Charles Heckscher. For Heckscher, the juncture that labor faces today is as pivotal as the one faced by workers in the 1920s and 1930s. He argues that the shift toward EI is as major a change in labor relations as the 1930s shift from craft unionism to industrial unionism (Heckscher, 1988). Beyond the challenges for workers and unions in transforming how work is organized, many also believe that EI is central to the economic prosperity of the nation. For example, Irving Bluestone and Barry Bluestone contend that "the cornerstone in the rebuilding of America lies in reshaping the fundamental relationship between employees and management and creating a new work culture" (Bluestone and Bluestone, 1992, xiii).

WHY EMPLOYEE INVOLVEMENT?

Corporate executives have not shown any willingness to cede control of their companies to workers. In fact, their aim is quite simple: to increase productivity and improve quality. Managers increasingly realize the need to tap the "unemployed self" of the worker, using the knowledge and insight of employees to reorganize the labor process. A few cases of EI have produced productivity improvements exceeding 30 percent, and some studies indicate that the results from change are almost never neutral or negative. Accordingly, a 1989 *Business Week* cover story on the payoffs of teamwork concluded: "When jobs are challenging, workers are committed and perform superbly" (Hoerr, 1989, 62). Other studies, however, show a more complex picture, particularly in light of the methodological difficulties involved in isolating the independent variable of teamwork (Kelly and Harrison, 1992). When teamwork and trust are real, the benefits are substantial; when participation is only a facade, the benefits are not apparent.

Nevertheless, this shift reflects a radical change for American managers and a rejection of scientific management or Taylorism. While many in the business and labor communities hail these efforts, including the National Association of Manufacturers and the *Labor Research Review*, an explicitly pro-union journal, the spread of EI has been slower than expected. A number of dissenting voices among militant workers argue that management's new face is a veiled effort to co-opt workers, speed up assembly lines, and destroy unions. Divisions in the labor movement over EI led the American Federation of Labor and Congress of Industrial Organizations (AFL–CIO) to kill an internal report that called for experiments with cooperation (Bernstein, 1993, 35). Meanwhile, some managers are ambivalent about EI because they fear it undermines their control (Hoerr, 1990, 57).

OPPORTUNITIES AND THREATS OF TEAMWORK

For unions, the struggle over EI must focus on redefining cooperation to include the right to participate in corporate decision making, specifically targeting the traditional prerogatives of management, including product planning and investment. If unions turn the new ideology of cooperation to their advantage and use management's desire to reorganize the labor process to empower workers, the new ideology of teamwork could herald a radical transformation in the working lives of millions of Americans.

Not only do moves toward "cooperation" offer workers an opportunity to participate in decision making, but they also offer the organized labor movement a chance to reverse its decline and expand membership. For many, this position may seen quizzical. How could teamwork, often used to co-opt workers and stifle unionization efforts, be an agent for the rejuvenation of organized labor? The answer is simple: union presence is central to successful EI. Bluestone and Bluestone (1992) argue that a comprehensive survey of existing EI programs shows that those that occur in a nonunion environment rarely succeed. In fact, they conclude that EI usually does not increase productivity or quality, contrary to much of its recent publicity. Only when it is done with real trust and job security—and in the presence of unions—are the benefits apparent. They cite six major reasons that the presence of a union increases the success of EI programs based on a 1989 U.S. Department of Labor forum.

For one, unions help weed out the bad plans up front; for another, they keep companies from reverting to old ways. In addition, they provide a mechanism for addressing a company's glitches in their EI procedures without throwing out the whole participation process, and they tend to be the only practical way to give workers a meaningful voice. Finally, unions have played a crucial role in educating workers to make informed decisions, and have provided a creative power and tension to the process that simply does not exist in a nonunion setting. (173)

In general these insights parallel the conclusions of Freeman and Medoff, who have long argued that union shops are more productive than nonunion shops (Freeman and Medoff, 1984). This information should be broadly disseminated by those trying to organize unions to convince both management and workers of the advantages of a union shop.

With under 16 percent of American workers represented by unions (43 percent of government workers and less than 14 percent of private workers, overall the lowest among Western industrial nations), the crisis affecting labor has reached epidemic proportions. The establishment of a North American free trade zone will only increase the pressure on American workers to be the most efficient and skilled in the world in order to keep their jobs. While the focus of this chapter is the private sector, public sector workers have a similar interest in EI because of the increasing demand to cut government budgets, bring down the deficit, and introduce businesslike "efficiency" to government programs.

POSTWAR LABOR ACCORDS

To understand the opportunities that the new industrial-relations ideology of EI offers, it is first necessary to sketch the outlines of the postwar labor accords. Then it will be possible to show why EI makes it feasible to reopen the issue of worker participation in corporate decision making. During the Great Depression, the tremendous surge of labor conflict centered on the most fundamental workers' issue of all: the right to bargain collectively. The first contracts won were relatively simple and focused on union recognition and wages. World War II interrupted the escalation of labor conflict, but it resurfaced immediately after the war. Coal miners were the first to win pensions and then health care. But the most pivotal battle involved autoworkers. Mike Davis argues that "it was the protracted struggle between autoworkers and General Motors that cast American labor relations in the postwar mold" (Davis, 1986, 111).

General Motors (GM) demonstrated its willingness to bear the costs of a long strike in 1945–46 when it refused to negotiate the prerogatives of management and resisted efforts to "open its books." The company was willing, however, to accept the union's demands for wage increases, which was a small concession for the auto giant in the long run. But GM drew the line there. To preserve its exclusive power over product and finance decisions, GM was willing to hold out for months despite huge pent-up demand for cars. Commentators at the time realized the significance of GM's victory. Of the five-year, no-strike contract signed in 1950, which came to be known as "the treaty of Detroit," *Fortune* magazine wrote: "GM may have paid a billion for peace [but] it got a bargain. General Motors has regained control over one of the crucial management functions in any line of manufacturing—long-range scheduling of production, model changes, and tool and plant investment" ("The Treaty of Detroit," 1950, 35).

With cost-of-living and productivity increases built into future contracts, benefits would grow each year. Workers would be better remunerated for their labor, but management retained exclusive control over essential corporate decision making. For the twenty-five years of the "American century," the strategy of exchanging shop-floor power for monetary benefits was financially beneficial for large numbers of workers. But union successes in obtaining lucrative benefits through business unionism sowed the seeds of labor's current decline. By ceding control over the labor process and corporate planning decisions, workers relied on management to chart the direction of their companies.

While American industries were insulated from the rigors of competition, the dangers of ceding control to management were not fully apparent. Decisions not to reinvest in new plants and equipment and not to pay careful attention to quality did not appear to have a long-term effect on sales or employment. Unemployment at that time was cyclical and short-term. For those unions that negotiated supplemental unemployment benefits, temporary layoffs were not particularly costly. With growing international competition, however, these shortcomings became fatal. With the end of American corporate hegemony, the labor movement found itself unprepared to cope with the changes in the global economy. By neglecting questions of technological change and product development, workers today suffer from the shortsighted and short-term decisions of industry officials ("Mismanagement," 1987).

A striking example of the shortsightedness of American corporate planners is the auto industry's long-standing antipathy toward compact cars. As the nation's largest industry, its failures have sent shock waves throughout the economy. Following World War II, Walter Reuther, longtime head of the United Automobile Workers (UAW), argued that the automakers should produce a small car. Industry leaders summarily rejected this suggestion, because, according to its often repeated dictum, small cars meant small profits. Moreover, the companies were unwilling to discuss the prerogatives of management with workers. Since the Big Three controlled over 90 percent of domestic sales, car buyers had no other choice but to buy large domestic cars. As a result, the automakers reaped large profits and ignored the small car market. In the long run, this decision enabled foreign producers to penetrate the American market with small cars. With a hold on the small car market, Japanese car makers, for example, expanded into other segments of the car market, including luxury vehicles. Today, there are approximately one-quarter fewer hourly auto-workers in the United States compared to the peak year of 1978.

Overall, deindustrialization and plant shutdowns have devastated the ranks of American workers and destroyed the fabric of community for countless others. Thirty percent of the plants in operation in 1969 were no longer in production by the end of 1976. Overall, in the 1970s, 32–38 million jobs were lost due to private disinvestment (Bluestone and Harrison, 1982). In the 1980s, the new jobs created were increasingly in the low-wage service sector, which offers few benefits.

GLOBAL MARKETPLACE

During the 1970s, American companies began to understand that the world had changed. The globalization of market competition brought an end to the hegemony of American manufacturers. Hardly known foreign producers were capturing large segments of various markets from traditional American powerhouses. Initially seen as an aberration that would soon disappear, foreign competition became a fact of life. In response to international competition, American corporate officials attempted to improve the bottom line by pursuing three major tactics simultaneously: squeezing labor, seeking reduced taxes and government regulations, and increasingly turning to what Robert Reich calls "paper entrepreneurialism" (Harrison and Bluestone, 1988, 25; Reich, 1983). By the mid-1980s, workers in virtually every firm with unionized workers negotiated wage concessions; among nonunionized workers givebacks were commonplace as well. Meanwhile, the Reagan administration slashed taxes and regulations, and the largest merger movement in American history was under way. At the same time, American corporations were in the midst of a historic internal transformation. In the 1980s, "firms [were] merged and acquired, downsized, deindustrialized, multinationalized, automated, streamlined, and restructured" (22).

NEW MANAGEMENT "COOPERATIONALISM"

Accompanying these political and corporate changes was the restructuring of the labor process. Many American executives saw the advantages of imitating the production techniques of worker involvement of the Japanese. They were faced with companies that were more efficient and produced higher-quality products with fewer defects. As the Japanese reindustrialized after the war, they developed a radically different form of workplace organization. In large part, this was a response to the circumstances in which they found themselves. Japanese companies lacked the capital of American corporations and did not have as large an internal market, and management's ability to lay off workers was restricted (J. Womack et al., 1990, Chapter 3). As a result, using their labor force more effectively became an overriding concern. In fact, in the most comprehensive study of automobile assembly ever done with full cooperation of the world's automakers, James Womack concludes that central to the "lean" production techniques pioneered by the Japanese are labor–management relations. Instead of a top-down model of control, they used quality circles—discussion groups to elicit suggestions—and EI in general to improve quality and lower costs.

Instituting more "cooperative" forms of labor relations by involving workers in organizing production represents a wholesale rejection of the traditional practices of so-called scientific management. Andy Banks and Jack Metzgar describe scientific management, the dominant method for organizing the labor process in the twentieth century, as the "rigorous and systematic control of all aspects of the labor process" by management. It is "trapped in an extremely top-down, command system of decision-making and communication . . . systematically suppress[ing] information and insight into the organization of work by those who do the work" (Banks and Metzgar, 1989, 6). In addition, as the 1973 U.S. government report *Work in America* noted, "alienation is inherent in pyramidal, bureaucratic management patterns and in advanced Taylorized technology" (Special Task Force, 1973, 22). Moreover, as Harry Braverman incisively demonstrated, Taylorism was, from the beginning, based on power, not science. Its goal was to deskill workers and to solidify management authority over the labor process (Braverman, 1974).

However, controlling the labor process from above adds to the cost of production. It requires closely monitored bureaucratic control. Managers have to keep track of output, organize every detail of production, screen prospective employees for favorable personality characteristics, and keep vigilant watch over workers. In fact, Bowles, Gordon, and Weisskopf observed that between 1948 and 1966, the ratio of supervisory to nonsupervisory personnel in American industry increased by almost 75 percent. "By the late 1960s, nearly twenty cents of every dollar of revenue paid to the private business sector covered the salaries of managerial and supervisory personnel" (Bowles, Gordon, and Weisskopf, 1983, 74). In addition, as managers designed and controlled production, the knowledge of those on the shop floor was lost.

Central to the changes loosely described under the label of EI is quality of work life (QWL). It covers a number of different innovations, including job rotation, job enlargement or horizontal loading (two or more similar jobs are combined), job enrichment or vertical loading (upgrading jobs to include greater skill), and autonomous work groups in which workers have greater collective responsibility for the organization of work. Coupled with these job design changes, QWL programs typically include some form of participation by workers in labor–management committees, described with various labels: employee involvement programs, quality circles, participative problem solving, team management, and labor–management participation (Wells, 1987, 2). QWL is usually presented as beneficial to all involved: workers make decisions and have input into the labor process, and management obtains productivity increases.

By 1987, some form of QWL existed in one of seven of all American firms with over 100 employees, two of five firms with over 500, and between one-third and one-half of all Fortune 500 companies (Wells, 1987, 4). It spread throughout a number of industries, including autos, aerospace, electrical equipment, electronics, food processing, paper, and steel, as well as financial services. By 1987, the range of well-known companies with QWL programs included

Alcan, Alcoa, AT&T, Atlantic Richfield, Bankers Trust, Baxter Travenol Laboratories, Bell Telephone, Bethlehem Steel, Borg-Warner, Citibank, Corning, Dana, Digital,

Eastern Airlines, Eaton, Ebasco Services, Exxon, Fireman's Fund Insurance, Ford, GE, General Foods, GM, Harley-Davidson, Heinz, Hewlett Packard, Honeywell, Hughes Aircraft, Inland Steel, IBM, Kaiser Aluminum, Kroeger's, Lockheed, Manufacturers Hanover, Metropolitan Life, Monsanto, Nabisco, Northrop, Pillsbury, Polaroid, Procter and Gamble, Prudential Insurance, Ralston Purina, Shaklee Corporation, Texas Instruments, 3M, Westinghouse, Weyerhauser, and Xerox.

Despite the rhetoric of participation, American corporations have not suddenly become laboratories of economic democracy. Cooperation, as defined by management, limits the issues with which workers are involved. As Banks and Metzgar note, "[t]he trick for management was to get the productivity increases without losing control" (Banks and Metzgar, 1989, 7). To accomplish this goal, managers developed the ideology of cooperationism. With management-induced participation, emphasis is put on "cooperation," "trust," and "working together," not on the empowerment of workers based on their knowledge and insight or sharing of real power over all corporate decisions.

Cooperationism as an ideology uses the terms *cooperation* and *participation* interchangeably to blur the differences between management-organized EI programs (which co-opt workers to work harder without giving them the opportunity to participate in planning decisions) and union empowering programs (which increase the role of unions in all levels of corporate decision making). Union acceptance of management's version of "cooperation" explains the objections raised by many militant segments of the labor movement. Cooperation is linked to passive unions, bargaining concessions, and management controlled "teams." In fact, two of the leading voices in this movement, Mike Parker and Jane Slaughter, see the recent history of team concept practices as an actual effort to bust unions and increase management's power. Parker rejects the claims associated with teamwork. "Rather than taking a step toward a new era of industrial democracy, the new participatory management schemes constitute an intensification, not an abandonment, of the essence of classical Taylorism" (Parker, 1993, 250).

CRITIQUES OF COOPERATIONALISM

Parker and Slaughter view the team concept as inseparable from its antiunion potential. It cedes power to management, weakens unions, and increases corporate profits, they argue, with only false promises of job security. Since management controls teams, workers actually have less control over their work. Moreover, without the contractual protections of seniority and job classifications, workers are left in a weakened position. Management typically decides which questions the teams consider. Workers are asked only to help fine-tune production or decide how to eliminate jobs. Yet, the language of "teams" implies that workers and managers share the same interest and should work together. But, Parker and Slaughter note, "team concept plants do not even pretend, of course, to give workers control over how *much* work is reasonable, let alone such basic decisions as production levels, technology, or product design" (Parker and Slaughter, 1988, 43). Because the real goal is to get employees to continually increase productivity, Parker labels it "management by stress." "By far the best way to deal with the team concept," Parker and Slaughter conclude, "is to keep it out of your shop altogether" (40).

Fears about the team concept are not groundless. In nonunion shops, the team concept can be an effective antiunion technique. It presents an unparalleled opportunity for "team leaders" to steer discussions against unions and to intimidate workers. Management may realize the explicit antiunion potential that "cooperation" provides and manipulate team discussions to suppress latent union support. Guillermo Grenier observed such an effort firsthand and subsequently documented it in detail (Grenier, 1988).

Unfortunately, Parker and Slaughter present an alternative that is based in the previous political economy. The new global economy forces labor to alter its goals and tactics. It is not an idle warning when management threatens plant shutdowns unless productivity increases. A retreat to a traditional adversarial labor–management conflict can no longer serve the best interests of workers or unions. Attempts to rigidify existing work rules and resist efforts to improve productivity ignore the fact that these practices arose and were successful only because they developed during a time of U.S. economic hegemony. Barry Bluestone stresses this fact, arguing that "no matter how militant its stance [a union] has little power to tame the global marketplace or for that matter reign in the multinational firm that moves its operations abroad or outsources its production to avoid the union" (Bluestone, 1989, 68). Taking advantage of the rhetoric of cooperation, on the other hand, offers workers and unions a viable strategy to battle for control of corporate decisions and to reverse the pattern of business unionism. Thus, militancy is appropriate, but with a new focus.

The form "cooperation" takes determines whether it becomes true worker participation. Since small group processes can be used by management to increase its control over production, it is imperative that unions control such a process. Thus, Banks and Metzgar stress that any shop-floor component of EI should structurally exclude management from a direct relationship with the rank and file. If unions control such a process, "cooperation" can become an empowering strategy for workers. Cooperation needs to be organized through union representatives, allowing unions to collectively control the knowledge and insight of their members. Workers must reject the use of "neutral" consultants to organize teams. They should, instead, use management's desire to increase productivity as an opportunity to obtain wage increases, job security, and union representation as the price for their knowledge and insight (Banks and Metzgar, 1989, 25).

Even GM, long one of the most bureaucratic and entrenched companies in the country, has embraced EI, particularly in its new Saturn division, seen as the most advanced effort at teamwork. Through the UAW, workers were involved in virtually every stage of the design of the physical plant, the technology used in it, the marketing and advertising strategy chosen, and the recruitment and education programs developed to train new workers (Bluestone and Bluestone, 1992, 24). Union representatives also sit on the board of directors. Saturn cars have quickly become the "highest-quality American-made brand" (Woodruff, 1992, 86). Sales have been so strong that Saturn is planning to expand to a second assembly plant. In January 1993, Saturn workers overwhelmingly voted to continue EI programs. Of the 5,200 workers, 3,321 voted in favor of participation, and 1,366 voted against it. However, a few months later, the local president committed to cooperation barely won reelection (Slaughter, 1993, 3).

GOVERNMENT POLICY

Government policy can play a vital role in encouraging EI. It could provide tax incentives for those companies that reorganize firms (Kochan, Katz, and Mower, 1984, 196). Labor–management boards could be established to certify which companies would be eligible and which firms merely paid lip service to worker participation. This would provide an additional role for unions and further strengthen their political power. Tax incentives could also be increased for employee stock ownership plans (ESOPs), particularly those that also had a form of EI in order to facilitate a transformation of workers into formal stakeholders of companies for which they work. From an analysis of both EI and ESOPs, Corey Rosen concludes that "when employee ownership is combined with participative management practices . . . substantial performance gains result. Ownership alone, however, has no clear effect; neither does participative management" (Rosen, 1991, 3). Through their unions, workers should also be legally entitled to sit on the board of directors of their companies, as workers in Germany already do.

In addition, Congress should clarify Section 8(a)2 of the National Labor Relations Act (Weiler, 1990). Its intent was in part to limit the right of managers to unionize and it was the basis for the *Yeshiva* decision denying the right to private college faculty to unionize because they exercise "management" functions.[1] Although EI programs have not been interpreted as transforming workers into managers and thus denying them the right to unionize, the law should be clarified to avoid any confusion. At the same time, however, the prohibition against management dominated worker organizations must continue. Of course, the law needs to be changed to end state right-to-work legislation and to prevent the permanent hiring of replacement workers. Finally, Congress should infuse new life into the

Department of Labor's Bureau of Labor–Management Relations and Cooperative Programs so that it can promote and assist EI efforts.

Key policy decisions for the future of labor–management cooperation are also occurring in the National Labor Relations Board (NLRB), underlining the need for clarification of the National Labor Relations Act. Two recent decisions[2] have struck down company-dominated labor–management committees, one in a nonunion and the other in a union setting. These decisions (as well as other pending cases and possible appeals) suggest that the character of labor–management relations will continue to be a matter of political and policy struggle. The current direction, away from management-dominated cooperation, could be expanded to deny cooperation more generally. Or it could lead to a reemphasis on the importance of unions, as suggested here and by Bluestone and Bluestone. Many have read the NLRB's recent decisions as clarifying little for the future because of the narrow issues involved in the particular cases. Overall, much will depend on the policy positions of Clinton appointees.

A clear indication of the Clinton admininstration's support of EI was made in March 1993, when Labor Secretary Robert Reich and Commerce Secretary Ron Brown announced the creation of a new commission to explore way to increase labor–management cooperation and EI in the workplace. Entitled the Commission for the Future of Worker–Management Relations, it is headed by former labor secretary John Dunlop and includes many of the leading advocates of cooperation. Two other former labor secretaries are on the commission, W. J. Usery and Ray Marshall, as well as former commerce secretary Juanita Kreps. The other members are former UAW president Douglas Fraser; Xerox president Paul Allaire; and a number of academics who have advocated EI: Thomas Kochran, Paula Voos, Richard Freeman, and William Gould. The commission's fact-finding report (Commission on the Future of Worker–Management Relations, 1994) was a springboard for proposals for expanded labor–management cooperation.

EI AND WORKPLACE DEMOCRACY

Team-concept labor demonstrates what advocates of workplace democracy have long argued, that workers have the ability and skills to organize their work sites. This is not to suggest that EI by itself will lead to a radicalized union movement or working class. The lessons Edward Greenberg draws from an in-depth study of workplace democracy in Pacific Northwest plywood cooperatives are instructive. Worker cooperatives did not stimulate attitudes and behavior consistent with "democratic, self-governing socialism or inconsistent with the prevailing social, political, and economic climate in the United States" (Greenberg, 1986, 169). However, Greenberg argues, this is not a reason to dismiss the progressive potential of workplace democracy. In nations where there are forces committed to equality and economic democracy, workplace democracy can have this effect. Thus, the agents of progressive political education, parties, social movements, and organized labor have an essential role if EI is to realize its full potential. In any event, Greenberg notes there is much that is admirable even in the U.S. experience: complex, modern operations can succeed on the basis of egalitarian principles; important aspects of alienation can be overcome; and participation in political life can be stimulated (Greenberg, 1986, 170). Moreover, the centrality of extending democracy to the workplace has long been emphasized by a number of democratic theorists. In an industrialized society, it offers the only meaningful democratic experience for the most people.[3]

CONCLUSION

Business unionism ceded control to management to operate unilaterally in the marketplace. Unions primarily focused on wages and job classifications. This position was enshrined in public policy. In the long run, this stance has proven disastrous for many American workers. By linking their livelihoods to the successful business practices of corporate officials, American workers now suffer from mismanagement and the shortsighted decisions of profit-seeking executives. It is impossible to shut out foreign producers and return to the system of monopoly capital that existed in the 1950s. Moreover, this would maintain the structural exclusion of workers from corporate decision making, leaving intact a system of alienating labor with debilitating psychological and physiological consequences.

Team-concept labor presents a fundamental challenge to the labor movement. Unions must choose between shaping the changes under way in American factories or standing by while management undercuts their power. If the number of job classifications continues to decline as corporations implement team production, and union officials do not organize the teams, the role of organized labor will diminish. Team concept programs and EI offer an opportunity to reopen the long-dormant debate over the prerogatives of management and significantly expand the rights of workers. In an era of global competition, corporate officials need the support and help of workers to succeed in the marketplace. Behind the rhetoric of cooperationism stands the fact that the key to real cost reduction, quality improvement, and productivity increases is genuine participation of workers in organizing and managing the labor process.

Workers must challenge the contractual prerogatives of management and fight to participate in all corporate decisions, including sales and marketing, purchasing, engineering, investment, and long-term planning. As Banks and Metzgar argue, "[I]n this situation, unions need more information, not less, more control over business decisions at the top levels, and a much more organized and cohesive workforce at the shopfloor level" (Banks and Metzgar, 1989, 22). The new labor relations efforts, spearheaded by management's desire to increase productivity and sometimes weaken unions, can be turned around and used as an opening wedge for real worker participation. It does not mean the end of organized labor in the United States, only an end to the narrow business unionism that has for so long dominated the labor movement.

Business unionism is dying of its own accord, having flourished at a time when U.S. corporations dominated the world. As American society faces the challenges of a new global economy and the post-Industrial Revolution, the labor movement should respond by battling for control over corporate decisions. Workers must concern themselves with productivity, or they will continue to see their jobs disappear. They also need to fight for job security and the right to participate in corporate decision making. The current transformation of labor relations will be crucial in shaping the distribution of power within American corporations. Whether American companies emerge as more democratic as a result, or organized labor yields to corporate efforts to co-opt labor at the work site will, in large part, determine the direction of American society for decades to come. The labor movement should focus on the policy changes recommended to maximize the opportunities now available with a Democratic president who appears to be sympathetic to labor–management cooperation.

EI does not guarantee that American companies will meet the challenge of the global marketplace. Increased funds for infrastructure, education, and social services are also needed. However, without a fundamental reorganization of labor–management relations based on full worker participation through unions, the economic decline of our country will likely continue.

NOTES

1. *NLRB v. Yeshiva University* 444 U.S. 672 (1980).

2. *Electromation, Inc.* (309 NLRB 163) and *E.I. DuPont de Nemours & Company* (311 NLRB 88).

3. See, for example, Robert Dahl, *A Preface to Economic Democracy* (Berkeley: California University Press, 1985); Ronald Mason, *Participation and Workplace Democracy* (Carbondale: Southern Illinois University Press, 1982).

III

Policy Issues in the Economy

4

Corporate Restructuring and the Decline of American Unionism

John Russo

Membership in American labor unions has declined dramatically in the last three decades. In the 1950s, union membership constituted 33 percent of the labor force while in 1993 it had fallen below 16 percent. In the private sector alone, the unionization fell to 11.2 percent in 1994, and there are projections that the rate may be as low as 5 percent by the year 2000 (Bureau of Labor Statistics [BLS], 1994; Hoerr, 1991).

Many factors have contributed to this decline, such as market forces (international economic competition, changes in exchange rates, and deregulation), union animus by employers, the changing industry and labor composition, and restrictive labor laws (AFL–CIO Committee on the Evolution of Work, 1985; Troy, 1991). Yet, perhaps the most neglected factor in the decline of unionism has been corporate restructuring.

Corporate restructuring is a catchall term used to describe a myriad of changes in corporate organization, practice, and financing. Broadly speaking, restructuring involves the reorganization of the financial and organizational assets of a corporation. Restructuring is justified as a natural response of the business sector to declining competitiveness and profit rates. However, unionists and critics of restructuring argue that, in practice, it is used for other purposes, which often involve unnecessary reductions in labor costs, capital flight, and union animus (Harrison and Bluestone, 1988).

Most union leaders do not object to corporate restructuring per se. Most accept, in principle, that corporations have the right to organize and shift assets in response to changing economic conditions and competition. Furthermore, it is understood that restructuring can reinvigorate and create new operating efficiencies in poorly managed and depressed enterprises through recapitalization, technological improvements, and the reorganization of production (U.S. Congress, 1987b).

However, union officials, as well as government and community leaders, have raised serious questions over the forms of restructuring involving conglomeration, corporate takeovers, and, especially, leveraged buyouts. Critics argue that these forms of restructuring are largely speculative and have not been economically beneficial in creating new plants, equipment, products, or jobs. In fact, critics suggest that restructuring has contributed significantly to reduced competitiveness, plant closings, deunionization, unemployment, the expansion of part-time jobs and underemployment, and the impoverishment of American workers (U.S. Congress, 1987a, 1986, 1989).

Despite the criticism, the Bush administration was largely insensitive to the criticism of restructuring. It took action only in the area of horizontal mergers (mergers between leading competitors in the same market) where there is evidence of reduced competition. Ironically, cases challenging horizontal mergers have often been lost before pro-business judges appointed during the Reagan administration who believe that most anti-competitive arrangements are short-lived and self-correcting (Greaney, 1991).

THE CONGLOMERATE ERA

In the last four decades, corporations have restructured and grown economically, largely through the use of mergers and acquisitions. In fact, the 1950s and 1960s were characterized by the greatest increase in mergers and acquisitions since the trust-building era in the early 1900s. This period also saw the introduction of a new form of restructuring—the conglomerate merger.

In part, the evolution of the conglomerate merger was the result of the government's antitrust policy. As a consequence of merger and acquisition activity in the 1950s, community and political leaders became worried about increasing economic concentration and potential monopolistic practices. This led to government-sponsored research studies and hearings, which resulted in an increase in antitrust cases (National Commission on Food Marketing, 1964). To avoid antitrust actions, corporations restructured and grew economically through the purchase of other businesses that were unrelated to a company's primary product market. This is known as conglomeration.

Soon, conglomeration became the corporate rage. For example, between 1953 and 1969, Litton Industries grew from a small electronics producer to a multinational conglomerate through the acquisition of 117 separate firms in five different industries. By 1969, Litton Industries had grown into the thirty-fifth largest corporation in terms of annual sales (Craypo, 1975).

Conglomeration was justified on the basis that diversification would protect corporate earnings from the vagaries of individual product markets. That is, a decline in business activity in one market could be offset by activities in another market. The goal was to balance sales and profits among diversified product lines and attain greater financial stability through the cross-subsidization of assets. Further, advocates of conglomeration assumed that managerial and administrative skills were easily transferable between businesses—to effectively manage one enterprise was to effectively manage any enterprise.

Unionists quickly found fault with both the justification and major assumptions associated with conglomeration. In practice, it was shown that, rather than cross-subsidization, conglomerates often "milked" assets and impoverished newly acquired companies. The classic example was the purchase by the Lykes Steamship Corporation of Youngstown Sheet and Tube (YST) in 1970 and the subsequent acquisition of YST by another conglomerate, Ling-Tempco-Vought Steel, in 1979. Lykes and LTV did not recapitalize or technologically improve YST. Rather, they milked the company of its assets and then closed its facilities between 1977 and 1979 (Lynd, 1982). The results were that 6,000 employees lost their jobs, secondary businesses were forced to close or move, bankruptcies skyrocketed, and the value of the Youngstown housing stock dropped as much as 23 percent in one year.

For unions, conglomeration often meant premature plant shutdowns, failed strikes, and a general failure of collective bargaining. The latter was caused by shifts in tactical bargaining strength resulting from conglomerates' operational mobility and financial power (U.S. Congress, 1978). For example, traditional pressure tactics such as strikes are ineffectual against conglomerates because conglomerates can easily subsidize operations from other divisions or shift production to subsidiary companies. Since each conglomerate subsidiary is considered separately under labor law, disputes are largely limited to primary employers (the subsidiary directly involved in the labor dispute), while expansion of strike activities to other subsidiaries can subject the union to secondary boycott provisions and damage claims. Using the conglomerate USX as an example, USX subsidiaries such as Marathon Oil could help subsidize a strike involving another subsidiary like U.S. Steel while, at the same time, steelworkers could not engage in a secondary boycott of Marathon Oil.

Unions also had to deal with operationally inept conglomerate managers who focused largely on financial matters. The penchant for financial wheeling and dealing caused conglomerate managers to encourage diversification away from core technologies and product markets (Hayes and Abernathy, 1980). Their organizational clones, who headed acquired companies, failed to understand the nuances of the production, marketing, and distribution of the products of acquired companies. The result was that employees had little confidence in conglomerate managers, who, they believed, lacked vision, leadership, and the capacity to compete and innovate.

The unions' and employees' complaints about the effects of conglomeration fell on deaf ears both within corporations and in the business press. Not until the 1980s were their charges of managerial incompetence vindicated, as conglomerates attempted to unload earlier acquisitions on the basis of "poor fits," and management was held largely responsible for the general decline in both the productivity and competitiveness of American industry (Magaziner and Reich, 1982; Hayes and Abernathy, 1980).

CORPORATE TAKEOVERS

A new era of restructuring began in the 1980s that was qualitatively and quantitatively different from the mergers and acquisitions of earlier periods. Specifically, this era saw the use of cash as a primary means of acquisition payment, mergers and acquisitions involving some of the nation's largest corporations, and the rise of hostile takeovers and defenses. The most controversial method of corporate restructuring was the leveraged buyout (Auerbach, 1988).

Prior to the 1980s, corporate financial operations were characterized by the selling of equity to stockholders, little corporate debt, paying shareholders dividends, and being largely invulnerable to corporate takeovers. In the 1980s, corporations began to purchase equity, greatly expand their debt (leverage), and pay shareholders the bulk of their return through the company repurchase of stock, and they became increasing vulnerable to takeovers. The dramatic changes in the financial structure of corporations and the growth of takeovers were the result of changes in the tax laws, the reduction in the costs of incurring bankruptcy, that is, changes in bankruptcy law, and the use of high-risk financial instruments such as "junk bonds" (Schoven and Waldfogel, 1990).

The changes in corporate finance facilitated corporate restructuring. Most mergers and acquisitions in the past decade have been friendly takeovers involving the consolidation of corporate resources and operations within the same industry for the purpose of enhancing competitiveness. While most friendly takeovers have been financed using traditional means, many were highly leveraged and have resulted in plant shutdowns and store closings. In some industries, such as the grocery industry, the result has been fewer grocery stores and increasing levels of economic concentration (Scheringer, 1988).

However, what makes the period unique were the rise of unwanted or hostile takeovers by "corporate raiders" and the defenses used to protect against them. Hostile takeovers involve the utilization of borrowed funds to purchase a controlling interest of publicly traded stock, replacing its management, and then restructuring the corporation.

Often the purpose of hostile takeovers is the opposite of conglomeration. That is, a company's assets are seen by corporate raiders as worth more broken up than as a diversified whole. Typically, hostile takeovers involve the purchase of a corporation's public stock using exotic financing schemes, often including the use of high-risk junk bonds. In turn, the new debt-ridden and highly leveraged owners begin to sell various assets (asset-stripping) to repay debt and run the company on a cash-flow basis. In part, the latter is made possible because of the reduction in taxes resulting from the replacement of equity with debt. Stated differently, tax money can be used to pay off the junk bonds, and/or the corporation can be asset-stripped on a piecemeal basis where the corporation is undervalued relative to the sum of its parts.

Hostile takeover defenses involve corporate management attempts to evade corporate raiders through the addition of unwanted debt (poison pills), seeking another buyer more acceptable to management (white knights), the repurchase of company stock at a higher price (greenmail), by selling assets or the purchase of the target company by its management using a leveraged buy-out LBO. For example, the Goodyear Tire and Rubber Company, in order to help finance its takeover defense against Sir James Goldsmith, closed three plants, sold off its valuable Aerospace Division, cut corporate research and development, and laid off almost 6,000 employees. All told, Goodyear incurred a $2.6 billion debt, on which the interest alone is $200 million a year (U.S. Congress, 1986, 219–390; 1989, 4–7).

Economically speaking, the takeover advocates justify the takeover struggle and huge borrowing on the questionable argument that huge debt forces management to be more efficient and that they are freeing trapped capital. At the same time, asset-stripping is often rationalized on the basis that some corporate divisions do not fit with the corporation's main business activity, and their assets can be used productively by another company to compete more efficiently. On balance, advocates argue that takeovers are characterized by the redeployment of assets for greater competitive and economic gain (Icahn, 1989).

As with conglomeration, trade unionists and critics of corporate takeovers provide a starkly different picture of takeovers and leveraged buy-outs. To them, corporate takeovers are nothing more than a shell game run for the benefit of paper entrepreneurs in which there is no economic or social gain for employees and communities (AFL–CIO Executive Council, 1987).

Specifically, critics argue that the "takeover game" has squandered the nation's industrial and economic potential. By taking money (both internal and external capital) away from critical investments in plants and equipment, many corporate takeovers have undermined the nation's competitiveness at a particularly crucial period in its economic history. At the same time, the enormous corporate debt makes the corporations, banks, and holders of junk bonds vulnerable to bankruptcies should there be a recession.

Critics also complain that the fear of a hostile takeover has caused corporate managers to become preoccupied with short-term profitability and protection against takeover. The result is inadequate human and capital resources devoted to research and development necessary for long-term product improvement. Likewise, the preoccupation with short-term profitability has caused corporate managers to "cut corners," and this has resulted in a deterioration in product quality and service.

Equally important, many corporate takeovers have had a devastating impact on employees and union members. As a result of asset-stripping, many employees have lost their jobs, regardless of the competitive position of their company. In the case of successful takeovers, the new owners are not obliged to rehire former employees or honor existing contracts. Consequently, older, high-seniority, full-time employees can be replaced by a new, younger, part-time workforce. When this occurs, unions can do little legally to stop such activities.

Alternatively, highly leveraged companies have asked workers to accept reductions in wages and fringe benefits in order to service the assumed debt. Given the debt structure and potential asset stripping, unions are forced either to accept concessions or, in the case of Eastern Airlines, to push leveraged companies into bankruptcy.

Corporate takeovers have also been used to gut "surplus assets" in employee pension funds (Ghilarducci, 1992). This has two purposes. In the first instance, corporate raiders terminate existing pension plans, use part of the pension funds to purchase annuities for employees at current benefit levels, and pocket the remaining pension funds to finance the takeover. Second, corporations have used employee pension funds to fend off takeovers through stock purchases, debt maintenance, and improved cash flow. Over $20 billion has been stripped from the 2,500 pension plan terminations involving restructuring since 1980. Consequently, workers receive only sixty-five cents for every pension dollar they would have received, had their pension programs not been terminated (AFL–CIO, 1989).

Critique of corporate restructuring can also be heard from the business community. A recent study of 1,005 companies that have been involved in some form of corporate restructuring found that fewer than 50 percent met their goals to reduce expenses, increase profitability, and improve cash flow (Bennett, 1991). That is, corporate restructuring often has been ineffective in reaching stated corporate goals. Other economic studies suggest that many mergers and acquisitions have led to greater inefficiencies and resulted in a significant drain on corporate resources, which have forced corporations to sell off the very companies that were so expensive to acquire (Greaney, 1991).

Likewise, corporate restructuring has been tied to the crisis in the banking industry. It is well understood that the deregulation of the banking industry permitted both commercial banks and savings and loan institutions to become involved in real estate speculation and the purchase of high-risk junk bonds used in corporate restructuring. A result was bank failures at depression levels that are estimated by the General Accounting Office to cost taxpayers as much as $500 billion or $5,350 per household. This will be a clear drag on future economic growth.

The debate on corporate restructuring also is closely tied to the debate over the deregulation of trade. For example, critics of corporate restructuring argue that the North American Free Trade Agreement (NAFTA) is not about issues of commerce between nations, but rather corporate restructuring on a continental scale free from social, economic, and governmental checks and balances. Put differently, NAFTA is an extension of the deregulation and corporate restructuring of the 1980s. Because it provides little protection for labor and environmental standards, NAFTA will probably result in American workers' and their unions' experiencing another round of plant closings, intrafirm reorganization and outsourcing, multitiered wages, and continental whipsawing involving working and environmental conditions (Moody and McGinn, 1992).

UNIONS AND RESTRUCTURING: POLICY CONSIDERATIONS

To briefly summarize, critics argue that there is evidence that corporate restructuring has proven inefficient, a drain on corporate resources, and has contributed to the crisis in the banking industry. At the same time, business restructuring involving conglomeration and corporate takeovers has dramatically undermined traditional union functions over the last thirty years. Restructuring in unionized industries has reduced union bargaining power and subverted its collective bargaining functions. Negotiations involving restructured companies are frequently reduced to holding actions involving defensive strategies to avoid concessions, plant closings, and pension terminations.

More specifically, the cumulative effect on unions is that they are often seen as ineffectual and as offering little to employees. This has contributed to the loss of union morale and membership, as well as to a general decline in the effectiveness of union organizing itself. As unions have been weakened by corporate restructuring, so has the labor movement lost much of its political clout and its ability to represent working-class issues.

Overall, during the restructuring of the last forty years, unions have become increasingly marginalized. In part, this is the result of their failure to find an adequate strategy to deal with the structural changes in corporate organization and functioning. Without a strategy, unions have taken a piecemeal approach in promoting legislation that merely attempts to curb the excesses involving restructuring and corporate takeovers.

Union leaders like Milan Stone of the United Rubber Workers have urged changes in security laws limiting hostile takeovers, limiting the extortion of "greenmail," and reducing severance payments (so-called golden parachutes) to outgoing executives of acquired corporations. Furthermore, Stone has also recommended that companies mounting corporate takeovers provide disclosure statements that include methods of finance, debt-equity ratios, and a five-year plan for plant closings, layoffs, and the termination of operations. Stone also wants to require economic impact statements that estimate lost revenues for local communities resulting from corporate takeovers (U.S. Congress, 1989, 16–20).

James Hatfield, president of the Glass, Pottery, Plastics, and Allied Workers International Union, has urged changes in the tax law that undermine the basis for corporate takeovers. For example, Hatfield has urged a 5 percent tax on all large stock transactions and a special tax on greenmail payments at a rate designed to make such transactions undesirable.

Furthermore, Hatfield suggests legislation that forbids companies emerging from bankruptcies to engage in takeovers for three years. This would affect companies like the Wickes Corporation, which, in 1986, emerged from bankruptcy and attempted a takeover of its former creditor, Owens-Corning Fiberglass. The successful takeover defense by Owens-Corning Fiberglass saddled the company with a $2.6 billion debt (U.S. Congress, 1989, 21–34).

Other unions and the AFL–CIO have proposed legislation that would protect existing collective bargaining agreements and pension plans. The bargaining legislation would require that existing contracts remain binding on corporate successors or new owners for the term of the contract. Consequently, new owners could not breach existing contracts and would be forced to bargain with the existing union. Suggested changes in pension law prevent the use of pension funds or "surplus assets" to retire debt assumed as a result of a corporate takeover (AFL–CIO Executive Committee, 1991, 2–3).

In the area of trade, unions understand that the lack of worker rights is a powerful inducement for corporate restructuring and capital flight. The labor community has been instrumental in passing legislation, such as the Trade and Tariff Act of 1984, that links trade benefits to worker rights. Currently, the Generalized System of Preferences (GSP) and the Overseas Private Investment Corporation (OPIC) link trade and investment incentives to worker rights. These rights include the freedom of association, the right to organize and bargain collectively, the prohibition on compulsory labor, child labor laws, and acceptable conditions of work (minimum wage, hours of work, and safety and health) (Cavanagh et al.,1988).

However, the enforcement of these laws regarding trade and worker rights has been minimal. In the 1990s, organized labor is lobbying the Clinton administration for enforcement of the present laws and their application to NAFTA and for the extension of worker retraining and adjustment assistance for workers displaced by corporate restructuring. Further, organized labor will be joining environmentalists in connecting environmental laws with trade policy. For example, some environmental and labor coalitions are demanding that a corporation's failure to abide by environmental and/or safety and health standards should be considered an unfair trading practice.

While all of the foregoing have merit, none begin to challenge seriously corporate restructuring or the inviolability of corporate decision making. Most certainly, this means challenging the efficacy of managerial rights and replacing it with more democratic and participatory forms of decision making.

For example, unions should explore new approaches, not unlike those used in European countries. European unions and national governments participate in major corporate decision making. In West Germany, managers must negotiate major plant decisions with worker-dominated works councils. In turn, these decisions are reviewed by a corporate board of directors that has been elected by workers. These participatory programs occur within a strict legislative framework that makes it extremely difficult to engage in the types of harmful takeover strategies evidenced in the United States.

To this end, American unions should begin to take advantage of the recent interest in worker participation programs by promoting the democratization of information and decision making. Workers are being asked to develop new production methods, judge the usefulness of new technology, assure quality control, and increase productivity. Workers should carefully consider providing this assistance without more corporate information and participation in decision making that encompasses the introduction of new technology, job design, and investment and restructuring decisions.

At the same time, unions should promote legislation that ensures workers a legal right to participation. For example, in 1976, the Swedish government passed the Act on the Joint Regulation of the Workplace, which largely abolished "management rights" clauses and permitted bargaining over work organization and personnel policy. This could be accomplished by amending the National Labor Relations Act to legally sanction the rights of workers to bargain over investment decisions and the organization of production.

Lastly, unions must gain control over their insurance and pension funds. Not only will this prevent the misuse of "surplus assets" and insurance reserves often used in restructuring, but the control of pension and insurance funds will be an important step toward a democratic investment program and control over investment priorities.

Many may consider these suggested reforms too radical, and, in the American context, they are. Further, these reforms would be difficult to implement, given the current political-economic climate and corporate power. The levels of unemployment and underemployment, the increase in low-wage foreign competition, the threat of technological dislocations, the organizational and financial dominance of global corporations and their control of the media, the ascendancy of individualism, and the decline of traditional progressive social coalitions—all exert socioeconomic and political forces that undermine the movement toward authentic democratic and participatory reforms in the workplace and society.

Furthermore, such changes would have to occur at a time when unions are under employer and political attack worldwide. Even in Sweden, which can boast of 81 percent unionization, a tradition of participatory management and mandated benefits that are the envy of the global labor community, employers' organizations have announced that they will no longer participate in the national boards that govern laws involving work-related activities and are asking for dramatic cutbacks in socialized benefits (Sparks, 1992).

In the 1992 presidential campaign, American labor unions did not insist upon any systemic reforms that would dramatically curb corporate restructuring. Rather, organized labor concentrated on obtaining political promises for ameliorative reforms, such as new retraining programs and assistance. Yet, in such a hostile climate, organized labor must not be satisfied with merely fighting holding actions and instituting incremental reforms, for it is doubtful that its incremental reforms currently under consideration will prevent the misuse of restructuring that has undermined union bargaining power and marginalized unions.

In order to overcome the impact of corporate restructuring, organized labor must begin to provide an alternative vision of economic democracy and organization that challenges private decision making. The key to the implementation of such a vision is building new coalitions with environmental, community, and social justice movements that share labor's concerns about corporate restructuring. Unless private decision making and managerial rights are seriously challenged, and new coalitions are built, it is fair to assume that the assault on organized labor, of which restructuring is a central aspect, will continue unabated.

5

Unions, Finance, and Labor's Capital

Peter Pitegoff

The more responsibility the labor movement assumes, the greater will
be its power.
—Sidney Hillman, Amalgamated Bank, 1927 (Josephson, 1952, 248)

The American labor movement today is in crisis, by any of several measures—declining membership, serious loss of political influence, inability to
stem the tide of jobs overseas (Heckscher, 1988, 3–6). Businesses in the
United States face the challenge of dealing with the new realities of technological change and global competition, and so does organized labor.

Echoing earlier struggles over managerial prerogatives and the scope of
collective bargaining (Atleson, 1983, 111–135), events in recent decades have
dramatized the need for labor attention beyond narrow issues of wages and
working conditions. In the face of widespread industrial disinvestment,
unions have been hard-pressed to protect the job status or employment
future of their members (Harrison and Bluestone, 1988, 48–52; Bluestone
and Harrison, 1982, 78–81). At the same time, the developing labor law has
narrowed the range of bargaining opportunities for unions to affect corporate decisions—the very decisions that result in job dislocations and corporate transformations (Stone, 1988, 74, 86–96). The effectiveness of strikes has
been undermined by growing use of permanent replacement workers, from
Ronald Reagan's assault on the air traffic controllers' union (Professional
Air Traffic Controllers' Organization [PATCO]) early in his presidency, to
the failed strike at Hormel, in Austin, Minnesota, by members of the United
Food & Commercial Workers Local P-9 later in the 1980s (Rachleff, 1990).
Unions, in some instances, cannot even assure retirees that they will receive

the pension and medical benefits already promised by corporate employers (Lynd and Lynd, 1991, 907–12).

To thrive in the coming decades, unions must carve out a new and expanded role. A critical component of an expanded labor role is for unions to exercise the rights of capital and to tread on traditional management prerogatives (Barber, 1987). With an active hand in finance and capital and a greater voice for rank-and-file workers in the process, unions can increase workers' say in shaping the changing workplace and the broader political economy (Hoerr, 1991).

Finance strategies by labor have become more common in the 1980s and 1990s. Investment banking, corporate acquisitions, targeted pensions, employee stock ownership plans (ESOPs)—more and more, these financial artifacts belong to organized labor. In this era of a global economy, of capital mobility and shuffling corporate ownership, union activity has broadened dramatically to encompass issues of corporate finance and capital control. From collective bargaining in the managerial domain to worker ownership, from labor banks and insurance companies to strategic investment of pension funds, the interplay of labor and capital is changing as the border between them opens.

This chapter introduces labor's forays in finance. For more than a century, American unions have ventured, from time to time, into the realm of capital, from worker cooperatives in the 1890s to the labor banking movement of the 1920s. Most of these efforts have been isolated and short-lived, with a few notable exceptions. It remains unclear whether today's wide array of financial activities by unions signals a new direction for the labor movement, but the scale and sophistication of finance institutions with a labor perspective suggest more than simply a momentary diversion.

After a brief historical note, the following pages describe some of labor's finance institutions and capital activity, beginning with pension funds as the largest single source of capital with potential for strategic investment directed by labor. Next is a description of selected initiatives in targeted investment by pension funds, both directly and by intermediary institutions. These intermediaries, such as union-initiated labor banks and a growing community of investment bankers and advisers, manage extensive pension investments and other worker or union funds and are a repository for much of labor's learning in finance. Finally, this chapter analyzes the surge of worker ownership of businesses since the 1970s and the evolution of enterprise forms that ultimately integrate labor and capital.

These developments raise a series of challenging questions. What happens when labor institutions essentially become capital institutions? Can an enterprise focused on asset value and the bottom line really retain a "labor perspective" over time? Will labor's finance activity be driven primarily from the top down, or will it reflect the views and meet the needs of rank-and-file workers? The answers rest with organized labor, faced with the challenge of building new, more accountable financial institutions as an integral part of today's labor movement and committed to the interests of working people.

HISTORICAL NOTE

The history of business and finance by organized labor in the United States stretches back to the eighteenth century. Striking carpenters in Philadelphia, for instance, formed a cooperative enterprise in 1791 to compete with local employers. In the 1830s, Philadelphia cabinetmakers, tailors, hatters, and saddlers operated in cooperative enterprises (Grossman, 1945). In the late nineteenth century, American labor organizations explored worker ownership nationally. The Knights of Labor, for instance, sponsored the development of worker cooperatives as a direct challenge to the employer/employee system, assisting in the creation of more than 200 small, worker-owned businesses (Grob, 1961). Small in scale, however, and with limited access to capital, these early ventures were unable to survive rapid technological changes or economic downturns (Shostak, 1991, 229).

A similar fate befell the short-lived "labor banking" movement of the 1920s, with few labor banks surviving the subsequent depression. Today, while new union banks have emerged, only two of the three dozen union-owned banks formed in the early 1900s still exist—the Amalgamated Bank of New York, founded in 1923 and owned by the Amalgamated Clothing and Textile Workers Union (ACTWU), and the Brotherhood Bank and Trust, founded in Kansas City in 1924 and now roughly 40 percent union-owned (Noble, 1992).

The term *labor bank* or *union-owned bank* refers to a bank owned by some combination of a union, its members, and, more recently, its pension or benefit funds. The rationale for the early labor banks was twofold—first, to provide access and affordable services to working people and, second, to support the union movement. Unlike conventional banks, labor banks in the 1920s enabled low- and moderate-income workers to open interest-bearing accounts, obtain inexpensive loans, and even transfer funds to family members overseas (Brown et al., 1929, 55). The Amalgamated Bank of New York, for example, served numerous immigrant workers by handling about 199,000 remittances to foreign countries in 1924 alone, totaling almost $7 million (Grant, 1983).

In practice, labor banks were best known for these consumer services, the banking activity most immediate and obvious to working-class depositors. But the origin of these banks was also explicitly strategic. On occasion, they would provide loans to employers whom they deemed friendly to labor, even stepping in with financing to rescue firms forsaken by conventional bankers and thus to save jobs of union members. Foreshadowing today's targeted investing by labor institutions, some labor banks of the 1920s invested directly in business development by and for union members.

That era of labor finance also gave rise to the Union Labor Life Insurance Company (ULLICO), founded in 1925 pursuant to resolutions adopted by the American Federation of Labor (AFL) at a special conference that year on insurance. The next year, the company sold three-quarters of a million dollars of capital stock to sixty international unions, six state federations of labor, thirty-four city central labor unions, 240 local unions, and 361 individual trade unionists. It issued its first individual life insurance policy in 1927. ULLICO is still thriving today, with an array of services geared to union members, labor organizations, and pension and benefit plans (UL-LICO, 1990).

The largest segment of "labor's capital" has emerged in pension funds. Employer-based pension mechanisms have existed in the United States for over a century. The American Express Company sponsored the first major industrial pension plan in 1875. Other large companies followed suit in the subsequent decade, and pension funds grew substantially just prior to World War I (Ghilarducci, 1992, 14).

During the early 1900s, a system of trade union pension plans, financed primarily by union dues, emerged separately from private corporate plans. The first union pension plan was formed in 1900 by the Pattern Makers of North America, followed by the bricklayers, carpenters, sheet metal and iron workers, electrical workers, railroad workers, and printing trade unions. The depression had a devastating impact on these pension plans and was a factor in the labor movement's support for federal Social Security. One lasting significance of this group of union plans, though, was that it formed the pattern for multiemployer plans that emerged on a larger scale in the 1950s (Ghilarducci, 1992, 30).

The Internal Revenue Code recognized pension plans in 1926, and Social Security was established in 1935. Not until the 1940s, though, did explosive growth of pensions signal a start to the formation of the huge pension regime of today. Immediately following World War II, employer-funded health, welfare, and pension plans expanded substantially, with unions administering a growing number of plans for their members. In 1947, however, the Taft–Hartley Act halted this nascent growth of union-controlled benefit plans funded by employers. The act prohibited employer payments to certain employee benefit trust funds unless, among other requirements, the funds were jointly administered by the union and the employer. Congressional debate at the time reflected some government resistance to benefit plans solely controlled by unions.

Multiemployer pension plans established after the 1947 Taft–Hartley Act were controlled jointly by boards of employer and union trustees. With an overriding goal of maintaining a safe investment portfolio to preserve the workers' retirement benefits, unions tended to defer to professional trust managers, often banks or insurance companies. A handful of unions—notably, the Amalgamated Clothing and Textile Workers, the International Ladies Garment Workers, the Teamsters, and the Mineworkers—looked beyond just yield and stability. They played an active role in managing pension funds for strategic purposes, foreshadowing today's activist targeting of pension funds by labor.

Single-employer plans were controlled entirely by management, despite attempts by the United Automobile Workers and other unions for joint control. Collective bargaining in single-employer plans focused essentially on benefit levels and sufficient funding of plans. After a period of union–management struggle over formation, funding, and form of pensions, bargaining over pensions reached relative stability in the 1950s. Despite continuing disagreement over the issue of control, employers generally funded the plans and received substantial tax benefits for plan contributions. Although the American Federation of Labor and Congress of Industrial Organizations (AFL–CIO) advisory council recommended in 1954 that unions negotiate for participation in pension decisions, most industrial unions accepted employer management of the details of pension accounting, investment, and distribution (Ghilarducci, 1992, 29). More recent growth in public sector employment and public employee pension funds created new opportunities for labor and public influence over pension investment.

FINANCE WITH A LABOR PERSPECTIVE

"The battle has shifted from the pavement to the boardroom," announced Jack Sheinkman, president of the Amalgamated Clothing and Textile Workers Union, referring to efforts by Health-Tex Inc. employees. In early 1991, pressure on banks by rank-and-file workers contributed to the survival of Health-Tex, at least temporarily, buying time for the clothing manufacturer to arrange a financial rescue by another firm (Swoboda, 1991, L1).

The late twentieth century has witnessed a resurgence of capital strategies by organized labor, changing with the times. Among these strategies has been the formation or expansion of labor's finance institutions. As in the 1920s, many critics charge that these activities divert valuable attention and resources from organizing and collective bargaining and are likely to undermine the commitment of union leaders to working people (Slott, 1985). Yet, while unions must continue to organize, they cannot opt out of the fundamental financial analysis and practice that shape the new labor–management environment (Weston, Whelan, and McBarnet, 1993, 95–97).

Many of labor's financial institutions resemble conventional firms—banks, insurance companies, pension and benefit funds with diversified portfolios, investment banking firms, and corporate businesses with ESOPs. The challenge for labor is to keep these institutions focused on broader goals and, in the process, to develop business expertise from a labor perspective. The attributes that distinguish these labor ventures from conventional financial entities are essentially threefold—the definition of their constituency, the nature of their control structure, and the strategic use of their capital.

A labor perspective is reflected in the definition of an organization's constituency, such as a bank or insurance company that concentrates its services on the needs of working people or a pension fund operated to benefit retired workers. More fundamentally, it is reflected by who controls an entity. Many a worker-owned company, for example, is technically owned by an ESOP trust and controlled not by the employees but by trustees who view the employees as passive constituents or beneficiaries of the trust. On the other hand, some worker-owned companies are also controlled, in whole or part, by their employees, with greater potential to influence the company operation and policy. Pension funds, too, are administered by independent trustees, although labor can exercise some influence over a fund's investment portfolio.

A labor perspective entails the strategic use of such institutions for affirmative purposes, from job creation and economic development to demanding corporate responsibility toward workers and communities. Labor's capacity in finance is built upon increasing union and worker control of business organizations and upon the sophisticated expertise required to translate that control into stable and accountable financial institutions.

Pension Potential

Finance from a labor perspective requires finance. Thus, pension funds are central to any examination of labor's finance institutions. Pension assets, essentially deferred compensation of millions of workers, total over two and one half *trillion* dollars (Ghilarducci, 1992, 118; Silvers, 1992, 44). Pension funds own about 25 percent of all stock in publicly traded corporations, a number that the federal Department of Labor predicts will reach 40 percent by the year 2000 (Zanglein, 1991, 772). Clearly, at that scale, those who control pension funds hold the potential for enormous influence over the economy and its impact on workers. From labor banks to worker buyouts, pension capital helps drive many of labor's new forays in finance with "targeted investments."

In May 1991, the AFL–CIO Executive Council adopted a policy statement on pension fund investments that includes an assertion that "all workers are entitled to equal participation with employers in the administration and investment of pension fund assets" (AFL–CIO, 1991). Yet, for single-employer plans in the private sector, workers seldom have a say in their pension fund operation. Pensions are administered by trustees or boards of trustees "for the benefit" of the workers, not "by" the workers, and the law does not require employers to have worker or union representation on single-employer pension trustee boards. Trustees are ordinarily professional money managers, often from large commercial banks or insurance companies. Unions can attempt to influence pension funds through collective bargaining, but attempts at negotiating joint union–management representation for single-employer plans have met stiff resistance from employers. In June 1989, Congressman Peter Visclosky (Democrat from Indiana) introduced the Employee Pension Rights Act, calling for employee representation on the boards of trustees for single-employer pension funds. Although reported to the House of Representatives by the Budget Committee, the Visclosky amendment was killed on the House floor and was never enacted (Visclosky, 1989).

Nonetheless, particularly since the 1970s, organized labor has battled over control of pension fund assets, including efforts to achieve union representation in single-employer plans. The more fertile ground today for union influence over pension investment is in multiemployer pension plans. These "Taft–Hartley Plans" typically are sponsored by a union and negotiated with several employers to cover workers in a given industry. By law, Taft–Hartley Plans must be administered jointly by employees and employers.

Similarly, public sector pension funds, which today constitute one-third of total pension assets or almost one trillion dollars, present opportunities for labor participation. The vast majority of public pension plans are administered at the municipal or county level for local government employees, although substantial assets are held by state employee plans. While administrative and governance structures vary widely among the many plans, decision making in public sector pensions tends to be more accessible than in private plans. In addition to collective bargaining, public employees can seek election to boards of trustees of some public funds or can organize collective voter action to influence pension investments. Highly publicized struggles for control of state pension plans, such as the California Public Employee Retirement System (CALPERS), led to a statement by the AFL–CIO Executive Council in early 1992 sounding an alarm about "power grabs" by state and local governments. "Their tactics," stated the council, "include . . . changes in the structure of public employee pension funds that weaken the role of employees" (AFL–CIO Executive Council, 1992).

Even in public sector or jointly administered plans, pension fund trustees are constrained by law in their ability to target investments. A pension fund is ordinarily structured as a trust, a separate legal entity that holds assets for the retirement benefits of workers covered by the pension plan. The workers have no say in the administration of the fund. Instead, a trustee or trustee board has the fiduciary responsibility to operate the fund for the exclusive benefit of the workers, or "participants." Strict standards for this fiduciary duty are defined for private pension funds in ERISA, the Employee Retirement Income Security Act, first enacted in 1974 to protect the interests of pension plan participants. Among these fiduciary standards is prudence in investment, including diversification to minimize the risk of large losses. Although public employee pension funds are not governed by ERISA, analogous fiduciary duties are imposed by common law, state statutes, and certain tax law constraints.

The fiduciary standards of ERISA severely limit trustees in the use of private pension funds for union goals, particularly if such collateral goals undermine the financial return on fund assets. Fiduciary standards for public employee funds impose similar, though slightly less stringent, limitations on trustees. Until recently, pension trustees generally administered pension fund investments without reference to social and political goals of labor, and union leaders tended to defer to trustees' cautious adherence to the prudence rule (Burroughs, 1985, 58).

In the late 1970s, however, organized labor responded to dramatic reports that pension funds were undermining union goals, from pension investments in unsafe or nonunion businesses to financing multinational corporations that were shifting jobs overseas. Earlier, in the late 1950s, some analysis of the potential of pension fund ownership was published and debated (Harbrecht, 1959; Tilove, 1959). But a combination of circumstances two decades later sharpened the issue. First, total pension assets had grown enormously. Second, employers were making increasing concession demands, often coupled with their moves toward union–management cooperation schemes that, at least by logic, might extend to pensions. Third, high unemployment and numerous plant closings suggested unmet social needs that might be addressed with pension investment, particularly when traditional union activities were failing to represent workers adequately in an increasingly complex political economy (MacDonald and Bingham, 1986, 124). In addition, by the 1980s, organized labor's accumulated experience in finance suggested both the potential and capacity for greater union participation in pension control and investment.

The potential for pension investment was underscored for labor, ironically, by management pundit Peter Drucker in his 1976 book describing a new brand of "pension fund socialism" (Drucker, 1976). Responding from a labor perspective, Randy Barber and Jeremy Rifkin in 1978 published a book documenting antiunion uses of pension funds and arguing for the potential of pension fund control (Barber and Rifkin, 1978). With vigor, organized labor accepted the challenge posed by Barber and Rifkin. Since then, union leaders increasingly have pressured pension trustees to avoid antilabor investments and to target investments that support labor.

Protecting the retirement benefits of pension participants is still paramount, as reflected in the legal dictates for fiduciaries to diversify investment, to manage assets with prudence, and to act for the exclusive benefit of plan participants. But pension investments also can be targeted for the benefit of union members, so long as such investment is not at the expense of overall performance of the pension fund (Wessel, 1986). The AFL–CIO Executive Council, in its 1991 policy statement, provides the contours of a labor perspective in pension fund management: pension trustees must balance financial factors (risk and return) and other direct interests of the pension beneficiaries with such broader factors as "promotion of local economic development," "job creation," "ensuring a safe and healthy environment," and "promotion of corporate responsibility to shareholders, employees and communities in which the company operates" (AFL–CIO, 1991).

How, then, has labor used its increasing pension clout? One way has been through pension trustees' participation in the governance of corporations, where the trustee acts for the pension as an institutional investor in a corporation. A second way has been through targeted investment of pension funds.

As part owner of a corporation, a pension fund has certain limited rights to a voice in corporate governance, access to information, and standing in litigation. Pension trustees can exercise their shareholder rights to influence corporate governance by sponsoring shareholder resolutions, voting their shares in resolutions and in election of directors, or simply negotiating agreements with management in the shadow of their shareholder power. Thus, for instance, the California Public Employees Retirement System, the largest public pension fund, convinced General Motors in 1991 to amend its bylaws to require a majority of its directors to be independent and convinced Avon Products, Inc., to hold semiannual meetings with its major institutional investors to discuss corporate performance and governance (Zanglein, 1991, 774).

Similarly, ACTWU worked with British public pension funds to influence North American activities of Marks & Spencer, a large British retail company. ACTWU represents workers at Brooks Brothers, a Marks & Spencer subsidiary, and pressured the company to improve management of its North American operations, with the explicit intention to introduce a resolution on the subject and to solicit proxies for voting at the company's annual meeting in London (Silvers, 1992, 43, 47). A 1991 ACTWU shareholder resolution at JC Penney strengthened the company's affirmative action policies, while a concurrent initiative at Sears Roebuck resulted in termination of Sears's sales of products made by prison labor in China (Industrial Union Department, 1992, 2). Here, with just a foot in the door, the shareholder role gives the union and its pensions access to corporate decision making and the legitimacy to affect corporate policy.

In large companies, internal corporate policy activity often takes the form of proxy fights, where management solicits proxies from thousands of shareholders. Shareholders ordinarily give management their proxies, with the right to vote according to management's preferences, although shareholders may direct their proxies to be voted differently. In certain circumstances, by law, management must include shareholder proposals with its distribution of proxy solicitation materials, and this has been the vehicle for growing shareholder activism since the 1970s. Pension funds as institutional investors are also in a position to influence corporate control contests. Thus, for example, players in recent takeover battles at Lockheed and NCR actively pursued the support of pension fund shareholders (Zanglein, 1991, 776; Stevenson, 1990).

The potential influence of pension funds as institutional shareholders in large corporations is part of a broader debate about corporate governance. In recent years, this debate has increasingly taken into account a variety of "stakeholders," including employees, who are affected by corporate decisions (Stone, 1991). The influence of stakeholders can take a variety of forms, including shareholder rights of institutional investors and statutory rights of workers and communities in plant shutdowns (Kerson and LeRoy, 1989). Yet, in large, publicly traded corporations, pension trustees' participation as shareholders is somewhat diffuse. Increasing activism by institutional shareholders, including pension funds, demonstrates the potential for strategic influence in corporate governance. Targeted investment, however, has been a more concrete and dramatic mechanism in recent years for strategic use of pension funds, using a portion of retirement funds directly in starting or supporting enterprises.

Targeted Pension Investment

Through the 1980s, Local 675 of the International Union of Operating Engineers in Ft. Lauderdale, Florida, pursued an aggressive strategy of targeted investment. Frustrated by the caution and poor performance of their pension managers and outraged by discoveries that their pension fund helped to finance such antiunion activities as the construction of the National Right-to-Work Committee headquarters in Virginia, the union leaders and pension trustees essentially redirected the pension investments to benefit union members and the local community. The small pension fund set up a program to make affordable mortgages available to union members and financed the development of Park Central, an office park with thirty buildings constructed with union labor and eventually leasing new headquarters to the union. Through Park Central and other construction projects, according to one estimate, Local 675 leveraged over $400 million of construction work for local building trades members (Banks, 1988, 39, 43).

Dennis Walton, as the business manager of Local 675 and chairman of the pension fund's board of trustees, was persistent in his mission to use the fund to create union jobs. The federal Department of Labor challenged Local 675 in 1981, arguing that the fund's trustees violated prudence rules and prohibited transaction rules of ERISA. The dispute wound its way through several years of federal court litigation in Florida, resulting in a federal district court decision in 1985 in favor of the union and pension fund officials (*Donovan v. Walton*, 1985).

Celebrated as a labor victory, the court decision in *Donovan v. Walton* held essentially that the pension fund investment in real estate, designed to create union jobs, was permissible provided that the trustees acted prudently (Shostak, 1991, 246; Chernoff, 1985). The precise meaning of "acting prudently" in the pension context entails a complex array of substantive and procedural guidelines, which nonetheless provide some room for discretion in targeting investments. That is, pension trustees can make investments that further union goals, but only with diligent investigation and careful analysis to produce adequate return on investment.

The saga of Local 675 and Dennis Walton illustrates one way that pensions and union funds can be targeted. It also demonstrates the potential downside of targeted investment, since capital control comes with risk. In an ironic twist, the labor-sponsored insurance company ULLICO initiated foreclosure proceedings in June 1990 against the operating engineers' pension fund as owner of real estate on which ULLICO held a mortgage. This legal action, followed soon after by a Department of Labor challenge to replace the pension fund trustees, signaled the end of several years of targeted investment by the fund (Chernoff, 1990, 1). By 1990, the local real estate investments had soured. Although diversified by product type and among five different properties, nearly all of the fund's assets were invested in real estate in one local geographic market. While the dispute continues, the Pension Benefit Guaranty Corporation is likely to take over the plan (Chernoff, 1991,1).

With the experience of the Operating Engineers Local 675 and other targeted pension investments, unions are seeking the appropriate balance of prudent management and social goals. While the Operating Engineers in Florida broke new ground in targeted pensions, other efforts continue and appear to be lasting. The Sheet Metal Workers National Pension Fund has a diversified portfolio of investment in companies that will employ its members, including investment in research and development in new solar energy technology (Bernstein, 1988). The Michigan State Retirement System is authorized to invest up to 5 percent of its assets in small business or venture capital firms, in order to enhance the state retirement system and expand jobs. Its venture capital portfolio exceeds $700 million, with a return on investment of 20–25 percent and roughly 3,500 jobs created (Zanglein, 1992, 116–17, 132).

Housing finance has been a long-standing focus of organized labor, dating back over four decades to the formation of the United Housing Foundation by a consortium of unions. This focus continues today, as with the California Building Trades' Pension Fund commitment of over $250 million to construction projects built with union labor (Shostak, 1991, 262). This emphasis on housing flows from goals of providing affordable housing to working people, creating union jobs in construction, and making investments that can be secured by real estate.

Operating since 1964, the AFL–CIO Housing Investment Trust (HIT) has pooled close to $650 million, much of it from pension funds, to invest in unionized housing construction. In 1987, the AFL–CIO expanded HIT's scope with formation of the Building Investment Trust (BIT) to invest in commercial and industrial real estate projects. The combined assets of the HIT and BIT programs total almost $1 billion (Coyle, 1993, 7). These HIT and BIT investments range from large-scale projects such as construction of a $5.8 million hotel complex in Taos, New Mexico, to home mortgage financing, such as the 1991 ProLoan program in St. Louis, and funding for renovation of inner-city rental housing in Washington, D.C. (Industrial Union Department 1991). In 1993, the AFL–CIO launched the National Partnerships for Community Investment program, designed to develop housing and commercial property in sixteen major metropolitan areas. Targeted toward inner-city neighborhoods, the National Partnerships initiative has projected investment of half a billion dollars in pension funds and creation of thousands of jobs and housing units over the course of five years.

In Boston, the B & L Non-Profit Housing Co., sponsored by the Bricklayers and Laborers unions, directs pension investment in certificates of deposit in an area bank. The certificates of deposit are federally insured, while the bank, U.S. Trust, provides construction financing at its own risk for local housing development that employs union members and provides affordable housing (Banks, 1988; Zanglein, 1992). This use of intermediary institutions—here, the nonprofit housing company and the local bank—can be a means for community-based pension investment. Rather than local investment directly by such a large financial institution as a pension fund, the use of local intermediaries is often more efficient and locally accountable. Thus, the targeted investment of pensions has helped generate a wider array of financial institutions related to labor—banks, investment funds, worker-owned businesses, and a growing community of experts in business and finance.

These financial institutions, in many cases, have arisen independently of any pension capital but share many of the same social goals and structural attributes as targeted pensions. Over time, these separate institutions may constitute a locally based infrastructure of organizations serving as a vehicle to channel pension capital to communities. For instance, driven by the need for housing assistance to low- and moderate-income union members in Boston, Local 26 of the Hotel, Restaurant, Institutional Employees and Bartenders Union formed the Union Neighborhood Assistance Corporation (UNAC). A separate nonprofit organization, UNAC is a community-based housing assistance effort that links jobs with housing, union members with community groups, and millions of employer and union dollars with affordable housing development. UNAC uses private and public funds to create new units of housing for union members and community residents. It also provides educational, financial, referral, and counseling services to participants, including a housing assistance trust fund (Davidson, 1990).

This multiemployer housing trust fund arose from a 1988 contract that Local 26 negotiated with Boston's unionized hotels. The trust fund is funded by a five-cents-per-hour contribution by employers. It is jointly administered by employer and employee representatives, providing participants with financial assistance for housing, such as funds to reduce down payments on home purchases, funds to assist in initial rental costs, or collateral for loans (Shostak, 1991, 251; Zanglein, 1992). In fact, the efforts of Local 26 helped to precipitate a change in the Taft–Hartley Act (Section 302[c][7]), explicitly permitting unions and employers "to bargain over the establishment and administration of trust funds to provide financial assistance for employee housing."

Labor Banks and Other Intermediaries

"We have to learn *management* as well as ownership," explained labor leader Sidney Hillman in 1927. "That is where labor banking comes in. . . . We have got to find a way for the introduction of democracy into industry" (Josephson, 1952, 320).

The Amalgamated Bank of New York, sixty years after Hillman's statement, apparently has heeded his advice, for its very survival as a successful banking institution is evidence of management savvy. At the same time, Amalgamated reaffirms its labor orientation within its cautious approach. For instance, it offered a variety of special services, including a loan program, for striking workers at NYNEX and at Eastern Airlines in 1989. In 1987, Amalgamated helped three New York locals of the Bridge, Structural and Ornamental Iron Workers Union to make some of their pension fund assets available as low-cost home mortgages for their members. In all, over $3 billion of Taft–Hartley retirement funds are managed by Amalgamated, suggesting huge potential beyond simply providing financial services geared to the needs of working people (Zemke and Schaaf, 1989).

In 1992, Amalgamated Bank announced formation of the Longview Fund, which will invest in the equity of the largest corporations. Much of the earlier social investing focused on negative screens, divesting or avoiding investment in bad corporate citizens, such as those that pollute the environment or treat their workers unfairly. The Longview Fund, instead, will invest in any large company and engage in active shareholder advocacy within these companies in accordance with AFL–CIO guidelines (Industrial Union Department, 1992, 2).

Harking back to the labor banking movement of the 1920s, a half dozen new union-owned banks or savings and loan associations have emerged in the late 1970s and 1980s. These include the First Trade Union Savings Bank in Boston, the United Labor Bank of California, Union Bank & Trust in Minneapolis, the Union National Bank of Colorado in Denver, Union Savings Bank in Albuquerque, and Union Savings and Loan in Phoenix. They join the Amalgamated Bank of New York, now in its seventh decade, in a reemerging cluster of union-sponsored banking institutions (Zanglein, 1992).

"Labor banks" are commercial institutions, savings banks, or savings and loan associations owned by a combination of pension funds, union funds, and/or union members. With the growth in pension funds, the new labor banks are owned, in substantial part, by multiemployer pension funds. First Trade Union Savings Bank, founded in 1987, is wholly owned by the Massachusetts State Carpenters Pension Fund and the Massachusetts State Carpenters Annuity Fund. United Labor Bank of California, acquired in 1991, is owned principally by the northern and southern California affiliates of the California Carpenters Pension Trust and by union members. In contrast, the older banks are owned substantially by unions themselves—Amalgamated (1923) is owned by staff funds of ACTWU, and Brotherhood Bank and Trust (1924) is 40 percent owned by staff funds of the International Brotherhood of Boiler Makers, Ship Builders, Blacksmiths, Forgers and Helpers (Industrial Union Department, 1986, 1). The difference in ownership is significant, in that the substantial pension fund involvement in the newer institutions implicates ERISA constraints on lending practices, from prudence and diversification requirements to prohibited transaction provisions. Still, with careful attention to these ERISA mandates in structure and operation, labor banks can integrate strategic social goals in administering their capital (Noble, 1992).

Like their predecessors, these labor banks offer consumer services to working people, from low-cost banking to financial counseling and loans. Moreover, some are investing their capital strategically with a labor focus, such as the First Trade Union Savings Bank's focus on the housing needs of the local community, including local commercial and real estate lending (Industrial Union Department, 1987).

These institutions, at least in conventional terms, are not typical banks nor typical labor organizations. With such a mix of goals, they grapple with tension between the demands of labor and capital in a single institution. The inherent ambiguity of a labor bank presents a challenge for the newer banks, a challenge met somewhat successfully by Amalgamated Bank of New York.

Of similar vintage to Amalgamated, the Union Labor Life Insurance Company (ULLICO) today has expanded well beyond simple life insurance policies, to a wide variety of insurance products offered by an affiliated group of corporations—a holding company with three insurance providers, an administrative services firm, and a trust fund advisory firm. At the end of 1990, its consolidated assets totaled almost $2 billion, and its annual revenue was over half a million dollars.

This family of corporations hardly looks like a labor institution, and, in fact, ULLICO resembles conventional insurance companies in many ways. How is it any different from Aetna or All-State? ULLICO's focus, much like the labor banks, was, and remains, affordable service to unions and working people, with a certain caution that limits strategic investment of capital. It differs from other insurance companies in its ownership structure, its market niche, and a small portion of its investment portfolio. In each of these three attributes and explicitly in money management and investment assistance to pension trustees, ULLICO is a vehicle for further development of labor's business expertise and practice.

Ownership of ULLICO is confined primarily to labor organizations and their members. Stockholders cannot sell their ownership shares without first offering them to the company for purchase at twenty-five dollars per share. In practice the company purchases all such shares and resells them at twenty-five dollars per share to labor organizations or individuals affiliated with the labor movement.

The union insurance company focuses its services primarily on Taft–Hartley benefit trusts, jointly managed by labor and management, in the health and pension area. By knowing the world of organized labor—unions' resources, abilities, limitations—ULLICO presumably is better able than conventional companies to target labor's particular needs. Thus, in the late 1980s, for example, a number of union leaders approached the company and complained that insurance carriers were abandoning the trustees of Taft–Hartley benefit plans. In a short time, ULLICO became the leading underwriter for fiduciary liability insurance in the Taft–Hartley market (Maher, 1991).

To a limited degree, ULLICO has targeted its investment for the direct benefit of union members. In 1977, it launched the J for Jobs Mortgage Account to channel pension fund investments into union-built construction. Endorsed by the AFL–CIO and the Building and Construction Trades Department, the J for Jobs program promises first mortgages to developers of income-producing properties. This provides the mortgage commitment, prior to construction, that a developer needs to obtain construction financing. A condition of the mortgage commitment is that all construction must be performed by contractors and subcontractors that have collective bargaining agreements with unions affiliated with the AFL–CIO Building Trades. Thus, touts a ULLICO brochure, participating pension plans earn a competitive return, union contractors get business, and union workers are employed (ULLICO, 1990).

With a more populist hue, the Crocus Fund in Winnipeg, Manitoba, offers a Canadian model of a labor-initiated finance institution focused strategically on local economic development (Kreiner, 1992). Created in 1993 by the Manitoba Federation of Labour, the Crocus Fund is a venture capital corporation designed to promote job creation and retention, support local ownership of businesses, and provide opportunity for investment and supplemental retirement benefits for Manitoba residents.

The Crocus Fund is capitalized primarily by investments from citizens of the province, including sales of fund shares to the general public and work site campaigns that facilitate payroll deduction plans or direct sales. The fund is an eligible retirement investment and a potential repository for Canadian equivalents of U.S. individual retirement accounts. As such, all return on individual investments is tax-deferred, and government incentives for investment are a 20 percent provincial tax credit and a 20 percent federal tax credit.

Additional government support for the Crocus Fund includes a $500,000 grant to the Manitoba Federation of Labour to cover a portion of start-up costs and investment in the fund by the provincial government in the amount of $2 million, with an additional $2 million to be triggered by certain performance criteria. Fund organizers projected a modest $5 million in capitalization in 1993, the first year of operation, with total assets of $76 million projected after five years.

On a much larger scale, the Quebec Solidarity Fund started in 1984 with a similar means of capitalization. It now holds assets totaling $600 million in a province with roughly ten times the population of Manitoba. Similar institutions include the Working Ventures Fund in Ontario and the Working Opportunity Fund in British Columbia. Only the Crocus Fund, however, serves, in part, as a vehicle for workers to gain equity in their own companies. The fund intends to serve as an equity partner in some worker buyouts, enabling employees to leverage financing from banks or other lenders. In other cases, the fund lends directly to worker-owned companies or to related employee benefit trusts analogous to American employee stock ownership trusts.

As a model for labor finance and community development, the Crocus Fund is significant in this combination of government, private, and grass-roots capitalization and more notably in its governance and in its targeted investment. The fund is governed by a five-person Board of Directors, with a three-member majority selected by the Manitoba Federation of Labour, a federation of provincial unions with 90,000 members. One director is selected by the provincial government, and one is elected at large by the individual investors.

Legislative guidelines and internal criteria require a substantial portion of fund assets to be invested in companies with less than $50 million in assets and with a majority of employees in Manitoba and further require that the fund make its best efforts to assure that a majority of its investments promote employee ownership or employee participation in governance. Thus, the Crocus Fund has combined the mechanism of a labor-sponsored investment fund with a vehicle for local development finance and equity for worker ownership of businesses.

Provincial and federal government policy supports the Crocus Fund to a degree that is literally foreign to many policymakers in the United States. Still, organized labor would do well to import selected elements of this Manitoba model across the Canadian border and adapt them here. At its recent convention, the Washington State AFL–CIO passed a resolution calling for creation of such a fund.

Investment Banking and Financial Consulting

The United States has no exact analogue to Manitoba's Crocus Fund, with such substantial pooling of public and private capital in a labor-controlled fund, combined with its targeted investment in local economic control and development. In early 1990, on a grander scale, the AFL–CIO Industrial Union Department unveiled plans for the Employee Partnership Fund, an investment vehicle for corporate acquisitions by workers. This initiative stalled in the recession years of the early 1990s, facing difficulties in capitalization and lacking the focused tax incentives available in Canada. Nonetheless, the attempt signaled recognition by the AFL–CIO of the need and opportunity for a labor role in equity financing in worker buyouts.

The Employee Partnership Fund was to be capitalized, in large part, by public and private pension funds, providing a pooled outlet for pension fund trustees to target investment of some trust assets. The fund was to serve essentially as an equity partner for workers attempting to buy the companies where they work. To leverage bank loans and other debt financing required for such buyouts, the fund was designed to purchase equity shares in cooperation with worker groups (Bernstein, 1990). Projected capitalization of between $100 million and $200 million, however, proved unfeasible in the midst of recession, and equity investment for worker buyouts tends to be structured instead on an ad hoc basis.

To start and manage the Employee Partnership Fund, the AFL–CIO had selected investment bankers Eugene Keilin and Ron Bloom, who are among an emerging handful of investment bankers with a focus on assisting organized labor (Kilborn, 1990). Before starting their own firm in 1990, Keilin and Bloom were at Lazard Freres & Co., a large New York investment banking firm. While there, Keilin and, later, Bloom assisted in a number of employee buyouts and attempted buyouts in the steel industry and the airline industry. With trust developed among key union leaders with whom they had worked, Keilin and Bloom won the bid for management of the

Employee Partnership Fund despite competing bids from larger and more established investment banking firms.

Primarily in the 1980s, a number of other investment banking and consulting firms emerged to provide business expertise from a labor perspective. Groups such as the Midwest Center for Labor Research in Chicago continue to examine and participate in an array of new strategies for labor, while the Center for Self-Help in Durham, North Carolina, has expanded its credit union activity to include statewide teachers' funds and strategic investing for local economic development. Randy Barber, since the 1978 publication of *The North Will Rise Again*, has continued to advise unions and influence policymakers on issues of pensions and capital through his Center for Economic Organizing. A long list of law firms, business consulting groups, public agencies, and labor institutions has become a key repository for development of sophisticated financial expertise on behalf of labor.

Aside from the pension arena, much of this activity has revolved around organizing worker-owned companies, with learning accumulated from hundreds of projects over more than a decade in groups such as the Industrial Cooperative Association (now the ICA Group, in Boston), PACE of Philadelphia (and now a related consulting group called Praxis), the Michigan Employee Ownership Center in Detroit, the Steel Valley Authority in Pittsburgh, Working Equity, Inc. in New York, the Northeast Ohio Employee Ownership Center, and others. Prolific in generating successful worker buyouts in the early 1990s has been American Capital Strategies, an investment banking firm in Bethesda, Maryland.

WORKER OWNERSHIP

"Employee buyouts are alive and well," announced a news release from American Capital Strategies (ACS) in late 1990. ACS, an investment banking firm for labor, had just completed its fourth ESOP leveraged buyout in less than a year. With ACS arranging the finance packages, two of the transactions resulted in 100 percent ownership by the employees and the other two in a majority of the stock employee-owned. The union played a pivotal role in three of the four deals—the Amalgamated Clothing and Textile Workers at Textileather Corporation, a vinyl plant that was formerly a division of GenCorp, Inc., in Toledo, Ohio; the United Steelworkers of America at the Erie Forge & Steel Company in Erie, Pennsylvania; and the Maryland Brush Company in Baltimore. Financing packages for the four transactions ranged from $5 million to $19 million (Wilkus, 1991).

These cases are neither isolated nor unique. But they reflect a subtle change, as unions increasingly take a lead role in worker ownership transactions, with a more entrepreneurial and less defensive perspective. In recent decades, as in earlier periods of American history, organized labor has reacted with ambivalence—or resistance—to the growth in worker ownership of businesses.

Overview and Critical Perspective

By the end of 1990, close to 12 percent of U.S. private sector workers were participating in employee stock ownership plans (ESOPs), with additional workers involved in other forms of ownership or management participation (Rosen et al., 1991; Heckscher, 1988). That growing percentage of employee ownership compares to the 12.1 percent of private sector workers in unions in 1990 (Hoerr, 1991).

Despite cutbacks in federal programs to support economic development, substantial tax benefits continue to exist for ESOPs and worker cooperatives, and many state governments have programs to support worker ownership. Even Wall Street has entered the fray, with investment banking firms and law firms clamoring for ESOP deals and ESOPs appearing in the 1980s takeover frenzy, often as defensive devices ("ESOPS," 1989, 116). Some unions are taking the offensive in takeover bids, becoming players in the highly technical and competitive world of corporate takeovers and reorganizations (Hyde and Livingston, 1989; Valente, 1989; Swinney, 1991).

As employee ownership has penetrated the mainstream economy, unions are reconsidering their resistance. Organized labor can ill afford to ignore the increase in number and complexity of worker ownership transactions, especially when coupled with decreasing union membership. With due caution and a critical perspective, unions can use worker ownership affirmatively as one ingredient in a mix of capital strategies.

An affirmative union strategy to use worker ownership, just as other capital strategies, requires a critical perspective. Worker buyouts, for instance, have saved jobs, but some of these jobs have lasted only a short time, while others have reduced wages and benefits, relaxed work rules, or threatened the security of pension plans (Pitegoff and Lynd, 1982). Too often, unions have faced the prospect of partial employee ownership in the context of concession bargaining (Metzgar, 1984). Complete and dramatic worker buyouts have been attempted in the crisis of plant closings, in some cases without adequate feasibility analysis in advance or with intensive internal tensions—and thus eventual failure (Lueck, 1987).

In other cases, workers' expectations of ownership rights have been dashed, due to structural obstacles to worker control. In 1975, the machine tool manufacturing South Bend Lathe Inc. became the first company owned 100 percent through an employee stock ownership plan. Five years later, the workers went on strike ("against themselves," according to newspaper headlines) because their corporate structure gave employees no voting rights as shareholders (Whyte et al., 1983). By law, worker ownership need not include worker control. ESOPs, when authorized by Congress in 1974, were designed as a tax-favored financing vehicle for business corporations and as a mechanism for employee benefits—not as a way for employees to govern corporate policy.

Employee ownership, clearly, is not always good for employees. One transaction, highly publicized as unfair to employees, was the attempt of Scott & Fetzer Company to go private in 1985. The corporation's management, along with investment banker Kelso & Company, proposed that an ESOP trust borrow $182 million to purchase 41 percent of Scott & Fetzer outstanding shares, while managers and Kelso were to pay $15 million for 29 percent of the shares, and General Electric Credit (also a lender to the corporation) would be given the right to purchase 30 percent of the company for $4.5 million. The upshot was that the employees would be paying over $44 per share for the same stock that the managers and investment bankers would be buying for $4 to $7 per share and that GE Credit could buy for $1.50 per share (Olson, 1989, 220).

Analyzing the proposed ESOP transaction, ACTWU found it particularly unfair to the employees and publicized its findings. Before the transaction was completed, the federal Department of Labor (DOL) intervened and claimed that the ESOP was receiving less than fair market value for the share price. In fact, argued the DOL, for the proposed prices, the ESOP should receive 67 percent of the shares, and management and the Kelso group should get only 3.3 percent. Despite company negotiation with the DOL, the transaction was not completed (Olson, 1989,221). The controversy over Scott & Fetzer ultimately led to DOL regulations several years later attempting to protect the rights of ESOP participants to get a fair price for the purchase of stock.

Since the South Bend Lathe and Scott & Fetzer experiences, organized labor has become more familiar with the technicalities of ESOPs, including subtle issues of stock valuation and the critical distinctions between worker ownership and worker control. The Industrial Union Department of the AFL–CIO has published guidelines to help unions assess ESOPs and maximize employee rights in such plans—to assure that employee ownership plans are structured in the interest of the workers, not to their detriment ("Guidelines," 1987). The United Steelworkers of America passed resolutions regarding employee stock ownership plans at its 1986, 1988, and 1990 constitutional conventions. These resolutions provide guidelines for selected and strategic use of employee ownership by the union. As of late 1990, roughly 50,000 members of the steelworkers union were participants in twenty-three employee ownership plans (Newman and Yoffee, 1991).

In one of the largest union-initiated worker buyouts to date, employees of United Airlines (UAL) gained majority ownership of their company in June 1994. In a transaction driven by the Air Line Pilots Association (ALPA) and the International Association of Machinists (IAM), the workers acquired a 55 percent stake in UAL, the parent company of United Airlines, in exchange for wage and benefit concessions valued at $4.9 billion over half a dozen years. About 54,000 employees of a total workforce of almost 76,000 were involved in the buyout, agreeing to more flexible work rules and to wage concessions ranging from 8 percent to 15 percent (Bryant, 1994). This was the fifth attempt at an employee acquisition of United over the course of seven years. It was heralded by Labor Secretary Robert Reich as "a major landmark in American business history" and a model for other large companies to restructure without resorting to large-scale layoffs (McCarthy and Quintanilla, 1994).

Four prior buyout efforts had failed at UAL and, at times, were marked by sharp divisions among ALPA, IAM, and the Association of Flight Attendants. Among these disagreements were questions of financial feasibility and finance strategy, as well as differing interests among the three unions and opposition to steep concessions (Valente, 1989; Bryant, 1993; Veverka, 1993). Even in the fifth and apparently successful attempt, the flight attendants opted out of the deal initially, unable to reach agreement with UAL management on concessions. Dissident members of the IAM have vowed to break away from the IAM and to affiliate, instead, with the Aircraft Mechanics Fraternal Association. The Teamsters Union, meanwhile, is attempting to represent United's 20,000 noncontract employees (Moore, 1994). Problems clearly persist, and the new owners of UAL face multiple challenges. By purchasing the airline company while it was still relatively healthy, however, they may have charted a long-term course that will maintain their jobs and give them more of a say over their economic future.

Some commentators maintain that firms owned and controlled by their workers are at a disadvantage in the market economy, due, in part, to the difficulty of establishing an efficient collective governance system for a diverse workforce (Hansmann, 1990, 1779–96; Jensen and Meckling, 1979, 475). Others, in contrast, promote worker ownership as a means of increasing productivity and broadening wealth (Rosen, Klein, and Young, 1986). Neither perspective applies neatly to all worker-owned firms, especially given the wide variation in form and context for worker ownership (Hyde, 1991).

Some union leaders resist worker ownership to avoid undermining the adversarial relationship at the core of collective bargaining or because they fear organizing themselves out of a role (Compa, 1992; Slott, 1985). Yet, unions can play a lead role in assuring that employee ownership is used selectively to increase the rights of workers, to benefit workers in healthy companies, and to strengthen (not weaken) organized labor (Hester, 1988; Swinney, 1985). Such has been the case in a wide range of industries and locales—from wood products in the Northwest to steel in the Midwest and garment manufacturing in the South and in the Northeast. In 1991, ACTWU Local 667A led a successful buyout of clothing manufacturer John Roberts, Ltd., financed by a creative combination of private equity and public investment and organized with broad community involvement. Known now as ACT II, Inc., the company employs 170 workers, who own a portion of the firm and have a voice in corporate decision making (Industrial Cooperative Association, 1991, 9–10).

A business owned by its workers tends to be more rooted in a local community, where the worker-owners live, than a business with distant owners. The local commitment can be all the more dramatic when the ownership structure includes an array of local institutions and builds on the identity of a long enterprise history in the area.

Worker Cooperatives

As a local ownership strategy, harkening back to union activism in the nineteenth century, some contemporary American unions have turned again to worker cooperatives. In 1979, the Independent Drivers Association (IDA) took the lead in a driver takeover of Denver Yellow Cab. A decade earlier, the IDA had separated from the Teamsters to form a strong and unaffiliated local union to bargain with a succession of company owners. Finally, through the buyout of an ongoing and profitable firm, IDA members formed the Denver Yellow Cab Cooperative Association, the fourth largest taxi company in the country at that time—a worker cooperative owned by over 900 drivers (Gunn, 1984, 152–56). Similarly, just a few years later, facing potential shutdown of two dozen A & P supermarkets in Philadelphia, the United Food and Commercial Workers Union, Local 1357, helped its members organize worker cooperatives as part of a strategy to save jobs (Kreiner, 1987).

In a worker cooperative, the corporation is owned and controlled directly by its workers, through democratic election of the Board of Directors. In addition to wages paid regularly as in a conventional firm, corporate profits and losses are allocated equitably among workers on the basis of the amount of work they perform. Worker cooperatives operate throughout the country in a wide variety of business sectors (Ellerman and Pitegoff, 1983).

Some of the most successful worker cooperatives tend to be in service industries, where the workers' direct stake in the success of the business may improve job satisfaction and thus the quality of service. This is clearly the case at Cooperative Home Care Associates, Inc. (CHCA), a worker-owned home care company in Bronx, New York, founded in 1985. The home health aides at CHCA are primarily African-American and Latina women, working in an industry notorious for low wages and high turnover. In contrast, CHCA has a relatively stable workforce of 170 workers who, after a trial period, become part owners of the business, with a say in corporate affairs and a stream of income in addition to basic wages. The successful model of CHCA is being replicated in other parts of the country (CHCA, 1992; Fried, 1989; Surpin, 1987).

Although the leadership of CHCA works in cooperation with organized labor in public policy and advocacy, the company's worker-owners are not unionized. This is due, in part, to the fact that the company operates in a segment of the industry in New York City—proprietary home care enterprises—that is essentially nonunion. But it is due, more fundamentally, to a mismatch between the needs of the workers and the benefits offered by the health care unions.

For the most part, unions lack either the expertise or the will to provide financial advice and support to members in worker-owned companies. Labor leaders appear reluctant to fashion special eligibility criteria or benefits tailored to worker-owners. As discussed later, unions can envision, and have envisioned, an important role in companies with employee ownership. But the CHCA example points to the significant adjustment in perspective and program required for organized labor to move to the center of worker ownership activity. Even in a kindred company such as CHCA, a labor perspective is not necessarily the perspective of organized labor.

ESOPs

Unions that are involved with worker ownership today are more often in companies with ESOPs than in worker cooperatives. This is due, in part, to scale, for worker cooperatives tend to be smaller, in general, than companies with ESOPs. Moreover, much more of today's activity in employee ownership involves ESOPs. An ESOP is a mechanism for employees to own all or part of the corporation where they work and for the corporation to obtain financing with favorable tax treatment. Despite concrete tax advantages for worker cooperatives under Subchapter T of the Internal Revenue Code, ESOP tax advantages are far more compelling, particularly by increasing access to loan capital. ESOPs were authorized by federal law in 1974. In the subsequent fifteen years, over 10,000 companies formed ESOPs (Blasi, 1988).

Business owners usually form an ESOP because it provides substantial tax advantages to the company or the owner, and employees stand to benefit by eventually receiving stock or cash if the company does well. Only in a small percentage of cases, however, do employees control a company through an ESOP. The National Center for Employee Ownership estimates that as few as 200 companies with ESOPs are controlled by their employees, with the anticipation of several hundred more (but still under 5 percent of all companies with ESOPs) planning for majority control by the employees in the foreseeable future (Snyder, 1992). This apparent irony of so few worker-controlled companies among the thousands with ESOPs is, in large part, because worker interests are not the predominant purpose of most ESOP arrangements. As a tax-favored means of company financing or a vehicle for an owner to sell company shares for cash, ESOPs ordinarily are designed by management without substantial involvement of the employees in the ESOP's creation or in its subsequent operation. Many ESOPs own only a small percentage of the company, while some ESOPs hold a substantial majority of the company stock but still limit the shareholder rights of employees.

The term *worker ownership* thus refers to a wide range of circumstances—from management-initiated benefit plans giving employees little or no say in corporate affairs, to corporations whose employees own a controlling interest and whose union plays an active role. Union leaders and members must be prepared to distinguish between various employee ownership plans and to advocate private and public policies that shape employee ownership toward forms that best serve their members and the community.

Basic structural questions about any worker-owned firm are (1) amount of ownership—what percentage of company stock do employees own? (2) breadth of ownership—how widely and equitably is stock allocated among the workers? and (3) amount of control—do employees have the right to vote on critical issues and in election of the Board of Directors? (Dawson, 1987). These structural questions are crucial for unions or workers assessing the potential ownership structure in a worker buyout of a firm or in negotiations with respect to the formation of an ESOP in an existing firm. Just as important, however, is the broader corporate culture, including labor–management relations and organizational history and norms. Thus, for instance, the garment workers in Maine who helped buy clothing manufacturer John Roberts, Ltd., and now own a minority share in ACT II, Inc., feel some pride in their company. This is due, in part, to saving 170 jobs but also arises from the goodwill engendered and persisting in the coalition effort for local ownership (ICA, 1991, 9–10).

Technically, an ESOP is a special type of employee benefit plan, governed by federal tax law (the Internal Revenue Code) and pension law (ERISA). It is somewhat similar to a pension plan because the employer provides a deferred benefit to its employees. A pension plan, however, makes diversified investments on behalf of the employees, and the employees' benefits are federally insured. Unlike a pension plan, an ESOP invests primarily in stock shares of the employer, and the employees' benefits are at risk of loss if the company fails.

To establish an ESOP, a corporation forms an employee benefit trust, subject to approval by the Internal Revenue Service and the Federal Department of Labor. The trust is a separate legal entity formed to hold company stock on behalf of the employees, although not necessarily controlled by the employees. A trustee, selected ordinarily by the company's Board of Directors, administers the ESOP and controls the assets (stock and cash) held by the ESOP. The ESOP borrows money from a bank or other lender, and these funds are used to buy some or all of the company's stock shares. The company can use the borrowed money for any corporate purposes, and some or all of the company is owned by the employees through the ESOP.

Each year, the company makes cash contributions to the ESOP so that the ESOP can repay the bank. Essentially, the company is repaying the bank loan, but the company also receives a tax deduction for the entire amount of the payments (interest and principal). A non-ESOP company would get a much smaller deduction (only interest) for repaying a loan. This "tax-favored financing" for companies with ESOPs is a major reason for the popularity of ESOPs. In addition, ESOPs have many other tax benefits. For instance, employees are not taxed on their benefits until they receive distributions out of the ESOP (usually upon termination or retirement). Even the bank that lends money to an ESOP gets a tax break in certain cases.

Aside from company tax advantages, the ESOP mechanism is important to unions and employees for another reason. As the company repays the loan through the ESOP, stock shares in the ESOP are "allocated" to accounts in the name of the employees. Generally, employees can withdraw their stock or the cash value of that stock upon retirement or other termination of employment.

The ESOP can be critical in defining the rights of the employees in corporate decision making. Ownership of corporate stock ordinarily carries the right to vote on a range of shareholder issues, including election of the corporation's Board of Directors. But in closely held corporations, where stock is not traded on the public market, stock held in an ESOP for the benefit of employees is ordinarily voted by the ESOP trustee, not by the employees. The law requires only that votes be "passed through" to employees on certain major corporate changes such as merger or dissolution of the company. Some ESOPs are in large corporations with publicly traded stock. In those companies, the law requires voting rights to be passed through to employees, but the employees' percentage of the corporation's stock and thus their portion of voting power are typically quite small. The vast majority of ESOPs are in closely held corporations, and the norm in these companies is to limit the pass-through of voting rights to employees.

The ESOP *can* be structured, however, to give the employees the right to vote as shareholders on important issues. One of the most important issues for voting is the election of the corporation's Board of Directors, since it has the authority to govern and oversee management of the corporation. Thus, a "majority ESOP" with the trust holding a controlling portion of company stock can be a mechanism for democratic worker ownership and control in a corporation (Kaufman, 1989; Pitegoff, 1987). Whether or not a majority of company stock is held by the ESOP trust, ESOPs can give employees a voice in corporate affairs.

Even in the most democratic of corporate structures, however, it is important to note the limitations of workers' rights as shareholders. By law, it is not the shareholders but the Board of Directors that governs any business corporation. In practice, especially in larger, conventional corporations, this separation of ownership and control is quite pronounced, with management playing a dominant role and shareholder rights and participation extremely limited (Berle and Means, 1932). In a corporation closely held by the employees, their rights as shareholders may be expanded through corporate charter, bylaws, and agreements, but the Board of Directors is still charged by law with responsibility for managing the corporation. In practice, even in worker-controlled companies, the governance rights that workers can exercise as shareholders are often limited to election of the directors and voting on major corporate issues.

Thus, corporate structure alone cannot make a company democratic. Worker ownership and control as shareholders may be a necessary, but not sufficient, element for a democratic workplace. For this reason, many worker-owned companies supplement the ownership structure with other mechanisms for employee participation and influence. The union and a collective bargaining agreement, in many cases, provide additional rights for employees to affect corporate activity. Programs may be established for shop floor participation or other shared decision making in operational matters. Management and board policies can reinforce a participatory system (Banks and Metzgar, 1989).

The ESOP, though, is the primary way that employees get rights *as owners*. Most ESOPs are essentially a tool for financing and a passive benefit for employees. Nonetheless, unions have the opportunity to use the ESOP for tax-favored financing *and* for participation in corporate affairs. One example is the Seymour Specialty Wire Company in Seymour, Connecticut. In 1985, members of United Automobile Workers (UAW) Local 1827 led a buyout of Bridgeport Brass from its parent company, National Distillers. For the next seven years, the wire manufacturing company was 100 percent owned by its 270 hourly and salaried employees, with a majority of the Board of Directors elected democratically by the employees. The company performed well for a number of years, with the local union leadership playing an active role (Hanson and Adams, 1987). Unfortunately, racked by the recession of the early 1990s, the worker-owners lost their jobs and their share, if any, of accumulated earnings when the company folded in the summer of 1992.

Union Role

Worker ownership will not eliminate the union role in such companies, unless organized labor ignores and avoids the growth of worker-owned firms. Unions can use worker ownership in selected circumstances as part of a long-term strategy to retain jobs and membership and to sustain a progressive voice in economic policy. Organized labor should prepare for both an internal role and an external role in worker ownership (Pitegoff, 1989).

The role of a union within a worker-owned company varies as the nature of the ownership changes. If, for instance, the employees do not have majority control of the company, the union's role as collective bargaining agent is likely to persist, as in a conventional company. Even in enterprises with a democratic corporate structure—with employees electing the Board of Directors and controlling the voting on important shareholder issues—the union has a critical role in assuring that the democratic process of decision making works. Similar to the "legitimate opposition" in parliamentary systems of political democracy, a union can provide a protected and informed voice to counter that of the management in a worker-owned firm (Ellerman, 1986). Experience has shown that, even in worker-controlled companies, disagreements and conflicts inevitably arise (Johnson and Whyte, 1977).

To a limited degree, the union can be a guarantor of free speech, as well as an institution to inform that speech with data and analysis developed independently from those persons managing the company or even from the groupthink of the majority. The union also can protect individual rights against unfair treatment, through a grievance system available to all employees in the firm (Whyte and Whyte, 1988, 276).

Externally, unions are of critical importance to their members in the context of worker ownership. Union members in worker-owned companies can turn to their union for benefit plans and political clout that require a larger institution than the particular company. Solidarity among union members in different firms arguably can help to reduce the tendency of worker-owned firms to compete to the detriment of one another or of workers in conventional firms.

Unions also can provide technical assistance in worker buyouts to avert shutdowns, and they can be especially effective, as in some of the steelworkers' efforts, by helping to anticipate potential shutdowns long before they happen. Proactive strategies can lead to worker-owned companies with greater potential for success than in crisis situations. In practical terms, an ongoing union role in a worker-owned firm is all the more likely if the union played a lead role in facilitating worker ownership in the first place. Unions can retain membership and better serve their members in some circumstances by playing an affirmative role in worker ownership strategies.

This vision of a new role for unions with worker-owned companies requires an expansion of traditional union activities and expertise, as evidenced by the absence of a union at Cooperative Home Care Associates. In order to help their members in worker buyouts or worker-owned companies, unions must become more familiar and comfortable with new disciplines beyond traditional labor–management relations and labor law.

This necessity is already apparent, as unions increasingly become involved in matters previously thought to be strictly in the managerial domain.

CONCLUSION: IMPLICATIONS FOR LABOR, CAPITAL, AND UNIONS

Today, with increasing expertise in matters of corporate finance and ownership, unions can use worker ownership to their advantage and for increasing worker control of enterprises. Worker ownership is one of several tracks that can help unions build their necessary expertise and mind-set for capital strategies and for a creative role in public policy (Barber, 1987).

Union activity has broadened significantly to encompass business planning, finance, and corporate governance, as well as bankruptcy, all too clearly evidenced in the lengthy bankruptcy proceedings at Eastern Airlines. Despite conflict among the pilots, machinists, and flight attendants at United Airlines in their employee buyout attempts, it is significant simply that their interunion disagreement was often over capital transactions and business judgment.

More positively, labor is playing an important role in the targeting of pension funds toward affirmative investments and in their exercise of shareholder rights as institutional investors in large corporations. Labor banks and other financial intermediaries are giving form to a nascent infrastructure of finance institutions with a labor perspective.

With the ever-changing interplay of labor and capital, however, questions persist. The frequency of failed initiatives by labor in business and finance, some recounted here, is a troubling reminder of the risk involved, particularly in crisis situations. But even where successful, can labor's finance institutions retain a labor perspective, as they compete in the marketplace and attend to the bottom line? Will forays in finance leave workers behind and distract unions from their primary goal of representing working people? Who, in particular, will be the constituents of organized labor in the years to come?

Despite these questions, the growing scale and sophistication of finance institutions with a labor perspective suggest that organized labor can expand its mandate and its constituency. In the context of global competition and technological change, unions will find it difficult to thrive without an active hand in capital strategies and finance. Organized labor faces a challenge, not only of building its own financial capacity and institutions but of assuring that these institutions remain broadly accountable and that labor's capital is deployed strategically for widespread benefit.

6

International Trade Policy: Implications for Employment and Labor Policy in the United States

Gerald Glyde

International trade expansion raises important employment and labor policy questions for the United States. While positive-sum benefits generally flow from trade accords, they may also lead to potentially significant intracountry redistributive effects. Like technological change, trade represents a double-edged sword. Or, as Deardorff and Stern suggest, "Trade policy is like doing acupuncture with a fork; no matter how carefully you insert one prong, the other is likely to do damage" (Deardorff and Stern, 1987, 39). In an increasingly multipolar and trade-sensitive world, employment and labor policy must be reexamined as an integral component of a more deliberate joining of domestic and foreign economic policy.

In this chapter only some dimensions of the many questions that relate to the trade, employment, and labor policy debate can be addressed. First, evidence of the recent increase in trade policy initiatives is noted. Second, several of labor's concerns over this trend are identified. Third, to illustrate that trade politics and economics are closely intertwined, the different motivations that led the United States, Mexico, and Canada into treaties such as NAFTA (North American Free Trade Agreement) and FTA (United States–Canada Free Trade Agreement) are explored. Fourth, four different American trade policy positions, along with their implications for workers, are identified. Finally, the issue of what U.S. trade policy should look like if it were more explicit and if it joined domestic and international dimensions, particularly in the employment and labor policy areas, is addressed.

INTERNATIONAL TRADE EXPANSION

The next century promises a continuation of the recent trend toward increased international trade via block or regional accords and by multilateral agreements such as GATT (General Agreement on Tariffs and Trade) (Belous and Hartley, 1990). On a regional basis, Canada and the United States commenced FTA in 1989; by January 1994, the trilateral NAFTA was in place, linking more closely the economies of the United States, Canada, and Mexico. Chile has already been invited to enter NAFTA, with official entry most likely in early 1996. Moreover, a recent summit meeting among the United States and thirty-three other Americas countries announced plans for a free trade zone by 2005 as part of the Americas Initiative commenced under President Reagan (Baer, 1993; Green, 1993).

The European Union (EU) represents another more established trading block (Wise and Gibb, 1993; Wilkinson, 1992). Integration has been slowed recently by an early 1990s recession, longer-term economic restructuring, the political collapse of both Eastern Europe and the Soviet Union, and German unification. However, the EU continues to lower economic and political barriers to integration and to consider new member countries beyond the current twelve. A recent referendum in Sweden resulted in a slight majority vote in favor of membership in the European block; Finland also elected to join, whereas Norway's referendum resulted in rejection of membership. The advisability of joining the EU club versus some other form of more independent association, which would provide more sovereignty, was a key point of contention in these decisions. The EU block represents both competition and a large potential market for U.S. goods and services.

Immediately after NAFTA was passed by Congress in the fall of 1993, the United States met in Seattle with fellow APEC (Asia–Pacific Economic Cooperation) members to discuss expanding trading relations among its eighteen member countries. APEC recently concluded its 1994 meeting in Jakarta, with members reaching a nonbinding agreement to work toward a 2020 free trade agreement. Moreover, the U.S. Congress recently passed into law the new GATT accord signed, in Marrakesh, Morocco, in the summer of 1994, by the United States and 123 other countries. Trade increases between the United States and NICs (newly industrialized countries) and Third World countries continue to proliferate. In short, trade now makes up about 20 percent of American gross domestic product (GDP), having been about 10 percent in 1960, and it is becoming a more important sector each year, particularly in the industrial relations context (United States Department of Commerce, 1993; Edwards, 1994; Gutchess, 1992; Yochelson, 1985). For NAFTA and FTA trading partner Canada, the international sector has always represented a larger share of its economy, at present being over 30 percent of GDP.

The new trading arrangements just mentioned are part of the institutional lubricant for increased global trade, for expanded informational and financial transactions, for increased direct and indirect foreign investment, and for growing activity of multinational companies. Properly conceived and implemented, trade accords offer positive-sum benefits where all countries can gain, and all citizens can share in the increased economic activity (Lustig, Bosworth, and Lawrence, 1992). Poorly conceived agreements may produce benefits for some countries at the expense of others and major redistributions of income among groups within countries. Redistribution problems exist, even if an overall trading arrangement produces positive-sum results.

Few scholars or practitioners would argue that trade is a bad concept; its benefits are largely understood. In our own economic lives, we specialize and trade with others as a matter of course, and it is clearly viewed as beneficial. But we also know from experience that some particular trades are not productive, even though trading is. Thus, comprehending the possible merits of international trade, even the more esoteric notions of comparative advantage, does not mean that an enlightened person should necessarily be in favor of any specific trading arrangement such as FTA or NAFTA. These block accords, for example, are discriminatory in concept; nonmembers are excluded, and thus the agreements are not really free trade, although they may be "freer" trade. Moreover, trade accords are institutionally negotiated arrangements, often with thousands of pages of regulations, new protections, and grandfather clauses, thus making permanent many trade-distorting practices from the past.

Particular trading agreements, therefore, reflect past trading regimes, the relative negotiating power of the countries involved, and the relative strength of intracountry interest groups (Lake, 1988; Przeworski and Limongi, 1993). Corporations and unions provide examples of these interest groups. Their interests may often overlap, and they may do so in trading matters, but they apparently diverged on accords such as NAFTA and GATT. Large corporations particularly supported these accords, while labor opposed them, although labor strongly supports the idea of trade (AFL–CIO, 1992; Carr, 1988). Canadian business and Canadian labor also clearly diverged in their view of the advisability of both FTA and NAFTA. But when the stakes are high in the international context, it is apparent that corporations can exert what might be called in this context "strategic choice," a choice that labor seldom can exercise (Kochan, Katz, and McKersie, 1986).

While trade is thus a commonsense notion that labor has no trouble endorsing, in its actual negotiation and implementation there is much room for legerdemain in the international trade forum (Liebeler, 1993). The label "free trade" attached to an agreement may be politically expedient, making opponents of it more easily characterized as being anti-free trade, as being unschooled in trade matters, or as being simply obstructionist. Workers and unions, like any other group, may indeed be obstructionist. However, labor opposition to accords such as NAFTA or FTA raises important points, issues that other important trading nations, for example, members of the European Union, have integrated as essential components into their common market accord (Deppe, 1992).

LABOR'S CONCERNS ON TRADE

Objections of United States labor regarding NAFTA and of Canadian labor over FTA and NAFTA would include reference to the following: unequal protections written into the accord; inadequate consultation with labor compared to strong input from corporations; inadequate consideration of the effect of trade-related industrial restructuring on industrial relations practices and policy; and inadequate employment policies (Glyde, 1993). While the benefits of the agreements may come in the long term in a trade trickle-down form, the costs of adjustment may be more immediate and concentrated on particular industries, occupations, regions, and workers (Prestowitz, 1992; Stokes, 1992–93).

Whatever the immediate effects of NAFTA, it will work to compound an already unfavorable industrial relations and employment climate. These labor market and workplace changes have confounded politicians. Their intractability seems to explain, in part, the 1992 election of President Clinton over George Bush on the issue of the middle class's well-being. In turn, the rejection of Democrats two years later in 1994 appears to be related to the same question. What has been happening to middle-class workers and their unions—and, by implication, to those less fortunate income earners?

First, strategic restructuring choices by employers over the last twenty years have contributed to the drastic reduction of unionization rates in the private sector to about 12 percent prior to the regional accords. The reduction in unionization has come about as a result of permanent layoffs, plant closures, and a reconfiguration in job creation toward nonunion sectors. Moreover, firms have prevented union organization by instituting positive human resource policies, using the law to the letter, and by breaking the law more often (Freeman and Medoff, 1984).

Second, real hourly wages in the United States have fallen over the last two decades. From 1973 to 1993, real hourly wages, in 1982 dollars, fell by a compound rate of .07 percent per year from $8.55 per hour to $7.39 per hour. This decline is in contrast to a compounded average growth in real wages (1982$) of .07 percent between 1959 and 1973, from $6.69 to $7.39 per hour (Council of Economic Advisers, 1994).

Third, for much of the last twenty years, particularly during the Reagan– Bush presidencies, government itself took an aggressive negative stance toward unions. The firing of 11,000 striking air traffic controllers invited private sector employers to toughen their bargaining behavior as local enforcers of a more general, government-backed, "get-tough" attitude toward labor. Presidential appointments to government regulatory and agency boards validated this message (Glyde, 1986).

Finally, the 1980s offered a supply-side, free-market, trickle-down domestic economic policy as a remedy for the country's economic stagnation, which began in the 1970s as "stagflation." The same policymakers then negotiated FTA and NAFTA, maintaining that international trickle-down effects would be positive; assistance in transition was not required, according to this view. Having already been buffeted by restructuring and firms' strategic choices that reduced union ranks, having faced concessions in pay and benefits, having already experienced aggressive supply-side domestic policy, and having been excluded as a domestic partner or participant in the trade talks, it is not surprising that labor did not support the regional accords, which potentially offered more of the same treatment.

Opponents on the trade question seem to line up on two identifiable sides of the issue. One favors almost any trade deal based on faith in free-trade theory principles (U.S. Congress, 1988, 1994). The other side is more focused on changing institutional arrangements and processes in the U.S. economy and reducing the negative redistributive effects that restructuring related to trade might have (Wilkinson, 1992). The problem is that economics and politics intertwine around the trade issue, with plenty of room for intercountry and intracountry struggle (Lake, 1988; Laxer, 1987; Liebeler, 1993). In this context we consider the motivations of three countries, Mexico, the United States, and Canada, for entering the NAFTA.

MOTIVATIONS OF NAFTA PARTICIPANTS

Motives of the three governments for entering NAFTA and FTA both differ and overlap. Important segments of each economy have been concerned with economic revitalization, including increasing productivity, lowering costs of production, and enhancing profitability in the private sector. The accords also reflect their political sponsors, Reagan and Bush, Mulroney of Canada, and Salinas, all strong advocates of free-market forces and privatization and all now out of political office. The labor movement in the United States was awakened in opposition to NAFTA, after being rather mute on FTA. Canadian labor coordinated strong, but unsuccessful, opposition to FTA, while NAFTA represented an extension of the FTA battle that had already been lost. In Mexico, the "official unions" of the Confederation of Mexican Workers, made powerful by their connection to the PRI (Institutional Revolutionary Party), the ruling party in Mexico for the last sixty-five years, supported NAFTA, while many of the "unofficial" or independent unions did not.

For most of the post–World War II period, Mexico was a hostile climate for foreign trade and investment, with high tariffs and import substitution rules. The policy was that Mexicans should be supplied by Mexican production and services where possible. American firms contemplating a Mexican location faced a loss of patent protection, rules on domestic content, and possible nationalization. In short, Mexico chose to promote economic nationalism. In the 1970s and early 1980s, this nationalist policy was to be funded by rising oil revenues. It borrowed large sums of money from U.S. banks at high interest rates for investment, projecting rapid income gains from rising oil prices to pay for it. As is now well known, oil prices and revenues fell, and Mexican payments at high rates of interest became past due.

By the early to middle 1980s, it became clear that Mexico needed to open its economy in order to provide for adequate modernization, to secure additional investment funds, and to make payments on its international debts. In 1988, the free-market-oriented and Harvard-trained Carlos Salinas de Gortari became president. While his election continued the PRI's political control since 1929, his economic direction was quite different. Prior to NAFTA, Mexico joined GATT, unilaterally lowered tariffs, began a period of privatization, and developed the tariff-free twin plants zone along the U.S.–Mexican border. In short, in response to "la decade tragica," Mexico pushed for increased trade, as well as increased indirect and direct investment prior to NAFTA, and gambled with Mexican sovereignty. But as made clear by the falling peso in early 1995, Mexico's economic problems are far from solved by NAFTA, and neither is the sovereignty question.

The Mexican policy reversal fit tongue and groove with a number of contemporary political and economic needs of the United States. In the cold war period, the United States required a stable and anticommunist Mexico, even if that country's economic strategies were protectionist, and it was relatively undemocratic (Orchard, 1993; Erfani, 1992). But, as has been pointed out, the U.S. economy's long-run performance, particularly during the late 1970s and 1980s, left much to be desired; trade deficits and the national debt rose (Laxer, 1987). Under these conditions, the country began to strongly encourage others to become more free-trade-friendly. What had been an acceptable trading regime at another time was no longer operative from the U.S. perspective.

The NAFTA and its overarching policy umbrella, the Americas Initiative, were consistent with these new U.S. needs. First, the objective was to begin a more aggressive posture toward countries like Mexico (and Japan) that had heretofore been allowed to restrict trade and foreign investment in return for assistance in Soviet containment. Second, since American competitiveness in the world appeared to be in relative decline, the trade accords provided a partial solution: encouraging exports of U.S. goods and services and lower domestic costs and prices in the form of imports—both consumer goods and production components as well as improved access for U.S. direct and indirect foreign investment. Third, the United States could now work toward the goal of encouraging internal free-market reforms and political restructuring in its image with its trading partners. There is, therefore, a "they should be more like us" element to the trade accords, and this has created opposition in both Canada and Mexico to the accords over sovereignty issues (Canadian Center for Policy Alternatives [CCPA], 1992; Carr, 1988). The concern of domination was also evident in recent APEC meetings, explaining, in part, the long time horizon given to working out more of the specifics.

Canada feared that it might become more subject to punitive U.S. international trade sanctions if it did not negotiate a special status or exemption. It had already become the object of numerous U.S. industry-originating unfair trade allegations; moreover, the United States at the time of FTA negotiations was preparing new legislation (known as Super 301 of the Trade Act) that would provide more rapid remedies to punish those countries deemed to be engaging in unfair trading practices. Given that U.S. trade complaints originate from the private sector and become very political in nature, Canada's nervousness was understandable, especially since U.S. industry was involved in long-term restructuring (Stein, 1992). Moreover, about 70 percent of Canadian exports have a U.S. destination, and about 30 percent of Canadian GDP is export-dependent.

Canada entered the FTA, therefore, to secure guaranteed access to the huge U.S. market and to avoid that country's protectionist proclivities. Another official reason for the Canadian interest in a trade treaty was to obtain economies of scale for its industry by encouraging longer production runs with access to the larger U.S. market (Glyde, 1993). In the end, Canada did not get guaranteed access or exemption from Super 301, and there is some question as to how important economies of scale are in this context. Most jobs created in Canada and the U.S. are in the services and are created by smaller firms. The FTA does provide for trade dispute panels, which have made judgments in Canada's favor, but on many key issues the panel's decisions require only that the United States follow its own laws.

Canada was not motivated to initiate NAFTA itself, but, once in FTA, there was not much choice but to sit at the negotiating table with the other two parties to the planned accord. Canada will also now be party to any expansion of NAFTA as part of the U.S. Americas Initiative. Canada and the United States are also members of APEC.

THE AD HOC CHARACTER OF U.S. TRADE POLICY

Given the importance of the emerging global economy, it is perhaps odd that the United States does not have a coherent trade policy. Rather, current policy is a "bubbling up" of public and private interests of varying political and economic strengths. The strength of the interest group and the merit of its claim may not be related, leading to unsound arrangements. But it is not surprising that there are divergent views on trade, given the possibility for positive-sum gains and important concomitant intercountry and intracountry redistributional implications. Trade questions also provide a forum where government noninterventionists clash with interventionists, as the following four nonmutually exclusive positions on trade policy illustrate. These views include those held by free-trade believers, free-trade pretenders, managed traders, and protectionists. Important and different implications for labor come from these partially overlapping and contrary positions. The four views are described, followed by their implications for workers and labor.

First is the noninterventionist free-trade believer position. The free-trade believer simply extends a strongly held view of free markets domestically, with minimal governmental interference and reliance on private decisions, to the international scene. It is a fundamentalist view of economy and starts with the position that, were it not for government efforts, the system would largely meet theoretically based, free-market standards. The benefits of comparative advantage, specialization, and exchange are no more difficult to imagine among countries than among individuals or firms within countries. The complexities of the real world do not change the fundamental truths of the free-market model, according to this view (Bhagwati, 1991, 1994). President Ronald Reagan appeared to view the domestic economy and the trade question from this perspective. In trade negotiations he called for a "level playing field" across countries.

The second view, that of the free-trade pretenders, fits in with the free-trade believer's policy position, but the pretenders see the economic world through very different lenses. As with the free-trade believers, this group supports governmental deregulation and the reduction of other countries' trade barriers. But they see in the residual benefits after deregulation and trade barrier reduction a potential increase in private corporate power rather than free-market competition. The hoped-for result is a much more concentrated type of competition, or market sharing. This contrasts with the free market believer, who expects a more atomistic-like competition as the obvious option to governmental interference.

The free-trade pretender position could thus be taken by powerful transnational firms that fully realize the oligopolistic and political power realities of trade relations. The pretenders can support the believers because the negotiation of reductions in barriers and the tamed regulatory trade environment mean, less constraints on oligopolistic and powerful corporations, enabling them to take advantage of weaker competitors in enlarged markets (Rugman, 1990). Not surprisingly, therefore, the most powerful corporations can support openly the idea of atomistic international and domestic competition, in full knowledge that the alternative to a more purposeful and government-regulated trade regime, including government involvement and barriers, may well be regulation via powerful private interests instead. This possibility concerns many smaller countries, should they lower their investment and trade barriers too quickly.

Complexity of real markets suggests a third view of trade: the managed-trade perspective (Jones, 1994; Cowling, 1987, 1994; Hazeltine, 1988). The benefits of trade are evident to managed traders, but they argue for a more interventionist trade policy. The policies coming from the managed-trade position could include assisting firms and industries in securing comparative advantage; obtaining economies of scale in financing and research and development; providing infant-industry assistance; arranging for temporary trade protectionism; providing resource and development assistance to potential "winners"; encouraging aggressive partnership arrangements among government, labor, and business; and improving research on the economics and politics of trade.

Moreover, the managed-trade position should include the crafting of adjustment policies for firms, workers, and communities facing restructuring as a result of trade polices. In the employment context, economic losers should receive compensation from the winnings associated with trade. Managed trade should also include economic, social, and environmental monitoring of corporate performance in international markets. Managed-trade policies can thus come in a variety of guises and can mean different things to their proponents and their detractors. Like industrial policy, managed trade ideas are often vague and, therefore, are poorly considered. As with domestic regulation, managed-trade policy can be good or bad, depending on what it is. In support of becoming more explicit in trade policy, one could argue that the United States has a managed policy already, but it is the worst kind; it is ad hoc, hidden, and based largely on private political power considerations. In this case, creating a more explicit policy requires getting past the vested interests.

A fourth position on trade is that of the protectionist, a position more clearly concerned with the immediate distributional and fairness aspects of trade relations and policy. A managed-trade position can be protectionist, too, for example, in cultivating a particular industry or in protecting an industry in the short run to assist in economic adjustment. Naturally, firms, workers, and unions do not wish to be subject to debilitating competition, whether that competition is considered fair or unfair, or whether there exist adjustment policies or not. The more extreme protectionist position is like the old mercantilistic view; that is, trade is a zero-sum game, and the goal is to export as much and import as little as possible with the help of barriers to trade (Reich, 1991). The protectionist view tends to exist because there is no enlightened managed trade policy to share the benefits of trade and the costs of adjustment. The protectionist position, therefore, is designed to prevent any change from taking place.

U.S. trade policy, in practice, combines aspects of all four of these views, even though the announced policy is usually free trade, NAFTA and FTA being examples. As mentioned, these accords are discriminatory and exclusionary agreements against nonsignatory countries; moreover, they contain all manner of grandfathered arrangements, qualifications, exceptions, and other concessions or demands that become part of the agreement—even though, overall, the accords represent a reduction in barriers to trade and investment. They are, in many respects, private sector-sponsored managed-trade arrangements, promoted as free-market agreements.

The implications for workers differ greatly under these four trade policy scenarios. Free-trade believers tend to view labor as a productive input much like any other input. Making the heroic assumption of flexible wages and full employment, they recommend few protections for workers from readjustment; protections only postpone the inevitable, in their view. The free-trade believer position has little sympathy for unions; they are simply viewed as obstructionist, from this perspective. It is not surprising, therefore, that during the Reagan–Bush years there were attempts to roll back union power.

The free-market pretenders, as noted, do not want to be regulated, either domestically or internationally; in fact, international activity generally reduces the ability of unions to deal with firms. Thus, the free-market believers' perspective combines with that of the private corporate sector to limit employment protection or participation of labor in trade arrangements.

Managed traders and protectionists tend to focus much more on institutions, processes, and implicit contracts involved in restructuring related to trade. Included in this institutional-process view of the world are unions, collective bargaining, unemployment, adjustment problems, labor standards, and distributional issues associated with changes in the economy due to global competition. The managed-trade view clearly has more "public" interventionist implications than does the free-market view. But the free-market believer and pretender combination provides for a great deal of "private" or "corporist" intervention, as well as de facto "statist" intervention, on the firm's behalf, with a de-emphasis on employment, community, and labor readjustment considerations.

COMBINING TRADE, EMPLOYMENT, AND LABOR POLICY

Given the importance of trade to the future welfare of the United States and therefore to the future of workers, unions should pose the following questions. Should trade policy be explicit? If so, what should that policy be? Should trade policy and domestic economic policy be joined? In particular, should there be a new effort to revise domestic employment and labor policy to reflect the new global realities of the economy? The answers to these questions, in this author's view, are as follows. Yes, there should be a more conscious trade policy; it should be a more explicit and participative managed-trade policy; domestic economic and trade policy should be more closely joined; and there is, in this spirit, a critical need to revise employment and labor policy to reflect not only the international economy but also its enabling complement, technological change.

Authors such as Paul Krugman believe that we unnecessarily worry about the international economy (Prestowitz et al., 1994; Krugman, 1994). He reminds us, as did Adam Smith in a much earlier era, that what really counts in a country's development is the rate of productivity growth of its domestic economy. All else, including the ability to compete, will take care of itself if domestic productivity growth is sufficient. Thus, according to this view, any economic policy focus should be on domestic issues and not on international competition as though it were a separate problem. Moreover, since trade is generally seen as a positive-sum proposition, with all trading countries winning, Krugman chastises those people who view international trade as a competition with winners and losers.

This focus on the domestic economy is consistent with Robert Reich's argument in his book *The Work of Nations* (Reich, 1992). While he previously leaned toward a corporate-industrial policy, he now suggests that we can no longer identify truly American companies to which such a policy would apply. Both foreign and domestic companies utilize the same global webs of production and services. These global webs comprise workers that Reich calls "symbolic analysts"—people who identify problems, conceive and implement the solutions, and market the results within the webs.

In this scenario, these elite workers, perhaps less than one-fifth of the current U.S. labor force, are the key resource to a country's wealth; firms come to them, contract out to them, or hire them. It makes little difference whether the firm utilizing these scarce labor services is a U.S. resident or not, or whether the firm is a foreign or domestic corporation, according to Reich. He suggests, like Krugman, that our focus should be on the domestic economy; moreover, this emphasis should be on education and training aimed at creating more symbolic analyzers as well as other technologically skilled workers. American and foreign firms progressively tend to look more alike, in Reich's view. Therefore, the United States should switch the focus away from firms, since they increasingly have no nationality and are more mobile across borders than ever before, emphasizing instead the quality of its workforce.

While Reich and others are persuasive about the importance of attention to the domestic workforce, their trade policy is incomplete at best (Prestowitz et al., 1994; Stokes, 1992–93; Wilkinson, 1992). Thurow, in his book *Head to Head*, argues that international trade competition can have winners and losers (Thurow, 1992). For example, the United States recently won a competition with the Europeans for passenger jet sales to Saudi Arabia. The Europeans did not leave their selling or production efforts to the free market only. Neither did the United States fail to utilize its geopolitical muscle or goodwill, generated as a result of the Gulf War, to enhance its marketing prospects. In essence, there were concerted efforts by the Unites States and Europe to obtain these sales, a tacit management of trade by the U.S. government, and an explicit effort on Europe's part.

Trade in this example was a win-win game for the United States and the Saudis, but at the same time it is win-lose between the United States and the Europeans, except in the indirect sense that both the Saudis and Americans, being wealthier from their trading arrangement, increase their demand for goods and services from Europe. One of these parties lost, for there were significant costs but few benefits. With further sales of aircraft and many other products hanging in the balance, it is appropriate for a state to develop a conscious trade policy to improve its competitive position. The Japanese government has already demonstrated the value of such policy. As noted earlier, the United States already has an ad hoc trade policy; the discussion here suggests that it should become more explicit, more deliberate, and more coordinated. The policy should be crafted to promote and protect U.S. (and all) worker interests in the new global economy.

One danger of a managed approach is that everyone will want special help, and the process becomes largely politically driven. For example, David Stockman, when attempting to implement reform in government during the first Reagan presidential term, became demoralized on finding that weak claims (for government assistance), promoted by strong claimants, won out over strong claims (for assistance), promoted by weak claimants (Greider, 1981). While this problem exists in all policy deliberations, that is not a reason to give up efforts to effectively manage trade. The answer is to empower weak claimants and to improve the hearing of all claims. Labor unions and community groups must become a stronger and more independent voice in trade policy bargaining. The Federation for Industrial Retention and Renewal (FIRR) is a successful example.

If managed trade can be an efficiency-enhancing approach, given that trade and trade competition will become more important to the country's overall welfare, it makes sense to coordinate domestic and foreign economic policy. In effect, the government should make sure that its domestic and foreign economic strategies are not in opposition to one another. It has been suggested by Stokes, for example, that the United States should create an Economic Security Council (ESC) to coordinate its foreign and domestic economic policy, in the same fashion as the National Security Council coordinates both foreign and domestic security matters (Stokes, 1992–93). The main conclusion of his analysis is that the United States requires a high-level government effort (the ESC) to craft trade and domestic policy. Another entity—he calls it DITI (Department of International Trade and Industry)—would coordinate the implementation of policy across various governmental departments and agencies.

This approach is consistent with being more explicit and analytical about trade and domestic economic policy; and that effort can then be evaluated in a more rational manner and adjusted accordingly from within a more rigorous framework. This is not to suggest that there is a rational, one-answer, scientific solution to trade and domestic policy questions. But being more explicit tends to reveal more effectively both the economic and political aspects of this issue. Moreover, the very process of policy formulation raises the level and quality of communication among interested parties and may bring in the important interests of groups that now tend to be excluded, including workers and unions.

Particularly in the labor market, there is a need for coordination and cooperation in the domestic and foreign economic policy arenas. New technology and deregulation at home, as well as increased globalization and trade initiatives, have moved firms to demand a new flexibility at the workplace. While there are obvious requirements for more adaptive structures, there are also risks for substantial redistributive effects as well. At the workplace, these effects can appear as layoffs, plant closures, replacement of full-time with part-time workers, contracting out, two-tier wages, union-free strategies, capital mobility, mergers, acquisitions and divestments, as well as firms playing communities and countries off against each other for locational inducements, the so-called whipsawing technique.

It is appropriate for workers to resist sudden life-changing economic events associated with the negative redistributive effects implied in the numerous restructuring actions previously cited. Moreover, unions, as representatives of employees, with a mission to provide members with job security, are required to attempt to slow down change of this type. The adversarial nature of collective bargaining is based, to a significant degree, on this redistributive economic struggle. If enhanced workforce skills, economy-wide, and workplace adaptability and flexibility are key to both domestic and global success, then there is a drastic need for review of U.S. employment and labor policy in an international, as well as a domestic, context. Workers and their unions should be important participants in the establishment of that policy.

Why is there so much resistance to what seems like such an obviously beneficial and economically forward-looking idea—that is, to address more effectively workers' income and job security concerns related to restructuring as a result of global and technological change and to take these concerns into the decision-making process, in return for worker and union cooperation to enhance adaptability, flexibility, and productivity (and pay)?

The problem on one level is that many policymakers are effectively free-market absolutists. Their position dovetails with the view of economists who tend to practice exclusively with hedonist-abstractionist models of economic behavior. From this perspective, the focus is on what is called "partial equilibrium analysis." If, for example, there is unemployment in an occupation due to declining demand for labor—say due to increased trade competition, the analysis simply identifies the unemployment as a temporary disequilibrium where the wage is now above the equilibrium level. Four things will occur: first, wages being sticky, unemployment will increase; second, workers will move to other expanding sectors; third, wages in the original sector with decreased demand will fall toward a new equilibrium level, with lower wages and less employment than before. Finally, in the expanding sector, equilibrium wages will be higher and employment larger than before. From this market process another full employment equilibrium emerges. The system has gone from equilibrium to disequilibrium and back to equilibrium without direction.

While this scenario identifies important tendencies, the partial equilibrium approach is more realistic in a full employment world where workers can transfer quickly to an equivalent or better-paying job, where effective and rapidly delivered training and mobility services are available to the displaced, so that they can visualize the outcome of their rational human capital-enhancing behavior. Particularly, however, if the unemployment is caused by an unusual, institutional, and process-wrenching, long-run change, as we appear to be in today, then there is a need to consider new policies to deal with labor market adjustment. This need is compounded, given that the Federal Reserve and others demand a 6 percent unemployment rate as a hedge against inflation. The partial equilibrium approach, in short, ignores the adjustment realities of the labor market.

Joseph Schumpeter termed the abstract partial equilibrium approach the "Ricardian vice" because it ignored important adjustment problems in the labor market (McNulty, 1980, 66). The focus is on the beginning and long-run end result of a free-market change and ignores what goes on in a process or institutional way between equilibria. Again, this might be appropriate for many cases where adjustments are relatively rapid, and underlying institutional changes are not involved. The approach may be wildly inadequate, however, when institutional capital and processes at the workplace are being fundamentally revised by firms. In this environment of upheaval, there are clear benefits to considering ways to ease the adjustment process and to evaluate more effectively in a public context the usage of human resources, the economy's most important asset.

In the 1930s depression, John Maynard Keynes noted that, while the classical economic model's predictions of a return to full employment via wage reduction might eventually take place, in the long run we are all dead. There was every reason, therefore, in extraordinary times for the government to be actively involved in assisting the private sector. While government involvement does not appear to be very popular in the middle 1990s, innovative ways to simultaneously encourage both economic flexibility and economic security in the labor market represent an important avenue for productive government attention.

LABOR MARKET FLEXIBILITY AND ECONOMIC SECURITY

If the focus of trade were among families instead of countries, the apparent anomaly between flexibility and security disappears. For example, a change in the division of labor of a household, as part of increased trade by that household, would not be seen as a threat to economic security by family members precisely because enhanced family welfare is a public good within the unit. Reordering of tasks (flexibility) does not require job security (a particular job) or employment security (a guarantee of some task at all times) since family members' economic security is not in doubt, funded automatically by the positive-sum reordering. The distributional issue is not a problem in the family context. The absence of economic insecurity leads to a willingness to change. Economic security and flexibility need not be at odds; one can complement the other.

It becomes clear that, when we move to the country level, the overall benefits of trade are not public goods in the sense that they are in the family example. Important redistribution or equity questions arise. What seems economically logical and fair in the family setting is suddenly lost at the more aggregate level. The absence of economic security engenders limits on positive-sum benefits, given the need for losing parties to prevent, to the extent possible, the imposition of losses. It is not surprising to see protectionist behavior. Developing coexistence between flexibility and economic security is at the heart of any new employment and labor policy, making protectionist behavior less necessary.

Given the increase in trade and attendant technological change, the debate is really over how much economic security is consistent with efficiency, flexibility, and fairness and what factors should come into that calculus. The free-market approach would limit direct economic security in favor of market-driven change. Trickle-down benefits would compensate the losers in this scenario. The managed-trade view, in contrast, would attempt to join more closely trade and domestic employment and labor policy so that flexibility and economic security are complementary. Moreover, under managed trade, economic security would be more up-front and direct, part of the package of change.

Abandoning the realities of institutional and labor market adjustment problems would be a grave mistake. From a worker and union perspective and from an overall efficiency view, employment and labor policy needs an overhaul as we approach the year 2000. Workers and their unions should be an important participant in the establishment of any new policy. The Dunlop Commission has made a start in this direction with its series of hearings, but the final results of the commission's work are uncertain, given the new Congress elected in 1994 (Commission on the Future of Worker–Management Relations, 1994). At least, the questions asked by the commission are a move in the right direction, even though actions taken are likely to be too timid.

Discussing detailed specifics of employment and labor policies that should be pursued is beyond the scope of this analysis (for more specifics, see Edwards, 1994; Leckie, 1993; Block, 1992), but three important directions must include, first, exploring domestic measures to enhance labor market flexibility, while simultaneously providing for more economic security (not simply a focus on narrow job security) for workers; second, revising collective bargaining law to encourage more cooperation between labor and management, including the possibility of requiring works councils as a method of empowering workers and solidifying employee involvement in change; and, third, joining domestic and foreign economic policy so that what the country negotiates internationally is consistent with domestic policy.

For example, it is not unreasonable to have international labor standards across trading countries of different economic wealth. Social charters providing for base worker standards and mechanisms for enforcement should be an integral part of trade negotiations—the Europeans have done a much better job on this than has the United States (Wise and Gibb, 1993; Wilkinson, 1992). Just as U.S. standards are often applied across its individual states to prevent unfair competition, so, too, can basic standards be applied across countries. The New Deal uplifted U.S. worker rights in the 1930s, and European workers obtained even more extensive rights; a global new deal for all workers by the year 2000 is a natural and worthy extension of these rights as trade increases.

Among the major industrialized nations, the United States relies most on the "layoff" as the solution for employment adjustment—the free-market approach. European countries rely much more on making layoffs more difficult (costly) for employers via public policy, in addition to fostering cooperation and requiring consultation with employees via collective bargaining and employee involvement laws (Leckie, 1993). In Germany, for example, this approach has resulted in a very advanced system of protection and vocational training, while the country has been able to maintain high, long-term productivity rates. While the United States should not simply copy another country, a major review of its employment and labor policy is in order.

CONCLUSION

International trade expansion is inevitable, including rising foreign direct investment by U.S. firms and more rapid technological change, offering positive-sum gains while simultaneously requiring economic restructuring. Efficient economic change requires that the winners must gain enough so that they "could" compensate the losers and still be better off than before;

otherwise, there would be no net gain in economic welfare. But this free-market economic rule does not require that any compensation of the losers take place. The distribution question is left largely unanswered, especially when it comes to trade policy and worker adjustment.

Revising employment and labor policy so as to accommodate change—allowing the economic pie to grow—while at the same time providing more of a cushion for those faced with adjustment, and paying for the cushion out of the proceeds of growth, as a family would, are a reasonable model for the U.S. economy. In order to develop a coherent trade and domestic economic policy, as we approach the year 2000, it is important that the country consider carefully an innovative employment and labor strategy that is both efficient and fair. While differences of opinion exist on the best direction, the "Band-Aid" approach will not do. Trade flows will continue to increase, along with associated domestic employment problems. A serious U.S. public policy attempt to reconcile the desire for economic flexibility with the need for economic security is needed. Ignoring the issues raised here would represent a grave error with costly implications for individual workers and for the overall prosperity of the nation.

IV

Policy and Democratic Politics

7

Toward More Perfect Unions: Public Policy and Union Democracy

Susan Jennik

Members fighting corruption in Philadelphia Roofers Local 30/30B have been yelled at, spat upon, ejected from union meetings, blacklisted from jobs, and physically assaulted. This harassment is remarkable not just for its relentless and violent nature but because it occurred while the local was under a court-supervised "decreeship" intended to return democratic control to the members. Thirteen officers of the local had been convicted of using violence, taking payoffs, embezzling from union benefit funds, and associating with the notorious Scarfo organized crime family.

As a result of a government lawsuit under RICO,[1] a federal judge appointed a "liaison officer" to oversee finances and report on union affairs. Some of the attacks on the dissidents occurred in the presence of the liaison officer, who then duly reported them to the judge. But no action has been taken to protect the dissidents or even punish their harassers. The members were forced to hire their own attorney, who filed another lawsuit seeking some relief from the violence and retaliation that occurred under the decreeship. Three years after the decreeship, the reformers felt worse off than when the lawsuit began.

The ideal of union democracy is extolled by union officers, employers, and government representatives, but when these ideals are put into practice by honest workers, the support for democracy dwindles. Labor leaders pay homage to union democracy in the abstract. As George Meany stated in the foreword to the AFL–CIO [American Federation of Labor and Congress of Industrial Organizations] Codes of Ethical Practices, issued in 1958[2]: "The American Federation of Labor and Congress of Industrial Organizations is committed by word and deed, to the concept that free, democratic trade unionism must be clean, honest trade unionism." But when faced with the prospect of criticism from their members, even many honest union officers react as though they are at war. Absolute loyalty is demanded to protect the union against the bosses; anything less is betrayal of the cause, subject to ostracism and worse.

The problem is a real one for union officers who may well believe in free speech and fair elections. However, when that speech involves an attack on their performance as an official that could result in losing their position, democratic principles often take a back seat. Even those who are hardworking and sincere in their dedication to the union justify undemocratic practices by a belief in their own infallibility: they know what is best for the union; if some irresponsible or inexperienced member is elected, the union will suffer; the members must be protected from themselves. This attitude can calcify into the belief that the official *is* the union. Criticism of union officers becomes tantamount to treason. Many supporters of the labor movement believe unions will be weakened by too much democracy. In fact, democratic unions perform better in collective bargaining and organizing campaigns (Goldfield, 1987, 236–38; Roth, 1975, 142–43, 150–53; Zieger, 1986, 196; Fiorito and Hendricks, 1987, 569; Maranto and Fiorito, 1987, 225, 238).

Corporate managers are eager to denounce union corruption, especially when facing a union organizing campaign. But employers are the hidden partner in labor crimes involving payoffs of union officials: it is much cheaper to give a few bucks to a few business agents than to pay all the workers according to the contract. Workers who complain can be fired by the employer and then must turn to the union officials to file a grievance protesting the discharges. Others will soon get the message and stay quiet. Action is rarely taken by government agencies against corrupt employers who collude with corrupt union officers to punish dissidents protesting this cozy relationship.

Fortunately, most union officials are decent, honest advocates for workers. But members of those unions dominated by crooked officials, like the roofers in Local 30, too often find that the courts and government agencies responsible for enforcing their rights are ineffective. Thousands of union members appeal every year to the National Labor Relations Board (NLRB), the U.S. Department of Labor, and the federal courts with complaints about poor representation and improper union practices.[3] Most claims are turned away, and those few that are deemed to have merit enter an interminable series of legal procedures. By the time relief is granted, many reformers have given up.

In spite of this lack of support, courageous union members continue to speak their minds, to protest contract violations ignored by their union representatives, and to run for office against the incumbents. Many members believe that their democratic rights will be enforced, and they take extraordinary risks to fight for them. They have been expelled from their unions, fired, blacklisted, threatened, and physically assaulted, and a few have even been murdered. They educate themselves, they read the labor laws, they exercise their stated rights, and when retaliation occurs, they turn to the government for protection. Too often they find themselves in a bureaucratic maze where everyone is sympathetic, but no one will do anything to help them. They are still waiting for the stated public policy favoring union democracy to become a reality.

LEGISLATIVE POLICY FAVORING WORKERS' RIGHTS

For the past sixty years, the explicit legislative policy of the labor laws has been to protect the rights of individual workers. The Norris–LaGuardia Act was a turning point in the government's attitude toward unions. Prior to its enactment in 1932, government, primarily through the courts, was hostile to union activity (Morris, 1971, 3–24; Gregory, 1946). Early on, leaders of strikes and boycotts were indicted for criminal conspiracy to set wage rates. Later, civil antitrust laws were used to enjoin strikes and allow steep damage awards to companies injured by successful economic action by workers. The Great Depression starkly demonstrated the unequal bargaining power of workers and employers. Finally, Congress acted to give some protection to workers forming unions. The substance of the Norris–LaGuardia Act prohibited the federal courts from issuing injunctions in labor disputes, subject to stringent exceptions. The public policy underlying the act stated, for the first time, the government's interest in the rights of workers to organize.

In Section 7 of the National Labor Relations Act (NLRA), workers were given the explicit right to "self-organization, to form, join, or assist labor organizations, to bargain collectively through representatives of their own choosing." In 1947, Congress amended the NLRA with the Taft–Hartley Act, also known as the Labor Management Relations Act, with the purpose of imposing some limitations on union activity. Many in Congress believed that the pendulum had swung too far and that unions were too strong. One of the Taft–Hartley amendments modified Section 7 to include the "right to refrain" from union activity that, though motivated by antiunion sentiment, strengthened the rights of the individual employee.

The act was amended again in 1959 by the Landrum–Griffin Act, officially named the Labor–Management Reporting and Disclosure Act (LMRDA), which combined two different purposes into one piece of legislation: the separate body of the LMRDA was intended to regulate internal union affairs; amendments to Taft–Hartley were intended to further restrict union activity. Liberal members of Congress informed union leaders that if they accepted the regulation of internal union affairs, they could perhaps defeat the destructive constraints proposed by management adherents in the Taft–Hartley amendments. Union officials rejected this advice and adamantly opposed both parts of the bill (Lee, 1990, 138'159). The union democracy section of the bill was largely drafted by the American Civil Liberties Union (ACLU), which supported the civil liberties of union members. The bill was passed by an odd coalition of civil libertarians and employer supporters, who favored further governmental regulation of unions (Walker, 1990, 166, 254–55). For the first time, union members were given statutory rights within their unions.[4]

In 1970, Congress added another weapon in its arsenal against union corruption when it passed the RICO Act. The influence of organized crime in unions was overtly one of RICO's targets.[5] A major innovation of RICO was that, in addition to criminal penalties, it provided for a civil remedy allowing federal courts to dissolve or "reorganize" an enterprise affected by a pattern of racketeering activity. The list of RICO "predicate felonies," of which two in a ten-year period are sufficient to establish a pattern, explicitly includes labor racketeering offenses (embezzlement of pension and welfare funds, illegal payments to labor unions, and bribery of union officials). The Department of Justice has used RICO to "reorganize" corrupt unions, usually by appointing some independent monitor to supervise certain union functions for a time, culminating in a supervised election of new officers.

Thus, the public policy of labor legislation, at least as it has been stated, has consistently sought to protect the rights of individual workers in relation to their employers, their unions, and organized crime. However, as each law has matured, institutional interests have gradually been favored over individual rights.

REGULATION OF INTERNAL UNION AFFAIRS

The three laws previously discussed—NLRA, LMRDA, and RICO—are the principal statutes used to regulate internal affairs of unions, though other laws may be used for certain purposes (Title VII of the Civil Rights Act to challenge discrimination by union officials; the Employee Retirement Income Security Act [ERISA] to protect workers' pension benefits). An examination of the operation of each of these statutes to assist union members who are working to democratize their unions shows that the laws are falling short of their stated purpose of protecting the rights of individual workers.

The Impact of the NLRA on Internal Union Matters

The NLRA primarily focuses on workers as employees, not as union members. There are, however, certain areas in which the NLRA can affect internal union matters. The most significant of these are (1) protection of the rights of employees to engage in internal union activity at their jobs;

(2) imposition on unions of a duty to fairly represent all employees in the bargaining unit; and (3) regulation of union job referral systems.

Protection of the Rights of Employees to Engage in Internal Union Activity on the Job

Section 7 of the NLRA protects employees from retaliation by their employer for engaging in protected, concerted activity. Thus, the law, at least theoretically, prohibits an employer from firing a worker for supporting a union in an organizing campaign. There are, however, serious problems with the ability of the NLRB to effectively enforce this right (Geoghegan, 1991). The board has extended the definition of protected, concerted activity to include not just support for a union but also internal union activity.[6]

But the board's defense of union members fired for protected activity has been inconsistent. NLRB policy is set by a five-member board appointed by the president. The appointments are overtly political, and the board's policy changes with each change in administration; President Reagan's appointees to the board reflected his antiunion and antiworker attitude.

On January 19, 1984, the board issued a pair of decisions that relinquished its authority to decide charges of employer retaliation filed by workers covered by a union contract. In the first case, the Machinists charged that United Technologies threatened a worker with discipline if she processed her grievance to the second step of the grievance procedure. The union filed another grievance protesting this threat but withdrew it before the final step of the grievance procedure and filed a charge with the board claiming that the threat of discipline for protected activity was clearly a violation of the act. The board overturned an earlier case, which would have allowed it to hear the charge, and applied a "pre-arbitral deferral" policy requiring the union to take the grievance to arbitration before it would make a determination.[7]

In the second case, Salvatore Spatorico, president of an Oil, Chemical and Atomic Workers (OCAW) local, was fired for participating in a sick-out protesting the suspension of two workers. The union grieved the discharge but lost in arbitration. Overturning another earlier decision, the board decided that it would defer to an arbitration decision if the grievance issue was factually parallel to the unfair labor practice issue, if the arbitrator was generally presented with the facts relevant to resolving the unfair labor practice, and if the arbitrator's decision was not "clearly repugnant" to the act.[8] Since Spatorico's claim that he was unfairly fired for participating in the sick-out was the same in both forums, the board refused to hear the case and let the arbitrator's decision stand.

By adopting its deferral policy, the board allows contractual grievance procedures to determine statutory rights that the board is responsible for enforcing. For union dissidents, the policy spells disaster. The dissident is often complaining about the failure of union representatives to enforce contract violations by the employer. This "troublemaker" is upsetting a very comfortable relationship between the employer and the union. Both parties want to get rid of this person, and they are exactly the same parties that control the grievance procedure.

The Elusive Duty of Fair Representation

In 1944, the Supreme Court, in a burst of sympathy for a fired worker, held that his union's failure to adequately investigate his grievance protesting his discharge violated the union's duty of fair representation.[9] This obligation was derived from the provisions of the Railway Labor Act granting the union status as the exclusive bargaining representative for all employees in the bargaining unit. The duty of fair representation constituted an exception to the general rule that the outcome of the grievance procedure was final. In 1953, this obligation was extended to unions regulated by the NLRA.[10]

A worker who has a complaint on the job *must* go through the union for relief. Workers have no absolute right for their grievance to be processed, and if it is, they have no legal right to overturn the result if they are dissatisfied. The union determines whether and how a grievance will be presented. Fired workers have no right to hire their own lawyer to represent them before the arbitrator, who will decide whether the termination violated the contractual requirement that workers may be discharged only for "just cause." Some unions allow workers to be represented by their own counsel, but the law and the courts do not require it (Goldberg, 1985).

The duty of fair representation (DFR) is supposed to protect workers from abuses by unions of their power to exclusively handle worker grievances. Although the theory sounds good, in practice it is extremely difficult for workers to win DFR cases. An employee must meet a very high standard of proof in order to win: that the union acted arbitrarily, discriminatorily, or in bad faith. Negligence in presenting a grievance or even gross negligence, such as missing a time limit for filing a grievance, is not a breach of the duty of fair representation. A union is not required to file a grievance at all unless a member makes a request, and a union may refuse to file or pursue a grievance so long as the decision is based on the merits. Union officers are generally knowledgeable enough to avoid making statements that will prove bad faith. In the absence of a "smoking gun," a union insurgent will find it difficult to win a DFR case.

Regulation of Union Referral Systems

Many construction industry workers get jobs through their unions under referral systems, which vary from informal telephone referrals to hiring halls governed by written rules. In any case, members of construction unions are at the mercy of the union officials for steady work. Shane Phelan,

Don Fitzgerald, and Mark Cotton opposed Plumbers Local 76 business manager Patrick Quinn. Jobs in the local's jurisdiction in Connecticut were scarce, but there was a nuclear power plant being built in the jurisdiction of neighboring Local 305 whose business manager, Terrence Quinn, was Patrick's brother. Unlike other members of their local, the dissidents were not referred to the steady jobs. They sued and won a $500,000 jury verdict against Local 305 and the Quinn brothers. That verdict was appealed and partially overturned but remanded to the trial court. Litigation continues as of this writing.

Most victims of hiring hall discrimination are not so fortunate. Claims for union retaliation in job referrals can be brought either before the NLRB or in court. NLRB charges can be filed without an attorney; the NLRB agents will investigate the charge and make a recommendation to the regional director, who determines whether the charge merits a complaint or whether it should be dismissed. Appeals from a dismissal can be filed with the general counsel of the board, but they are rarely granted.

The board has developed a distinction between "exclusive" and "non-exclusive" job referral systems. Exclusive systems require employers to hire all, or a fixed number or percentage of, workers through the union referral system. Unions operating exclusive referral systems are subject to stringent requirements: they must have written, objective rules; they must provide information about referrals to members, upon request; and they may not discriminate against applicants for employment because of their union membership or activity. Only the prohibition against discrimination applies to unions operating nonexclusive systems.

Thus, the first hurdle faced by an out-of-work union reformer is to prove that the referral system is exclusive. Sometimes this is easy, as in New York City Carpenters Local 608, in which the contract explicitly requires employers to hire 50 percent of the workers through the union. Many unions, however, well aware of the ramifications of operating exclusive systems, take pains to write vague contract language and enforce exclusivity informally. Union officials then solemnly declare that members may solicit their own work, and employers are free to hire off the street. In reality, employers clear every prospective worker with the union, but both parties to this collusive relationship will deny it if questioned.

Even if the hiring hall is exclusive, the member must still prove discrimination. Members complain that favorites of the officials receive the best jobs through "the back-door"; those jobs and the names of those referred to them are not even entered in the hiring hall records. Another ploy is to refer the critics to the most dangerous and undesirable jobs in the hope that the members will turn them down. Under many systems, refusing three jobs puts the member at the bottom of the list. On occasion, job dispatchers blatantly inform the reformers that they will not be referred to work; those are the easy cases.

Workers in unions with nonexclusive hiring hall systems have an even harder time proving discrimination. They do not have access to records, and there are no rules. Anytime the worker points to someone who was referred ahead of her or him, the union official says that person was more qualified, the employer requested that person by name, that person got the job on his or her own, or some other explanation.

There are other disadvantages to the NLRB procedure. There is a six-month time limit. Workers are often reluctant to file a charge against the union; they wait until desperation forces them to act. If more than six months have elapsed, their damages will be limited to the six-month period prior to the filing of the charges. The procedure is long and tedious, and in the end the damages that may be awarded are limited to back pay minus any interim earnings. So, the diligent worker who goes out and finds other employment receives little or nothing in damages. Victims of union or employer unfair labor practices do not receive any damages for emotional distress, medical expenses, or punitive damages. They may have lost their homes, their families may have suffered or even broken up, they may have developed an ulcer or emotional problems, but they can recover only the back pay that they actually lost.

Lawsuits in federal court do not have the same limits on damages or time within which to file, but they present different problems. Although some workers do file cases on their own, most seek legal representation. It is difficult to find attorneys with expertise in hiring hall discrimination, but it is even more difficult to find an attorney who will take such a case without payment of a substantial fee, and blacklisted workers are notoriously short on cash. Although attorney fees may be granted to successful plaintiffs, few attorneys are willing to take such cases on a contingency fee basis because they are difficult to win and will take years to litigate. As discussed later, union officials who can use dues money to pay attorneys to defend them will not hesitate to file motions and appeals to postpone recovery. Then, when the award is granted they criticize the worker for costing the union so much money.

Recommendations

Congress ought to explicitly overturn the board's deferral doctrine and prohibit the NLRB from relying on a determination of statutory rights by any other forum. Arbitrators and joint grievance panels should be limited to their area of expertise: interpretation of collective bargaining agreements. The NLRB ought to maintain its exclusive jurisdiction to determine whether an unfair labor practice was committed.

The problem of the duty of fair representation requires a revision of the standard to which union representatives are held. Instead of requiring union members to prove bad faith or collusion with the employer, the standard should be similar to that used for attorney or medical malpractice cases, which would allow recovery for gross negligence of union representatives. Another approach would be to enact a national employee wrongful discharge statute that would permit arbitration of any employment discharge.

A very simple change in the law could improve the fairness of hiring hall systems overnight: unions should be required to adopt rules for job referral systems and post those rules along with information about job referrals. Exposing the process to the view of the membership would result in self-enforcement without need to resort to litigation or unfair labor practice charges.

Under current NLRA provisions, workers who are illegally fired from their jobs or discriminated against in job referrals receive only "make whole" damages, that is, the amount of wages that they lost less any wages they made from other employment. The employer or union, thus, has little to risk by violating the law; damage awards are generally small.

This problem could be corrected in one of two ways: (1) an "innocent until proven guilty" procedure that would require the NLRB to seek an injunction ordering an employer to reinstate a worker if the NLRB's investigation found probable cause that the employer had violated the law[11]; or (2) a provision for compensatory damages, such as loss of a home, emotional distress, or medical expenses caused by the termination, and provision for punitive or double damages.

The Impact of the LMRDA on Internal Union Matters

Congress took another step toward strengthening the rights of individual workers when it passed the LMRDA, which regulates the union as an institution and grants civil liberties to members. Since the law was passed in 1959, the state of union democracy has vastly improved over the situation described in the McClellan hearings that prompted the act (see U.S. Congress, Senate, 1960).

Although embezzlement of union funds, employer payoffs, and violence against dissident members continue to occur, the frequency of labor racketeering has decreased as federal courts have enforced members' rights.

Rights Provided by the LMRDA

The heart of the LMRDA is contained in Title I, the "Bill of Rights for Union Members," which guarantees equal participation in union affairs; free speech and assembly; votes on increases in dues, initiation fees, and assessments; the right to sue the union for violation of rights; due process in disciplinary actions; and a copy of the contract governing the members' working conditions. Retaliation by the union for exercising protected rights is prohibited. Provision of these basic rights is essential to union democracy, but there are loopholes in the law and obstacles to enforcement that need to be addressed.

The coverage of the law does not extend to members of public sector unions, that is, those employed by state and local governments, a group that now makes up approximately 25 percent of the labor movement. Rights of federal employee union members are protected by the Civil Service Reform Act (5 U.S.C. @ 7120), which adopts the principles of the LMRDA. Members of unions composed exclusively of public employees do not enjoy the democratic rights provided to members of private sector unions. They are limited to the rights provided in the union's constitution or bylaws which are enforceable in court, if a lawyer can be found to take the case.

No section of the LMRDA or any other law requires membership ratification of contract proposals. Union members have the right to vote on the contract provisions that regulate their wages, hours, and working conditions only if the union constitution gives them that right. When members do have the right to ratify their contracts, some courts have held that the Title I right to equal participation in union affairs gives members the right to an informed vote on union issues, including contract proposals. Rank-and-file Teamsters have used that right to obtain copies of a proposed contract two weeks before a vote to allow them to disseminate their views about the proposal to the membership.[12] In other cases, however, courts have held that the law requires only *equal* treatment and have not found a violation when all members are equally deprived of a meaningful vote by being denied information, or even by being given inaccurate information, about contract proposals.[13]

Title I of the LMRDA also includes a requirement that labor organizations inform members about their rights under the act (29 U.S.C. § 415). Most unions disseminated information about the law to their members when it was first passed in 1959. Since then, few unions have given their members any information about their rights under the LMRDA. Most of those who were members in 1959 have retired, and new members are not regularly provided with the information. The Department of Labor (DOL) takes the position that it has no authority to enforce that section of the act.

Regulation of Union Officer Elections

Title IV of the LMRDA regulates elections of officers. Local unions must elect officers every three years, intermediate labor organizations every four years, and national labor organizations every five years. Local union officers must be elected directly by the members; officers of intermediate and national labor organizations may be elected either directly by the members or by delegates at a convention. Use of employer or union resources for the benefit of a candidate is prohibited.

The provisions of Title IV are enforceable almost exclusively by the secretary of labor after members go through any internal postelection protest procedures. The Department of Labor requires not just that a violation has occurred but that the violation may have affected the outcome of the election. Thus, violations count for more in close elections. If the DOL finds that a violation may have affected the outcome of the election, it must file a lawsuit in federal court seeking to overturn the election and scheduling a new one supervised by the DOL.

The remedy of a supervised election is welcome but too often comes too late. Jerry Tucker's experience in the United Automobile Workers (UAW) is typical: in 1986, Tucker ran for regional director and lost by a margin of less than one vote. His protest to the DOL was upheld because union resources were used to support his opponent, the incumbent. The union stonewalled, and when the election was finally ordered rerun in January 1989, there were only six months remaining in the term of office. Tucker won the election supervised by the DOL but lost the next election, which was run by the union without supervision.

The one exception to the general rule that violations can be challenged only after the election is the right to use the union mailing list to send campaign literature to members. In 1990, the extent of this right was somewhat clarified by the Supreme Court. Timothy Brown, a candidate for president of the Masters, Mates & Pilots (MM&P), requested a mailing of campaign literature. He was told that the union allowed such mailings only after the nominating convention, which was held thirty days before the ballots were mailed to the membership. MM&P members work on ships that travel around the world and are often away from home for many months, making a thirty–day campaign period insufficient. Brown filed suit and won the right to mail his literature. On the union's appeal, the Supreme Court held that the relevant question is the reasonableness of the request, not the reasonableness of a union rule restricting access for campaign purposes.[14] The extent of this decision will certainly be litigated. As of this writing, candidates for office can assume that a union cannot put a time limit on how long before an election a mailing can be required.

Recommendations

The LMRDA should provide the same protection to members of public sector unions as it does to those in the private sector. Congress has already extended rights to public employees under other federal statutes, such as the Fair Labor Standards Act and Title VII of the Civil Rights Act. It should amend the LMRDA to grant democratic rights to members of public employee unions.

Contract ratification votes should be required by all unions. Setting the terms of working conditions is probably the most important function of a union, and that important decision should be subject to membership approval. The law should explicitly entitle members to an informed vote on contract proposals by requiring unions to distribute a copy of the proposed agreement prior to the vote.

Congress should put some teeth into the requirement that unions inform their members about their rights under the act. At a minimum, the DOL could adopt regulations specifying how unions may comply with the requirement, which should include notification to all new members and periodic notification to all members.

Many of the defects in unions result from the lack of a vibrant political life in the union. A requirement that all union officers be directly elected by the members would increase leadership responsiveness to membership concerns and would increase membership involvement in their unions. While direct elections alone will not cure corruption, they are a necessary prerequisite to change in unions dominated by organized crime. In addition, direct elections could prevent unions from sliding into corruption by holding officers accountable to the members.

As in other organizations, incumbent officers enjoy advantages when running for reelection. Many of these advantages are unavoidable, but some changes in the law could level the playing field for opposition candidates: unions should be required to provide equal space in the official union publication for all candidates for office; all candidates should have equal access to campaign on employer property; and elections should be run by an independent agency, not an election committee appointed by incumbent candidates.

LMRDA rights are enforced either by individuals' filing federal lawsuits or by action of the Department of Labor. Both enforcement methods have difficulties. Individuals who seek to enforce rights in court require the services of an attorney, a problem that can be insurmountable for both political and financial reasons. Labor lawyers, who are preferable because of their knowledge of the law, are generally divided into two camps, union and management, neither of which is usually interested in representing union dissidents. A small network of dedicated lawyers throughout the country has developed expertise in union democracy law, but even these lawyers, motivated primarily by idealism, must be concerned with how they might get paid for their work. Although large damage awards have been won in egregious cases involving long-term blacklisting or physical violence, the typical free speech violation is usually remedied by an injunction, but not the kind of money award that can induce an attorney to take a case on a contingency-fee basis.

The Supreme Court softened this harsh reality a bit by allowing attorneys' fees to be granted to union members suing to enforce their rights. That decision has been watered down bit by bit. Many courts do not grant attorneys' fees if a member is awarded financial damages, on the assumption that attorneys' fees will be paid out of the award. The entitlement to an award of attorneys' fees should be made as explicit in the LMRDA as it is in the Civil Rights Act.

Even if the union may be held liable for fees, union officers using the members' dues money to pay the union attorney have little to lose and much to gain by avoiding settlement of lawsuits filed by dissidents. Union members who win a Title I case establish the right to continued dissidence for themselves and all other members, thus encouraging increased criticism of the union officers. The successful plaintiff in a Title I case also wins an important political victory, weakening the reelection prospects of the incumbents. The litigation can drag on for years, wearing down the member and his or her attorney who, if handling the case on a pro bono or contingency-fee basis, is wondering how his or her practice will survive while awaiting payment of fees.

The solution to this endless litigation is to require the union officers responsible for the violation to pay an attorney to represent them individually. Union officers have been held individually liable for unlawful acts under Title I. Professor James Pope described the conflict of interest when the union's attorney, hired to represent the members, defends the actions of the union officers accused of violating the members' democratic rights (Pope, 1989). In such cases, union attorneys should be disqualified from representing the union officers. Requiring the union officers to pay their own attorneys deters officers from committing violations and promotes settlements when lawsuits are filed.

The Department of Labor is responsible for enforcing the filing requirements, trusteeship provisions, and election standards of the LMRDA. However, the Department of Labor has another function that conflicts with its enforcement responsibilities: to serve as a liaison between the administration and the labor movement. To effectively carry out this function, it is important to maintain good relationships with labor leaders. Its other function, to enforce the provisions of the LMRDA, sometimes requires legal action against these very officials. It is not difficult to imagine that the secretary of labor may feel uncomfortable suing those with whom he or she is attempting to build a cooperative working relationship. Some commentators and practitioners have suggested that the enforcement functions of the DOL ought to be transferred to the Department of Justice, which does not have the same conflict of purpose (Summers, Rauh, and Benson, 1986).

The Impact of RICO on Internal Union Affairs

The most significant labor event since the wave of industrial organizing in the 1930s was the Teamster officer election in December 1991, won by Ron Carey and his reform slate. The election was supervised by court-appointed officers in settlement of a RICO lawsuit brought by the government to end the long-term organized crime influence in the Teamsters. Although highly controversial, the use of RICO to restore membership control of the union proved more successful than decades of traditional law enforcement methods.

One of the main goals of RICO was to address the inadequate remedies for union corruption provided by the NLRA and LMRDA (Tilles, 1989). RICO is a complex statute that provides criminal and civil remedies to reorganize enterprises that have been subject to a pattern of racketeering defined as commission of any two acts, from a long list of state and federal crimes, within a ten year period. RICO is a powerful tool for prosecutors because it allows them to pursue all those who have participated in the racketeering activity, even if not the specific acts. The civil remedies are similarly strong: the government may seek broad injunctive relief to reorganize the enterprise, and individuals harmed by the racketeering activity can seek treble damages.

The Use of RICO for Union Reform

The use of RICO in the business world has been hotly disputed, but there is little argument that RICO was intended to be used to combat union corruption.[15] For decades, the Teamsters union had been dominated by racketeers. Hundreds of officers from the local through the international level were convicted of crimes ranging from embezzling union funds to murdering rank and filers who dared oppose them. But the removal of convicted officers only resulted in their replacement by new corrupt officers. Change seemed impossible. Former president Roy Williams testified about organized crime influence in the Teamsters union: "[The mob] was here a long time before any of us ever got here, and they have got pretty powerful. And you fellows [the government] haven't been able to do nothing with them either."[16]

The use of RICO to combat union corruption caused an uproar even before the government filed its lawsuit. The AFL–CIO Executive Council passed a resolution opposing government trusteeships over unions, a position echoed by 264 members of Congress.[17] On July 4, 1988, one week after the government filed its RICO lawsuit, a group called Americans against Government Control of Unions took out a full-page ad in the *New York Times* denouncing the lawsuit. Teamsters for a Democratic Union (TDU), a persistent rank-and-file reform group, also opposed a government trusteeship but advocated a supervised election of officers. Previously, Teamster officers had been elected by delegates at a convention that was tightly controlled by the incumbents.

On March 14, 1989, on the eve of trial, the government and the union settled the lawsuit with a consent decree that allowed the officers to maintain their positions while three court-appointed officers prosecuted misconduct charges, oversaw the union's finances, and supervised elections of convention delegates and international officers.[18] The settlement of the lawsuit shook the union from top to bottom. With the ink barely dry on the consent decree, the Teamsters began fighting every detail of its implementation. A rift developed within the general executive board, with one faction accusing the other of selling out to the government to save its own skins.

Carey, president of a New York City local representing United Parcel Service workers, had a reputation as a militant and honest Teamster official (Brill, 1978). He announced his candidacy for president in September 1989, and over the next two years he was an indefatigable, effective candidate who forthrightly attacked corruption in the union and promised to end it. Although not a member of TDU, Carey won its endorsement. TDU was founded in 1976; by 1989, it had an impressive network of 10,000 courageous and experienced rank-and-file activists who had led campaigns for better contracts and against dishonest officers (LaBotz, 1990). That network went into high gear for the elections for delegates to the convention and for the general officer election.

The union's 1991 convention, which had customarily been held in Las Vegas, was moved to Orlando. In addition to nominating three slates of candidates, the delegates voted on amendments to the constitution. Although Carey supporters constituted only 15 percent of the delegates, they held the balance of power between the other two slates headed by incumbent vice presidents R. V. Durham and Walter Shea. Several amendments that had been proposed by TDU delegates and overwhelmingly defeated at past conventions were adopted in Orlando: strike benefits were increased from $50 to $200 per week; an Ethical Practices Committee was established; members were given a separate vote on local supplements to national contracts; and the union's fleet of jets was to be sold. Reform became the ideal that all candidates soon espoused, but the incumbents could not shake off their association with the Old Guard, and Carey's slate won the membership election with 48 percent of the vote. While vestiges of organized crime influence remain in certain Teamster locals, the use of RICO to provide a supervised election gave the members a chance to regain control of their union through the democratic process.

RICO suits brought against local unions have had mixed results. The first use of RICO for union reform was in Teamsters Local 560, the New Jersey power base of the Provenzano family. For decades, brothers Tony, Salvatore, and Nunzio Provenzano divided their time between prison and union office; they were convicted of labor racketeering charges, including embezzling union funds, loan-sharking, pilferage, taking kickbacks and payoffs from employers, physical assault, and murder of a challenger to their positions. In 1986, U.S. district judge Harold Ackerman ordered the officers removed and appointed a trustee to run the local. After two years of trusteeship, the candidates supported by the former union officers won a court-supervised election. However, an opposition movement grew in influence and, in February 1992, the president and two members of the executive board resigned and were replaced by supporters of the opposition. It is not surprising that it would take many years to overcome the long history of corruption in the local. Without government action, there would have been no change at all.

RICO actions have also been filed against the Philadelphia Roofers local described before; Cement and Concrete Workers Local 6A in New York City; Teamsters Locals 295, 814, and 851 in New York City; the Carpenters District Council of New York City; International Longshoremen's Association locals in New York City; the United Food and Commercial Workers Local 359 in New York City; and Hotel Employees and Restaurant Employees Local 54 in Atlantic City. The suits have resulted in the appointment of trustees or administrators to oversee union affairs until a court-supervised election can be held. It is too early to tell whether the RICO strategy will be effective in all cases, but so far the failures, such as the Philadelphia Roofers local, have been caused by inadequate government action to protect dissidents who could form an alternative leadership. Without that protection, the former leaders or their replacements will simply come back into power when the government leaves.

Recommendations

RICO is a powerful weapon that can be remarkably effective against union racketeering. Unions have expressed concern that the broad remedial authority of RICO will allow too much government intrusion into internal union affairs, an especially alarming possibility with an antiunion administration. However, the government's use of RICO to date does not justify those fears. RICO has been used only in the worst locals in which officers have already been convicted of labor racketeering crimes, and the parent organization has taken no corrective action. Trusteeships or administratorships have been imposed for limited time periods with the goal of returning the union to membership control through the electoral process. The use of RICO for union reform is consistent with the already developed public policy of protecting the rights of individual workers and should be continued in the most extreme situations when nothing else has worked.

However, mere appointment of a monitor to sit in the union office for a period of time will not result in a more democratic union. To be effective, the court-appointed monitorships must have three elements:

1. The rights of members must be carefully protected. In construction unions, job referral systems must be supervised to ensure that opponents of the officers are not blacklisted. Acts of intimidation or violence must be dealt with quickly and forcefully. Supporters of the removed officers should not be allowed to dominate meetings; scrupulous adherence to rules of democratic process should allow all members to participate in meetings free from intimidation.

2. The cost of the court action should be kept to a minimum. In many cases, the union treasury has been depleted by payments of excessive salaries and benefits to the officers and sometimes by embezzlement. Court-appointed overseers who bill at corporate attorney rates will not be appreciated by rank-and-file members seeking to rebuild their union.

3. The goal of the government action should be to return control of the union to the members. In a union dominated by organized crime elements, members who want a democratic union are excluded from union positions and do not have the experience needed to run a union. To be successful, a court monitorship must educate members in the skills needed to administer the union, for example, grievance procedures, labor laws, contract negotiations, rules for union meetings, leadership development, rights of union members, responsibilities of union officers, and union structures. Another effective method of training is to create membership advisory committees to make recommendations on bylaws' revisions, grievances, contract proposals, a newsletter, organizing, or other union functions. Without intensive membership involvement during a court monitorship, it is likely that supporters of the former officers will return to power when the monitorship is lifted.

CONCLUSION

Perhaps it is understandable that union officials resist government regulation of internal union matters; no one likes to be monitored. However, there is a readily available, but largely unused, solution to government intervention: unions can police themselves. The AFL–CIO could revive and enforce its Codes of Ethical Practices. National labor organizations have the power to discipline officers guilty of misconduct and to impose trusteeships over corrupt locals but this power is rarely used. Instead, union officers mount campaigns to defend the worst among them from the consequences of their crimes against the members. There should be no place in the labor movement for those who would debase it by using the union for their own self-interest. Union officials as a group may be no more corrupt, as they argue, than representatives of government or business, but there are, and there will always be, those who seek to take advantage of a position of power. The problem will be resolved not by denying its existence but by making structural changes to prevent misconduct and to take corrective action when it occurs. The establishment of independent bodies, such as the UAW's Public Review Board, to oversee decisions of the union officers would go a long way toward obstructing criminal activity within a union. Unless unions themselves take action to combat labor racketeering, members will continue to need the protection of government.

NOTES

1. The Racketeer Influenced and Corrupt Organizations Act, 18 U.S.C. 1961–68.

2. The Codes of Ethical Practices are no longer published by, or available from, the AFL–CIO; the committee established to enforce the codes no longer meets. A copy of the codes can be obtained from the Association for Union Democracy.

3. For example, in 1990, 6,289 unfair labor practice charges were filed against unions alleging coercion of members. Of all 9,684 charges filed against unions (including charges for picketing violations), the NLRB issued 346 complaints. The *median* time between the filing of a charge to the issuance of a decision by the board was 774 days (*Fifty-Fifth Annual Report of the NLRB for the Fiscal Year Ended Spet. 30, 1990*, 1992).

4. Some earlier state court decisions had granted rights to union members under various common law theories. See Summers, 1960.

5. *Measures Relating to Organized Crime: Hearings before the Subcommittee on Criminal Laws and Procedures of the Senate Committee on the Judiciary*, 91st Cong. 1st Sess. 62 (1969).

6. *Tracy Towing Line, Inc.*, 166 NLRB 81 (1969), enf'd, 417 F.2d 865 (2d Cir. 1969). See also National Lawyers Guild, 1992.

7. *United Technologies*, 268 NLRB No. 83 (1984).

8. *Olin Corp.*, 268 NLRB No. 86 (1984).

9. *Steele v. Louisville & Nashville Railroad*, 323 U.S. 192 (1944).

10. *Ford Motor Co. v. Huffman*, 345 U.S. 330 (1953).

11. The NLRA includes a procedure requiring the board to seek injunctions to stop union picketing violative of the act; it also authorizes the board to seek injunctions on behalf of discharged employees, but that authority is rarely used. 29 U.S.C. @ 160.

12. *Carothers v. McCarthy*, 705 F. Supp. 687 (D.D.C. 1988); *Bauman v. Presser*, 117 LRRM 2393 (D.D.C. 1984).

13. *Talbot v. Robert Matthews Distributing Co.*, 961 F.2d 654 (7th Cir. 1992); *Ackley v. Teamsters, Western Conference*, 958 F.2d 1463 (9th Cir. 1992)

14. *Brown v. Masters, Mates & Pilots*, 111 S.Ct. 880 (1991).

15. Unions have been legitimately concerned about attempts to apply RICO in strike situations, but, for the most part, those attempts have not been successful. See Brown, 1988.

16. Deposition of Roy L. Williams by the President's Commission on Organized Crime, September 13, 1985.

17. Letter to Attorney General Edwin Meese, III, dated December 10, 1987.

18. *U.S. v. Teamsters*, 88 Civ. 4486 (Edelstein, J.).

8

Combating Plant Closings in the Era of the Transnational Corporations

Bruce Nissen

PLANT CLOSINGS: THE BACKGROUND

Unionized jobs, particularly those in manufacturing, have become increasingly insecure in the past twenty years. Unions are faced with wholesale job loss as older unionized plants in multiplant corporations close while new plants open either nonunion or abroad, or both. Many of the major industrial unions in the United States lost between 25–60 percent of their members in the massive restructuring that produced closed facilities across the United States in the 1980s.

Before examining union responses to this onslaught, it is important to recognize why this has occurred. Wholesale plant closings are the result of major changes in the economy in the post–World War II period. The United States emerged from this war as the dominant economic power in the Western world. American businesses extended their foreign operations rapidly in the following decades.

In the 1950s and 1960s, the increasingly transnational character of U.S. business was not perceived as a threat by the U.S. labor movement. Domestic production increased at a rapid rate throughout these two decades; despite periodic recessions, unemployment remained relatively low by historic standards. Incomes rose steadily throughout this period. Despite a slow but steady decline of the percentage of the overall labor force represented by unions, the U.S. labor movement was winning substantial compensation packages from U.S. employers. Thus, both the labor leadership and many of the rank and file were relatively complacent through the 1960s about the movement of capital and jobs abroad. There were significant exceptions: unions in the electronics, clothing, and shoe industries, for example, encountered major losses in membership by the 1960s due to foreign product imports and the export of jobs abroad. These unions sounded the alarm much sooner than unions in industries less immediately threatened by job loss, but their concern did not become widespread throughout the labor movement until the late 1970s and the 1980s.

By the 1970s, however, the worldwide nature of "big business" in the United States was obvious. Books such as Richard Barnet and Ronald Muller's *Global Reach: The Power of the Multinational Corporations* documented the degree to which U.S. workers and U.S. policymakers faced a global network of capital that transcended national boundaries.

Closely related to the internationalization of capital was the shifting geographic location of production within the boundaries of the United States. Companies increasingly located their new production facilities in the South or in rural locations without a history of unionization. The southern states have long histories of hostility to unions; most are "right-to-work" states with laws forbidding the union shop. These states have the lowest rate of unionization in the country; union organizing drives are difficult and, in the past, were often outright dangerous for the organizers attempting to conduct them.

The new "rural" plants are usually equally difficult to unionize. The workforce is unfamiliar with unions, industrial wages seem generous compared with traditional income sources, and the workers are so geographically dispersed that organizing is logistically difficult.

The internationalization of capital and the geographic dispersion of production were facilitated by similar factors. Advances in communications and transportation made mobility increasingly easy. Technological change simplified the tasks necessary for many types of production, lessening the dependence of corporations on the highly skilled (unionized) labor force located in the traditional U.S. manufacturing centers. Government tax, trade, and industrial policies encouraged the flight of capital and production abroad and south.

One final factor turned the internationalization of capital and the geographic dispersion of production into widespread plant closings of unionized facilities. Following a long period of undisputed dominance over the capitalist world marketplace, the United States lost ground to European and Japanese competitors in the 1970s and 1980s. In industry after industry, Japanese- and European-produced products captured a larger market share of worldwide production from U.S. producers.

The response of U.S. producers to increased competition was to "emigrate, evaporate, or annihilate." "Emigrate" meant more and more production located or relocated outside the confines of the United States. "Evaporate" meant closing operations and shifting to easier sources of quick profitability, such as stock market manipulations and paper asset shuffling. "Annihilate" meant destruction or near destruction of the union in those facilities where it was impractical to relocate or withdraw but feasible to take on the union. "Union busting" became a multimillion-dollar industry in the 1980s.

Emigration and evaporation created the phenomenon known as "deindustrialization." In their pathbreaking book *The Deindustrialization of America* (1982), Barry Bluestone and Bennett Harrison documented the wholesale abandonment of manufacturing communities in the United States. By the 1980s, plant closings were widespread in their occurrence and devastating in their impact.

UNION RESPONSE

Union responses to plant closings have traditionally fallen into rather limited patterns. The most frequent response has been the negotiation of severance benefits for the affected workers. The union local also may play a role in the retraining and job search programs that may be available to displaced workers. In particularly hard-hit industries with production facilities around the nation (such as the auto industry), the union may negotiate job transfer rights within a particular corporation, in this way protecting employment opportunities for the most senior employees.

Union locals sometimes offer concessions in compensation rates or work rules in the hope of thus preserving jobs. On rare occasions this offer is accepted, and on even rarer occasions jobs are actually preserved for a significant period of time. However, the general picture shows no consistent relationship between union concessions and job preservation; concessions are not generally an effective method for saving jobs (Craypo, 1990, 24).

On the political front, unions have attempted to deal with plant closings in a variety of direct and indirect ways. Organized labor lobbied for the law that went into effect in 1989 mandating sixty days' prenotification to workers in larger facilities of an impending closure. It has also lobbied for a variety of tax, trade, tariff, "domestic content," monetary, and fiscal (reindustrialization) policies that it is hoped would lead to a climate of greater domestic economic stability and thus fewer plant closings. While it is difficult to measure the ultimate effect of all these efforts, it is clear that none of them have been highly successful to date.

Whether in the political or the industrial arena, however, unions have seldom challenged a corporation's right to close facilities when it chooses to. Because of its support for an economic system based on private property rights, the U.S. labor movement tends to defer to corporate managers and owners in the larger decisions impacting on the enterprise as a whole. This is true both within the collective bargaining system and in the political arena.

The "management rights" clause in virtually all union contracts is the clearest expression of this deference. It cedes to management exclusive rights to all decisions governing the overall operation of the enterprise.

Only the specific clauses of the contract governing wages, hours, and terms and conditions of employment (i.e., *personnel* issues) constrain management's absolute control. In all other matters the union has no legitimate right to contest management's decisions.

In the political arena the absence of an independent voice for labor (such as a labor party) underlines the same secondary role. The U.S. labor movement has been content to mount no political challenge to corporate control of the economy.

RECENT BATTLES OVER PLANT CLOSINGS

However, there were increasing numbers of struggles over plant closings in the 1980s. The devastation to some industrial communities was so severe that resistance was generated to specific shutdowns. Some struggles originated from within the labor movement; others, from community or religious organizations.

Virtually all of these efforts began at the local level. The national unions have, for the most part, played no role at all or took a back seat in the effort. National publicity has attended the effort to resurrect Youngstown Sheet and Tube in Youngstown, Ohio; a battle to save the U.S. Steel plant "Dorothy Six" in Pittsburgh; the preservation of Morse Cutting Tool in New Bedford, Massachusetts; and the long campaign to save a General Motors plant in Van Nuys, California.[1]

Most, but not all, of these efforts have failed to reverse a plant closing decision. For that reason and because the larger national and international context is so crucial to the new mobility of capital, one might question the importance or usefulness of struggles of this nature.

In this chapter, I argue that such thinking is wrong for several reasons. It is certainly true that national and even international controls over capital will be necessary before the job insecurity brought on by shutdowns will be effectively addressed. It is equally true that national measures, such as a "superfund" for retraining of dislocated industrial workers, are needed. The many national measures that have been grouped under the term *industrial policy* can decisively affect the incidence of plant closures. There can be no doubt that local plant closing efforts and local labor–community coalitions lack the resources or means to affect the larger forces making shutdowns so common today.

Given all these limitations, what is the importance of local resistance to plant closures? Much of the answer will emerge from the case studies presented later in this chapter, but a preliminary answer follows. First, every struggle of any consequence of this type has resulted in appreciable gains for the workers and the community, even if the ultimate goal (prevention of the closing) was not achieved. Second, complete victories *are* possible, even with the limitations listed earlier. Third, national efforts are unlikely unless preceded by widespread local activism to change the terms of the national debate over the issues. Finally, local campaigns are much more likely to initially engage workers and the public than are national efforts to change public policy in the absence of local struggles.

The more successful campaigns to prevent shutdowns or to reopen closed plants have relied on unconventional methods. Approaches beyond collective bargaining or legal requirements were employed. Virtually always, a broad coalition of forces was used to bring pressure to bear on corporate decision makers. Organized labor, relatively powerless when facing the corporation alone, finds new strength when allied with social partners pursuing the common goal of job retention.

Across the country, a sizable number of organizations and coalitions dedicated to job preservation developed in the 1980s. Organized labor played a greater or lesser role in these developments, but virtually all such organizations have, or are attempting to develop, close ties with, or an organizational base within, unions in their local area. Many such organizations have formed a national umbrella group, the Federation for Industrial Retention and Renewal (FIRR). [2]

One such organization is the Calumet Project for Industrial Jobs, based in northwest Indiana. The Calumet Project has been in existence since 1984 with a staff of 1 1/2 to 3 1/2 full-time positions. Both organizations and individuals are members of the project, but the organizations are most important. A majority are local unions, followed by churches and community organizations. A Board of Directors, elected from the various constituencies and most heavily weighted toward labor, oversees the project. Funding comes mostly from private foundation and religious grants, union contributions, and occasional research grants.

The Calumet Project has engaged in a number of plant closing struggles jointly with the affected union locals. It also engages in economic development and public policy issues from a labor–community perspective. However, the following case studies will focus exclusively on plant closing campaigns by the Calumet Project. The intent is to evaluate the possibilities and limitations of efforts like this and to draw some lessons from the experience. These case studies represent a sampling of Calumet Project plant closing campaigns.

BLAW-KNOX CAMPAIGN

The Blaw-Knox foundry was located in East Chicago, Indiana. It produced extraordinarily large castings, in addition to normal sizes. Employment in the fall of 1984 stood at 800, down from over 2,000 approximately a decade earlier.

Blaw-Knox had been bought by White Consolidated Industries (WCI) in 1968. WCI primarily produced home appliances but also was in a wide array of other products. Throughout the 1970s, WCI shifted the Blaw-Knox foundry's product mix from 85 percent commercial castings and 15 percent military to 85–95 percent military and only 5–15 percent commercial.[3]

By the 1980s, the main Blaw-Knox product was castings of turret and hull armor for the M-60 tank. In the very early 1980s, the U.S. Army began phasing out the M-60, replacing it with the M-1, which is fabricated and does not require similar platings. After 1983, only foreign orders (through the U.S. military aid program) remained.

Meanwhile, WCI was investing virtually nothing in the plant. New investments did occur, but all were financed by the U.S. government, and all were for military production. The huge machine shop received no new equipment after 1968.

While the product line was being narrowed, and investment was minimal, WCI was "milking" enormous profits out of the facility. Financial data later given to prospective buyers show that the company earned approximately $80 million profit from this facility between 1980 and 1984.

In May 1984, a Calumet Project staff researcher noted press accounts that WCI might divest itself of all steel-related facilities. United Steelworkers Local 1026, which represented Blaw-Knox production workers, was notified immediately, but local leadership was reluctant to act. Employment continued to decline throughout the summer as the company turned away some orders; finally, in September, after prodding from the Calumet Project, the union local president sent out a memo to the mayor, the state governor, a congresswoman, local economic development officials, and others warning of a possible sale and/or plant closing.

Response was quick. In October, representatives from a broad array of political and community forces met and formed a permanent Blaw-Knox Steering Committee to try to save the plant. The company denied any intent to sell and then announced less than two weeks later that it was for sale.[4] The Blaw-Knox Steering Committee began efforts to develop a feasibility study to see what could be done to preserve jobs.

The Calumet Project and an allied community organization cohosted a community meeting with the union local in December that brought out 200 people. Publicity and community pressure were high at this point, directed at both the company and politicians. The message was clear: job preservation must be at the top of the agenda.

In January, Arthur D. Little, a Massachusetts consulting firm, was chosen to do a feasibility study of prospects for saving the plant with $50,000, which had been raised from state, union, city, and company sources for such a study. Over the course of the spring and summer, the Arthur D. Little researchers faced unrelenting pressure through community and union meetings to keep job preservation foremost.

The Little report was released in July 1985.[5] It noted that continued reliance on military production would mean certain extinction for the plant.

However, a product switch to smaller commercial castings, supplemented by limited large commercial castings, would make the facility viable. The cost, however, would be high. Total employment would drop from 800 to 300; state-of-the-art equipment and proposed parking lots and a "business incubator" use of vacated buildings would require $20–$24 million in private capital supplemented by $4.6–7 million in public assistance.

The community and union pressure on A. D. Little and the public source of most of the funding for the study resulted in two very unusual recommendations. Little recommended that the Blaw-Knox Steering Committee closely monitor any sale to see that the public interest in job protection was secured and that the city of East Chicago consider buying and brokering the plant to an acceptable ultimate buyer.

Neither the city nor the Blaw-Knox Steering Committee would follow these suggestions. The city refused to consider buying the plant, absent an immediate buyer.[6] The Blaw-Knox Steering Committee faced an internal struggle over its future role. Calumet project director Lynn Feekin, who served on the steering committee, suggested that it adopt four goals: (1) new buyer commit to East Chicago location, (2) new buyer reinvest to keep the plant viable, (3) new buyer retain current employees, and (4) new buyer recognize the union. Based on these goals, she recommended that the steering committee interview both seller and potential buyers about a business plan to keep the facility viable. The A. D. Little findings and recommendations could be used to push for conversion to commercial production.

If the owner refused or had no business plan, Feekin recommended pressuring the city to use "eminent domain" to buy it at A. D. Little's recommended sale price: liquidation value. The chair of the steering committee, a regional economic development official, refused to call any more meetings and refused to allow these proposals to be discussed. A firm believer in the "business climate" approach to economic development, she felt that any such "meddling" in the "private" business affairs of the company would harm the region in its efforts to attract new business.

In September 1985, WCI sold the Blaw-Knox foundry to a private group of investors for an undisclosed sum. At this time the chair disbanded the Blaw-Knox Steering Committee, considering its tasks ended. Calumet Project proposals were never discussed. Within the steering committee, the union local's representative, the local president, failed to take an independent role; instead of backing Feekin in her efforts to save his members' jobs, he remained completely on the sideline and played a totally passive role.

In early 1986, the Egyptian government canceled a tentative order for more M-60 tanks. Realizing that tank orders would end at least a year before they had expected, the Blaw-Knox management reconvened the Blaw-Knox Steering Committee *minus the union and Calumet Project representatives* in

February. The plant manager now chaired; only one item was on the agenda: lobbying the Defense Department for more tank orders. The congresswoman, city and regional economic development officials, and others wrote letters and flew to Washington, D.C., to ask for reconsideration from the Egyptian government and the Pentagon.

Meanwhile, the congressman insisted that the union and Calumet Project representatives again be included on the steering committee. The company next produced prewritten letters and petitions that employees, citizens, and taxpayers were to send to the Defense Department requesting more tank orders. The letters and petitions appealed to the issues of patriotism and "belief in the American way" of the workers, a purported Soviet threat, the alleged tax savings of the M-60 over the M-1, and the harm to the regional economy of a closing.

The union and community forces on the steering committee refused to carry out this company-sponsored "public awareness" campaign. They insisted that conversion to commercial work was the only viable answer, as the A. D. Little report had noted. At this point the steering committee fell apart, never to meet again. The company insisted it needed tank orders, while the Calumet Project and the union insisted on concrete conversion plans.

On October 28, 1986, the plant officially shut down. The last few months were spent in wrangling between company and union over management demands for massive concessions. The company had consistently maintained that it intended to convert to commercial work but just needed more time and tank orders from the Pentagon. But a former manager later told me in an interview that this was untrue: "from day one" they only intended to "run the armor work out to the end, and then dump the joint."[7]

HAMMOND LTV BAR MILL CAMPAIGN

In August 1986, LTV announced it was "idling" its cold drawn bar mill in Hammond, Indiana, which employed 150 workers at the time (down from 300 approximately a decade earlier). In November, it announced that the closing was permanent.

Members and leaders of the union, United Steelworkers Local 6518, contacted the Calumet Project in December. They formed an activist committee called the Alternative Ownership Committee (AOC) and embarked on a joint quest with the Calumet Project to reopen the plant.

With support from the national union and intervention with the company by the local congressman, a "quick look" feasibility study of the facility was arranged. Locker Associates, a union-oriented consulting firm, conducted a brief study and reported in May 1987 that the plant was indeed very viable if left intact. However, LTV was planning to remove the most valuable equipment (the #3 drawbench) to its Massillon, Ohio, plant. Minus this unique piece of equipment, the plant was much less attractive to any prospective buyer. Furthermore, LTV did not want to sell the plant, even without the #3 drawbench, because a reopened Hammond plant would compete directly with LTV's nearby Gary bar mill. Therefore, Locker and Associates thought the prospects for reopening rather poor.

The AOC and the Calumet Project immediately formulated a three-part plan. First, LTV must be prevented from moving equipment. Second, a suitable owner must be found. Third, LTV must be persuaded or forced to sell.

A suitable owner was found. Canadian bar company Union Drawn Steel expressed strong interest. It was also willing to rehire former workers and recognize the union. It had good relations with its Canadian union locals.

Preventing equipment removal and inducing LTV to sell were more difficult. Two tactics were unsuccessful. A legal brief filed in bankruptcy court where LTV was reorganizing argued that an *intact* sale was in the best interests of creditors, but it was withdrawn when its expense and slim chances of success were apparent. Secondly an attempt to find a market not competitive with LTV's Gary mill for the output of the Hammond mill was also unsuccessful when a possible Chinese market failed to materialize.

The AOC and the Calumet Project organized public pressure on LTV. A September meeting of 150 union members and community residents brought charges that LTV was pretending to find a buyer while privately informing Union Drawn that it could view the premises but all the best equipment was not for sale. City councilmen, religious leaders, workers, and others addressed the meeting; press coverage was extensive.

The Hammond city council passed a resolution asking the city's mayor to issue a lien on the mill's equipment preventing sale or removal until the company paid a $90,000 back-tax liability. It also asked the Hammond Economic Development Council to look into invoking eminent domain if necessary.

The combination of bad press, threats of a lien, threats of eminent domain, and intervention with the company by the local congressman brought LTV to the bargaining table. At a November bargaining session with the AOC and the Calumet Project, LTV pledged to aggressively market the plant.

But the company still wanted to move the #3 drawbench to Massillon, Ohio. A November 23 showdown occurred when an Ohio contractor sent to remove the equipment met a union picket line, which he chose not to cross. A rally before the plant was addressed by the Hammond mayor, AOC spokespersons, and local clergy.

A marathon negotiating session resulted, where LTV met with the AOC, the Calumet Project, the Hammond mayor, and officials from the United Steelworkers district office. The AOC/Calumet Project and its allies had only limited leverage over the corporation in these negotiations. The threats of eminent domain or a lien were useful, but they were unlikely to be used. The Hammond mayor was a Republican who would definitely want to avoid such "extreme" measures. Bad publicity could hurt the company, but only in a very minor way; furthermore, the company could counter this with its own considerable media contacts and expertise. Political pressure against the company would be limited; all politicians from the congressman on down adhered to a subservient "business climate" conception of government–corporate relations. None would be willing to pose a militant Left or populist challenge to the company's right to run "its own affairs." The picket line before the building was probably a dubious deterrent over the long run. LTV could attempt removal in the middle of the night, with an antiunion contractor who was willing to cross any picket line. Maintaining a picket line for weeks on end was also problematic, and the Hammond police would probably aid removal of equipment in the event of a physical confrontation.

One full day's negotiations produced a compromise. LTV was allowed to remove the #3 drawbench but had to (1) actively seek buyers for the plant, (2) retain a qualified appraiser and advise the union of the appraisal result, (3) cooperate with the AOC and the city in selling efforts, (4) attempt to sell *as a steel-processing unit*, (5) encourage the buyer to rehire former workers, (6) retain all remaining equipment, and (7) allow the AOC to do plant inspections. These efforts would continue until a buyer was found or March 31, 1988, whichever came first. (The March 31 deadline was later extended to April 30.)

December through April were difficult months of the campaign. Union Drawn Steel withdrew from bidding when it became clear that the #3 drawbench was being moved. LTV dragged its heels on marketing efforts for the plant. In January, a public meeting was addressed by the mayor, the AOC, the Steelworkers' district director, and others, where LTV was denounced for bad-faith dealings. In February and March, a major campaign for public support swung into motion. Almost 5,000 fliers were distributed throughout Hammond; letters to the editor in the region's two newspapers appeared weekly or more often; a thirty–minute video on the effort was shown on local cable television and was used in community outreach meetings.

In the end, no buyer materialized. In July 1988, LTV sold the remaining equipment, apparently dashing all hopes for reopening the plant as a steel processing unit.[8] However, in the fall, a steel tubing company based in Minneapolis expressed interest. Metal-Matic negotiated a buying price, agreed to rehire the former workers and recognize the union, and moved over forty truckloads of equipment into the plant.

However, LTV announced in November 1988 that the site was contaminated with PCBs.[9] Further tests in December revealed that the contamination was widespread, and in January Metal-Matic pulled out of the deal.[10]

The AOC obtained a city council resolution of support for back taxes collection and retraining assistance. A public meeting was held, but this two-year phase of the battle had ended. In 1989, AOC members joined environmentalists and community residents in an effort to force LTV to clean up its toxic dump.

Under pressure, LTV did agree to clean up the site. By the spring of 1991, extensive ground decontamination had been completed. In the summer and fall, a new buyer, Alpha Steel, surfaced. Alpha agreed to give job preference to former workers and indicated it is not antiunion. Alpha eventually did open in the facility, and ex-LTV employees were hired for some of the jobs. The long struggle eventually had reached a small measure of belated justice for those few workers still needing a job five years later.

LASALLE STEEL CAMPAIGN

LaSalle Steel is a subsidiary of the Quanex Corporation, a Houston-based producer of specialty steel products. Its main facility is a cold-drawn bar mill in Hammond, Indiana, whose 350 workers are represented by an independent union, the Progressive Steelworkers Union.

A thirty–day strike in early 1990 was followed by summer rumors that the company was considering relocation of the turning and grinding department. Because this department is considered the "heart of the mill," many workers feared that its loss would jeopardize the entire mill, not merely the fifty jobs directly at stake.

In late October, the union initiated contact with the Calumet Project at a training session offered by the project to help trade unionists discover "early warning signs" that a plant closing may be imminent (see Feekin and Nissen, 1991). In November, the union local joined the Calumet Project and began joint meetings to strategize how to intervene to save the department and possibly the plant.

Three special union committees carried out the necessary work. A corporate research committee systematically gathered information on Quanex and LaSalle to determine corporate strategy and vulnerabilities. The workforce committee surveyed the entire membership for demographic information and religious/community ties for outreach purposes. The workplace committee gathered detailed information on customers, suppliers, products and product mix, work-flow patterns, and other matters.

In mid-November, LaSalle plant manager and Quanex vice president Richard Treder wrote to union president Zed Rixie confirming rumors that a departmental relocation was being considered. Treder also stressed that no final decision had been made and requested the union to please hold its concerns until a final evaluation was completed.

At the end of November, Rixie responded by requesting that the union be included in all meetings and consultations on the possible move, because "the union has information, expertise and opinions which would be of value to the company in making this decision."[11] At about the same time, union department representatives wrote a letter to Quanex chief executive officer (CEO) Carl Pfeiffer exposing bogus-quality records being used by Treder to discredit the grinding department. (Inferior subcontracted work was being erroneously charged to the department.)

Treder responded with a November 30 letter giving official notice, as contractually required, that a tentative decision to relocate had been made; a final decision would be given within thirty days. On December 5, the union called a widely publicized press conference detailing the situation. Treder reacted angrily, accusing the union of "sensationalizing the situation by going public before a meeting between the company and the union could be arranged."[12]

At a subsequent private meeting with union leadership, Treder berated them for applying public pressure, claiming it was a mistake. He also revealed that Frankfort, Indiana, (about 110 miles south) was the intended alternative site for the department, complete with a new $2 million piece of equipment. He also refused to share copies of studies comparing costs at Frankfort and Hammond. Most significantly, he withdrew the relocation notice, claiming more time was needed.[13]

On December 10, the union/Calumet Project hosted a public meeting attended by the Hammond mayor, city councilmen, a state senator, the local congressman's aide, and over eighty workers and community supporters. All politicians pledged full support for efforts to preserve jobs; the congressman's office and the state senator promised to intervene to prevent the use of public money to lure the department to Frankfort. The Calumet Project and the union had to intervene to prevent the Hammond mayor from engaging in the "bidding war" against Frankfort over who could offer the greatest tax abatement.[14]

Despite Calumet Project's urging to the contrary, the union then chose to take no further action. Some of those on the union executive board feared "pushing too hard" or "going too far." Thus, the union lost the initiative.

Union silence ended when Treder notified the union on January 25 of a tentative decision to move the grinding department and an additional department, the "short cuts" line, to Frankfort. A final decision would be made within thirty days.

Company figures supplied to the union showed higher costs in Frankfort in all areas (transportation, construction, and so on), except labor, which would be nonunion and allegedly at approximately half the Hammond scale. Net savings at Frankfort were estimated to be $600,000—$700,000 per year. Treder intimated that massive concessions from the union might save the jobs at Hammond.

The union held mass educational sessions for all members; over 200 attended, and many signed up to work on the campaign. The union and the Calumet Project developed a six-point strategy:

1. reject all concessions;
2. expose glaring errors and inadequacies in Treder's figures;
3. develop a preliminary counteranalysis;
4. call for a neutral party to do a feasibility study of how jobs could be retained in Hammond;
5. "persuade" or induce La Salle to cooperate with those doing the feasibility study and to postpone a final decision until the study was completed and considered;
6. keep unrelenting pressure on Treder through media exposure, political pressure, religious and community support, and the like.

During February, this plan was carried out with precision. Calls from local public officials, news accounts, public/community entreaties, and communiques to higher Quanex officials hit Treder.

Three events were particularly noteworthy. A major daily local newspaper wrote an editorial endorsing union proposals and chastising the company: "LaSalle apparently has forgotten loyalty is a two way street. The employees have been loyal to the company, but the company is ready to run off to Frankfort and leave its Hammond workers in the dust. . . . The company should consider a feasibility study for expanding operations at the Hammond plant."[15]

Second, the Calumet Project revealed in major local news stories that LaSalle had received a $97,500 tax abatement in 1989 *for the very equipment in the "short cuts" line it was planning to remove to Frankfort*. A Calumet Project spokesperson labeled this a "clear betrayal of public trust": "They took tax abatement money for installing equipment and now they're threatening to pull it out. This is not a show of good faith to the community. . . . They promised to retain jobs and these are the very same jobs they're moving."[16] By this time, Treder was so angry at press coverage of the unfolding campaign that he refused to speak to the media anymore.

Third, the Hammond city council president and the mayor wrote their counterparts in Frankfort requesting that no public subsidies be given LaSalle and that a "bidding war" be avoided.[17] The Frankfort mayor told the press he sympathized with the request and could not see giving any incentives to LaSalle.[18]

At this point, Treder's original plan to relocate the grinding department was in shambles. He had achieved:

- union hostility and an active union-led campaign against the move
- community opposition, most visibly spearheaded by the Calumet Project

- a unanimous wall of opposition from elected public officials at all levels
- a large amount of unfavorable publicity
- less than enthusiastic reception at Frankfort, the intended recipient site
- higher corporate officials alerted by the union to closely oversee his conduct on this matter

If put into effect, Treder's plan now faced major problems, both because it had risks built into it from the start and because the union/Calumet Project campaign had ensured negative consequences from going forward.

In early March, Treder announced a reversal of previous plans. Citing a worsening economy and lower corporate profits, a prepared statement said: "While the new turning equipment we have purchased is scheduled for delivery in August, we are not at present making plans to install it anywhere, because demand for the product has dropped and prices are soft.... If the situation improves and the decision is made at some later date to install the new equipment, we would prefer that it be located in Hammond."[19]

The purported reason was clearly a face-saving gesture. The new equipment would be installed somewhere; *where* had nothing to do with the given reasons.

A few months later, Treder was quietly replaced by a new plant manager, who emphasized his desire to cooperate closely with the union and to maintain good relations with the press and community. In the fall and winter of 1991–92, the new equipment was delivered to, and installed in, the Hammond plant.

The union emerged entirely victorious. Not only were the jobs secured, but the individual who was the source of the antiworker, antiunion threats had been deposed.

LESSONS FROM THE THREE CASE STUDIES

These three case studies reveal the power dynamics built into struggles over plant closing decisions in the United States today. Corporations hold most of the resources. They, and they alone, have the legal and "legitimate" right to determine investment and plant location decisions. Neither the collective bargaining system nor the legal system affords workers or unions any important influence over these decisions.

Corporations use secrecy to further their agenda; "private" business decisions are kept from even such significant stakeholders as unions and workers until it is to the company's advantage to reveal them. Normally, political officials and related economic development officials defer to corporate wishes and conceive of themselves as merely the nurturers of a "good business climate" for the corporation.

Unions can challenge this corporate dominance only by using unconventional methods. Local labor/community coalitions like the Calumet Project are one important approach, among others. Despite the limitations, sources of power are available to the union and its allies. The contrasting patterns of defeat and victory presented by the three cases are examples of differences both in objective circumstances and in the effective use of this power.

Union influence depends on (1) piercing the corporate veil of secrecy—obtaining vital information and forcing the company to publicly respond to community and worker interests; (2) political pressure—making a supportive political environment for the company completely dependent on its responsiveness to worker/community needs for secure, well-paying jobs; (3) public and community opinion—a broad consensus favoring the union's position; and (4) strategic and tactical vision and expertise—fitting the pressure to the points of vulnerability of the company.

Ultimately, the union needs major changes in public policy to obtain a stronger institutional position (Nissen, 1990). But until such major changes occur, battles such as those previously detailed above must be fought. In fact, I argue that major public policy changes will happen only after numerous battles like these have forced the issue repeatedly onto the public agenda, so it cannot be ignored.

It is not accidental that the *later* struggles previously detailed above were more successful; early, losing Calumet Project battles (such as Blaw-Knox) prepared the public atmosphere in the region so that, by the time of the 1990–91 LaSalle struggle, the public officials, the media, and the public at large were very receptive to quickly aligning themselves with an antishutdown consensus. Also, many LaSalle workers were ex-LTV employees who were veterans of the LTV bar mill struggle; their consciousness had been permanently altered by the earlier experience. They consistently led the push within the LaSalle union to take a militant proactive stance. Such a response would not have been possible in the mid-1980s, because previous battles had not prepared the ground.

This means unions need to broaden their vision beyond their traditional concentration on conventional collective bargaining. They need Calumet Projects or the equivalent, all over the country. They need to be actively involved in "early warning" monitoring to foresee possible future closures. They need broad-based coalitions. In the preceding three cases, the broadest and most active coalitions were invariably the most effective. Within these coalitions the union *must* take the leading role; this is one tragic lesson from the unsuccessful Blaw-Knox campaign. Deferential or timid union behavior can result only in the corporate agenda's being dominant. The unions and their allies must force the politicians to put jobs and worker/community interests first. Unless this happens, they will inevitably bow to the "business climate" approach and to corporate dominance.

Permanent institutional gains giving organized labor more clout can come only from alterations in the public arena within which the battles are fought. It is not hard to list a number of appropriate public policy measures: mandated disclosure of corporate financial data and corporate plans to employees and their unions; requirement of much longer prenotification of closing than the federally mandated sixty days; closure of the loopholes in the present law that allow a majority of companies to give *no* notice; local governmental support for "early warning" activities; more stringent requirement of a "payback" to the community for any public aid given corporations for economic development; national controls over the unrestricted export of capital; a foreign policy and foreign aid requirements that encourage union rights and worker rights abroad, a worker-oriented federal industrial policy, worker and environmental protection controls on free trade agreements such as the North American Free Trade Agreement (NAFTA), and others.

Yet, few, if any, of these measures will be enacted unless a social movement forces union/community concerns to the forefront. That movement, if it is to occur, will not likely grow at the national level in the absence of local struggles such as those described in this chapter. The terms of the national debate must be changed, and local and regional movements and labor/community coalitions around the country may be necessary predecessors of such a change.

Even at present, partial and full victories for local plant closing struggles are possible, as demonstrated by the LTV Bar Mill and LaSalle Steel examples. It is important not to exaggerate the power of purely local or regional struggles. Alone, they cannot alter the global and national realities making rapid capital mobility and frequent plant shutdowns a fact of life. But it is equally important not to discount their importance or potential accomplishments.

Well-conducted local plant closing struggles, such as those engaged in by the Calumet Project, can win real victories; engage large numbers of union members and community residents in a struggle to defend their interests; expand horizons and education about the forces at work in today's economy; greatly improve union-community relations and ties; and change the atmosphere of public concerns in so many regions of the country that the national terms of debate begin to be altered dramatically and permanently. These are no small accomplishments. As labor confronts the twenty-first century, labor/community coalitions and plant closing struggles hold an important place in efforts at revitalization.

NOTES

1. On Youngstown, see Thomas Fuechtmann, *Steeples and Stacks: Religion and Steel Crisis in Youngstown, Ohio* (New York: Cambridge University Press, 1989); see also Staughton Lynd, *The Fight against Shutdowns: Youngstown's Steel Mill Closings* (San Pedro, CA: Singlejack Books, 1983). The battle to save "Dorothy Six" in

Pittsburgh was carried in much of the national media. The Morse Cutting Tool experience also received some national publicity; see Barbara Doherty, *The Struggle to Save Morse Cutting Tool* (North Dartmouth, MA: Southeastern Massachusetts University Labor Education Center, n.d.) for a good account. Eric Mann's *Taking on General Motors* (Los Angeles: University of California Institute of Industrial Relations, 1988) details the earlier, successful phase of the Van Nuys struggle, which ultimately ended in failure.

2. FIRR is located at: 3411 West Diversey, # 10 Chicago, Illinois 60647. As of July 1994 FIRR had 32 affiliates across the country.

3. "Blaw-Knox Likes East Chicago Location," *Hammond Times*, November 9, 1969; Arthur D. Little, *Reuse of the Blaw-Knox Castings and Machining Mill*, June 1985.

4. Nancy Winkley, "East Chicago Plant Up for Sale," *Gary Post-Tribune*, October 25, 1984.

5. All the information in the following paragraphs on the A. D. Little report is taken from Little.

6. Nancy J. Winkley, "$24 Million Needed to Convert Blaw-Knox," *Gary Post-Tribune*, July 21, 1985.

7. Fall 1989 interview with an ex-manager from Blaw-Knox who requested anonymity, a request I am honoring.

8. Nancy J. Winkley, "LTV Sells Bar Plant Equipment," *Gary Post-Tribune*, July 15, 1988.

9. Chris Isidore, "Hazardous Wastes Fund at Closed LTV Steel Mill," *Gary Post-Tribune*, November 3, 1988.

10. Chris Isidore, "Bar Mill Menace Spreads," *Gary Post-Tribune*, January 12, 1989.

11. November 26, 1990, letter from Zed Rixie to Richard W. Treder (copy in the author's possession).

12. Laura Viani, "Steelworker Union Seeks Info on La Salle's Plans for Its Grinding Division," *American Metal Markets*, December 10, 1990. For further expression of disappointment at the publicity, see Chris Isidore, "Meeting on LaSalle Move," *Gary Post-Tribune*, December 7, 1990.

13. Nancy Pieters, "LaSalle Steel Withdraws Closing Notice," *Hammond Times*, December 9, 1990.

14. In letters to the mayor, the congressman, state senators, and others, the union set out a series of conditions, or "strings," that should be attached to any public aid.

15. Editorial: "Big Pay Cuts Aren't the Best Way," *Hammond Times*, February 14, 1991.

16. Nancy Pieters, "Group Blasts LaSalle Steel on Tax Abatement," *Hammond Times*, February 15, 1991.

17. Letter from Hammond city council president Robert Markovich to the Frankfort city council, dated February 25, 1991 (copy in the author's possession); Howard H. Hewitt, "Plant Relocation Causing Stir," *Frankfort Times*, March 2, 1991.

18. Hewitt.

19. Nancy Pieters, "Grinding Department Moving Plans on Hold," *Hammond Times*, March 6, 1991.

9

Public Sector Unions and the Ideological Struggle for the State

Lawrence G. Flood, William Scheuerman, and Sidney Plotkin

Struggles over the proper role of the state are a regular feature of American politics. But for the past fifteen years the public sector has been the focus of especially intense controversy. President Reagan blamed government for American economic problems and worked to weaken it on a number of fronts. President Clinton, less hostile to government, still announced the need to "reinvent" it. The Republican congressional majority elected in the fall of 1994 began immediately in 1995 to carry out an antistate "contract with America," generally with the support of the president (House Republican Conference, 1994). At the state and local levels, political leaders, confronted with increasing social problems, recession, and taxpayer resistance, have struggled to get more for less from government while subsidizing the private sector. Friends and foes of the state have had common targets in their plans for change: public sector workers and their unions.

Through much of American history, public workers have been rather passive recipients of high-level state decisions, with little impact on policies that determined their livelihood. In the recent period, however, state workers and their unions became important players in the conflict over the role of the state and the meaning of public life. They helped shape, as political actors and practitioners, the public policies that resulted from those conflicts.

This chapter concerns the continuing controversy about the role of the state. After a brief discussion of continuing state fiscal troubles, it focuses on the ongoing ideological struggle over the proper role of the public sector. It then presents an analysis of past public union responses to this struggle and makes suggestions for future interventions.

THE FISCAL ROLLER COASTER

Reagan-led efforts to control inflation included tax cutting, promotion of unemployment, and reduced assistance to states and localities. The immediate result for states was fiscal crisis. Costs continued to rise, but revenues declined. In response, the states raised taxes, cut employment and services, and negotiated givebacks and speedup from workers. Modest national economic recovery then left the states with budget surpluses. But the happy period ended abruptly with the decade's second recession. By 1990, even significant tax increases could not offset huge deficits in most states. The early 1990s were a budget nightmare. Public workers were forced to accept no-raise contracts, lowered health and pension contributions, and reductions in force. Several states even declared temporary shutdowns of all but essential government services. Credit ratings of states and large cities declined. According to the Center on Budget and Policy Priorities, state programs for the poor were cut more deeply in 1991 than in any of the Reagan years, with forty states cutting or freezing Aid to Families with Dependent Children (AFDC) benefits, and many other programs weakened (Schneider, 1991). Cuts in programs for the poor continued (Claiborne, 1993).

During the early 1990s, many states did not cut total employment. According to a study by the Rockefeller Institute of Government, only sixteen states—mostly in New England and the Mid-Atlantic and Great Lakes regions—cut state employment. But as the study notes, the aggregate figures hide a significant shift in employment toward more corrections and elementary-secondary school employees. Further, most of the states with public employee growth were also states with greater-than-average population growth. Finally, it is not clear how much of the addition is in part-time employees' replacing full-time employees (Ritchie, 1993).

An analysis by the AFL–CIO Public Employee Department concluded that the states employed three tactics to close their budget gaps, each accounting for about one-third of the deficits: new taxes, service and job cuts, and ad hoc onetime-only actions such as use of pension funds or sale of public property (AFL–CIO Public Employee Department, 1993, 1–2). The situation was so bad that the June 1992 issue of *State Budget and Tax News* was printed in all-red ink ("Blotting Out the Red Ink," 1994). But the roller coaster ride continued. The June 1994 issue of the same journal was published in all-green ink: a symbolic recognition that most states were bringing in more money than projected for fiscal 1994. In part in response to recovery, state revenues were up, and Medicare and AFDC costs were not as high as predicted. But this "boom" did not continue.

January 1995 saw newly elected Republican governors and legislators leading a new charge against taxes and public spending. New York, New Jersey, Wisconsin, Michigan, California, and other states struggled with rising demands, probable loss of federal support, and tax-cut promises. The public unions again found themselves mobilizing to protect jobs and programs.

Meanwhile, of course, the president and Congress had engineered the largest government deficit in history. This affected state and local fiscal conditions as the federal government both reduced expenditures and cut into the state tax base in order to raise new funds (Henderson, 1993). Further, federal policy debates came to be dominated almost always by considerations of cost rather than need. Balanced budget conservatism, as two of the authors of this chapter argue elsewhere, became the dominant approach to national legislative discussions (Plotkin and Scheuerman, 1994).

Public sector crisis is not a new phenomenon. A collection of articles published in 1981, *Crisis in the Pubic Sector: A Reader*, analyzed 1970s difficulties in terms that remain relevant today (Fox, ca. 1981). But more than a decade after the beginning of the "Reagan revolution," further into the postindustrial economy and well after the collapse of communism, the terms of the crisis have changed. Unions are weaker, the international economy is more competitive, and the proper role of the state in capitalist society is more controversial. The new situation is summarized clearly by MacEwen and Tabb:

The changes in the international economy are placing severe and contradictory pressures on governments. On the one hand, the instabilities and social dislocations created by international change lead to demands that governments provide protection for their own citizens and industries. On the other hand, internationalization has enhanced the power of capital and reinforced theories of conservative political forces demanding reduction of government interventions and controls on economic life. (MacEwan and Tabb, 1989, 17)

Squeezing the Public Worker

The continuing state fiscal crises have many roots. These include a changing international economy, deindustrialization, the rise of service sector economies and related changes in tax bases, long-term recession, reduced federal government support, state and local tax reductions, increasing demands for state services, increasing health care costs, and persistent poverty. But such complexity is hard to convey in politics, and those in power seek resolutions to the crises that will leave them in power. Thus, there is a temptation for politicians and political commentators to seek scapegoats, which for this crisis are public sector workers and the public sector itself.

Attacking Workers

Confronted with state deficits, politicians and business leaders easily identify state workers as the cause of the problem. The obvious first solution becomes reduction in the number of workers on the public payroll. Workers

are described as overpaid, slothful, underproductive, and overprotected
bureaucrats (Noah, 1991). Layoffs are the way to eliminate much of this
waste, and that is where the squeeze on public labor began.

The second phase of the squeeze is to get more work out of the remaining
civil servants, through tighter discipline and control from above. Public
sector managers have chosen to move backward toward early twentieth-
century principles of scientific management that treat workers like ma-
chines. Supervisory levels face fewer cutbacks and new work rules are
demanded by state employers. The unfortunate offshoot of this, as contemporary management experts have discovered, is inferior products. Improved efficiency, as noted later, is a sensible value; the attempt to achieve
it through speedup and rigid control of workers is a poor means to the goal.

An excellent example of this approach is found in a recent proposal of
the Buffalo New York Financial Plan Commission (Buffalo Financial Plan
Commission, 1993). This private sector group, cochaired by two top bank
officials and established through the Chamber of Commerce, produced a
202-page document on the future of the city. Its main proposals were minor
fee increases, major reductions in the fire department, privatization of
garbage pickup, reduction of city worker health benefits and time off, and
lengthening the workday by one hour. In other words, squeeze the public
worker.

Attack on the Public Sector

A concerted attack on the public sector per se began in the late 1970s
under President Carter, expanded during the Reagan administration, and
may have reached its peak in the period of the "victory of the market over
socialism." During the Reagan years, government—taxing, spending, and
regulating—was identified as the primary cause of American economic
difficulties. Remove government from the economy, it was argued, and the
marketplace would generate an economic boom.

Tax reduction had the dual effects of reducing the amount of money
available to be spent and reducing the ability of the government to perform.
Regulation reduction removed government workers and made the government appear less the protector of citizens.

In addition to tax and regulation reduction, the primary proposed response to government ill effects has been "privatization." All levels of
government in the United States have begun the process of subcontracting
service performance to the private sector—usually to low-paid, nonunion
workforces. This reduces the size of the government workforce and takes
political leadership out of the service production. But it still requires tax
dollars, and the services are paid for by government (Savas, 1987; for a
critique of privatization, Starr, 1987).

IDEOLOGY AND THE STATE

Public versus Private

The distinction between public and private life is a major theme in American political culture, but, as John McDermott argues, "[t]he simple facts of the case fly in the face of an absolute public-private distinction" (McDermott, 1991, 108). The blurring of sectors is a matter of debate among students of public administration (Moe, 1987, 1988; Bozeman, 1988) as well as theorists of the state (Block, 1987, esp. Chapter 1). Today, tasks and funds are shared between the sectors, bureaucratic structures and management and labor relations are comparable, and the public sector touches all aspects of society. Courts have rejected efforts to identify certain functions of government as "traditional" or "integral" and thus clearly distinct from private activities (*Garcia*, 1985). So-called public-private partnerships abound. Ronald Moe of the Library of Congress critiqued this as the creation of "crypto, pseudo, quasi" agencies (Moe, 1987, 456), but a more dominant view suggests that all organizations are public (Bozeman, 1987).

This is not the place for a full analysis of the public-private distinction. However, certain differences between the sectors are quite meaningful for public sector unions, the subject of this chapter.

The public sector is preeminently political. In the words of David Lewin and his colleagues, "[t]he political nature of government is the key feature from which flow most of the important differences between public and private sector labor relations" (Lewin et al, 1988, 4). While the private sector produces commodities for private use through a form of market system, the public sector produces goods and services to meet politically defined social needs and does so through a legal/administrative/political structure (Johnston, 1988). Private sector employers are shielded from public view and are finally responsible to themselves or to stockholders seeking profits. Public employers are held accountable, through elections and public debates, to voters seeking achievement of interests.

The debate on distinctions between public and private sectors continues, with many points of contention unresolved. But public sector workers and their unions recognize the distinction easily, because they work under labor law and ideology quite different from those pertaining to the private sector. Public sector labor law is highly decentralized, operating at the federal and at fifty state levels. Some states *require* union representation for public workers; others essentially *deny* it. Historically, public sector labor law ideology, reflected in a long history of state and federal court decisions, has been hostile to unions (here we draw on the insightful analysis of Fox, 1985). It has argued that unions attack sovereignty—the basis of the state—by delegating power to a nonelected group. A strike against the state is seen as an unacceptable limitation on sovereignty. Public unionism is also seen as weakening democracy because it gives power to "private entities" rather than the properly elected public officials (Summers, 1980, 5). Typically, public unions are denied the right to strike, and the range of issues on which they may bargain is often quite narrow. This is not a matter of the jobs being done (such as garbage collecting or policing) but is simply a matter of government as employer. Thus, privatization of current public jobs is a clear threat to public unions.

Ideology

"Political struggles are ultimately struggles over ideas" (Block, 1987, 18). Thus, *ideology* sets the context for actions by public sector unions. As Johnston puts it, "[T]he public organization is particularly vulnerable to discursive challenges appealing to or redefining public needs" (Johnston, 1988, 58). This is quite well understood by conservative critics of the state, but perhaps less well understood by those working for it.

State actions are shaped, in part, by ideology, and thus public unions engage in ideological battles. But the role of ideological struggle in shaping state actions is "extremely unpredictable"(Block, 1987, 19).

The "New Public Ideology"

In the 1970s, problems developed in the U.S. economy that state actions appeared powerless to resolve. These included declining productivity and profitability and increasing inflation. A limited political debate developed over the proper role of the state in the economy. Corporate liberals, especially those associated with the Democratic Party, such as Robert Reich, now U.S. labor secretary, urged the development of national industrial policy (Magaziner and Reich, 1982). They proposed formation of a partnership among the national government, business, and labor to reconstruct American industry. This model would have promoted the national government into an even more central position in the organization of economic life. In this setting, "[t]he business community responded by mounting a campaign to shift the focus of blame for the macroeconomic problems from business to government" (Block, 1987, 24). They tapped patriotic feelings, antitax traditions, and pro-business attitudes to promote a public philosophy of the marketplace. The "message was pounded home through paid advertisements, op-ed columns and hundreds of studies produced by conservative think tanks" (Block, 1987, 24–25). The victory of what might be characterized as the new public ideology came with the election of Ronald Reagan in 1980.

The new ideology does not appear in a single source, nor, indeed, is there only one version of it. It has seen a variety of expressions between the late 1970s and today. A useful early statement is the Reagan administration's 1981 economic proposal to Congress, entitled "America's New Beginning:

A Program for Economic Reform" (White House, 1981). The Bush administration (and conservative critics of Reagan) later developed a "new paradigm" that attempted to distinguish itself from previous statements (Sawicky, 1991). A recent and more global view was presented in a much-debated article by Francis Fukuyama, "The End of History" (Fukuyama, 1989). Fukuyama argues that the final victory of political liberalism and consumerism has occurred and that all that remains for future politics is technical economic maneuvering. These several statements differ in important particulars, but, for the purposes of this chapter the key shared principles are more important: economic life must be based on domestic "free markets" and international "free trade," unhindered by government; government must live within its means (within tax revenues); decision making should devolve to the state and local level (where vigilant antitaxpaying majorities may be found); empowered, choice-making individuals should be the prime decision makers for the economy; and political competition, not accommodation, should determine who wins and loses in public policy. Finally, the public sector should be reduced in size and scope, and, where possible, its duties should be performed in the private sector (Plotkin and Scheuerman, 1994). Then federal budget director Richard Daran indicated in 1988 that *privatization* is the central ideal of this entire position (Sawicky, 1991, 4).

The end of the Reagan–Bush era was not the end of this attack on the public sector. In 1992, the American Legislative Exchange Council (ALEC) provided a state-by-state comparison of public and private incomes to conclude that public employees received "excess compensation." It characterized state and local workers as a "protected class" because they are independent of market forces. It displayed data that led them to conclude that public pay had gone up much faster then private pay and that, if public and private pay scales were comparable, the states would save billions of dollars (Cox and Brunelli, 1992; for a thorough rebuttal, Belman and Heywood, apparently 1993).

Shortly after the Clinton inauguration, the Institute for Policy Innovation issued a report concluding that "by all measures, federal, state and local government have grown far faster than the economy's ability to support them." Such growth, the institute argued, had three negative effects: a more bureaucratized, less citizen-oriented government; less efficiency, with costs up and quality down; and impeded economic growth as government shut out "productive " sectors of the economy (Institute for Policy Innovation, n.d.).

The initial Clinton Economic Message to Congress made clear his commitment to deficit reduction as a first order of business—and he began by cutting White House staff. He promised further job cuts and wage freezes as well. His attack on the problem would begin as an attack on public sector workers.

Reinventing Government

After a decade of dominance in public policy debates, the "new" public ideology got old. Splits among its supporters, head-on electoral confrontations, and continuing economic weakness in the United States posed clear challenges. The early 1990s saw a renewed ideological struggle for the state.

Of course, what we have called the new public ideology was not entirely antistate. Rather, it promoted a particular view of how to *employ* state power. The "Reagan revolution" reduced social programs, lowered taxes for the top income earners and business, and eliminated many regulations. But it also demanded great increases in military spending and was interventionist in international affairs. It also promoted government involvement in personal life on such issues as abortion rights, birth control information, gay schoolteachers, distribution of "pornographic" materials, and state-level rules on drinking age. Selected regulations, such as those checking the power of labor unions, were promoted. It supported capital punishment, surely a significant power of the state. By withdrawing from needed social programs, it also forced the states to expand government at the local level. The state did not wither away under Republican leadership.

A resurgent movement against the new public ideology developed at numerous points. The savings and loan bailout was hurried through Congress with rather little public debate, remarkable given the costs. The long-term and continuing recession raised strong critiques of federal government inactivity. Despite upbeat rhetoric from the Bush White House, average citizens were aware of chronic unemployment, decline in available good jobs, and weakened workplace protection. Parts of the business community also complained about the costs of failure to invest in the infrastructure, which is necessary for private sector growth. They pointed out that infrastructure expenditure is associated with higher productivity (Aschauer, 1990; Blinder, 1991). As early as 1988, a *Business Week* article reported a "growing sense in economics that the free-market paradigm, built around a belief in individual rationality, market equilibrium, and pure competition, often gets a big fat 'F' when it comes to explaining what is really happening in the economy and the markets" (Farrell, 1988).

The movement for national health care was another indication of change in perceptions of the proper role of the state. Even corporate leaders began to promote some version of a universal health care system. High and spiraling costs and poor distribution of health care services led to demands for state intervention from a broad spectrum of society. The *format* of the system is a matter of great debate, but its *need* is nearer consensus.

President Clinton's first acts signaled a more activist government and a more pro-labor administration. Robert Reich, the new labor secretary, made statements supporting unions and indicating their importance for the U.S. economy. Clinton's signing of the Family Medical Leave Act and lifting of two Bush restrictions on unions were promising. His Economic Message to Congress promised government commitment to economic improvement.

As the Clinton era progressed, there were further positive signals for public employees. In August 1993, Clinton lifted the employment ban former president Reagan had placed on the Professional Air Traffic Controllers' Organization (PATCO) workers. While the move was largely symbolic (few workers would actually be rehired), the AFL–CIO Public Employee Department praised it as "bringing a measure of justice" (AFL–CIO Public Employee Department, Fall 1993, 3). Hatch Act reform allowing a broader range of political action for federal employees was also passed, and with Clinton's prior endorsement. Finally, the president created two public sector task forces, one relating to federal employees and the other to state and local workers. Each was expected to promote positive labor–management relations and cooperative problem solving (AFL–CIO Public Employee Department, Summer 1994, 1).

The most significant signal of a change in ideological perspective came with Clinton's announcement of the National Performance Review (NPR)—a study with the goal of "reinventing" government. Clinton's expressed goal was not to eliminate government or to privatize it but rather to make it less expensive and more efficient while moving the bureaucracy toward initiative and empowerment. The result of the NPR became known as Vice President Gore's Report on Reinventing Government (Gore, 1993). The issue, said Gore, was not what government does (a major Reagan theme) but rather how it works. The root problem, he concluded, was industrial-era bureaucracies attempting to be effective in an information age, and his lengthy report proposed dozens of major changes in federal government practice. The "reinvention" metaphor became a dominant structure for discussion of state-level changes after the Gore report, with state and local governments and employees debating cost cutting and efficiency improvements. Within six months, 80 percent of Gore's proposals were "in progress," according to the National Performance Review (National Performance Review, 1994).

One year after the National Performance Review was released, the Brookings Institution presented an analysis of its accomplishments (Kettl, 1994). Brookings concluded the NPR had produced "impressive results" and had proven to be "one of the most lively management reforms in American history." But from the perspective of workers, not all was well. The "Clinton administration's eagerness for quick savings . . . led officials to shrink employment first and let the management improvements follow." This quickly alienated many government workers who "saw the downsizing as yet another explicit attack on their jobs and behavior." Public workers and unions were cooperating with the reinvention efforts, but warily.

PUBLIC SECTOR UNION RESPONSE

Faced with genuine state and local budget deficits and a dominant public philosophy attacking public workers and the public sector, unions representing the workers respond. The challenge is to survive the attacks and to redirect public debate to focus on quality of public life. This is a difficult task, but it is essential to the future of public workers and, indeed, to meaningful democratic practice.

First Responses

Public sector unions are a dynamic force in the union movement today (Freeman and Ichniowski, 1988; Freeman, 1986). They have improved the terms and conditions of work for government workers at all levels and established a record that includes many progressive innovations (Feuille, 1991). In this time of difficulty they must now outdo past performance.

The union movement *has* responded. The national and state-level American Federation of Labor and Congress of Industrial Organizations (AFL–CIO) organizations reorganized and strengthened their public sector divisions. Those departments (working with private sector unions) are leading the fight against privatization and for protection of public services. The national Public Employee Department publishes a newsletter, a privatization update, and individual studies of attacks on the public sector. Of course, individual unions have also been active in every state. Without these public efforts by unions, privatization and the dismantling of the public sector would be even more developed than they are.

Further, they have reacted quickly as individual problems arise. For example, the American Federation of State, County, and Municipal Employees (AFSCME) provided a paper entitled "Fact versus Fiction," which debunked the ALEC report on public sector pay and demonstrated its poor mix of data and unsupported conclusions (American Federation of State, Municipal and County Employees, n.d.). The National Treasury Employees Union described Clinton's approach as "dis-inventing government" and promised to form a coalition with other federal unions to persuade Congress and the president that "pay punishment" for employees could lead only to reduced efficiency and the loss of experienced workers. Public sector unions were prepared to respond as they had not been in the early years of the Reagan attack on government.

A problem for public sector unions, however, is that they commonly rely on a version of "business" or "service" unionism. In the words of one expert in public labor relations, "For all the attention on the 'political' dimension in public labor relations, it is apparent that public unions put most of their efforts (money, staff time) into the two time-honored collective bargaining processes (borrowed from the private sector) of contract negotiation and contract administration (Feuille, 1991, 354).

This approach reflects Samuel Gompers's often misquoted call for "more, more, and more." Its essence is provision of member services and avoidance of controversy. It focuses on narrow areas of agreement among union members, usually translated into demands for better wages and working conditions. These demands appeal to union members but are often poorly understood or rejected by those outside the union. Support for wages and good working conditions *is* an essential responsibility for unions. But standing by itself, this form of unionism gives credence to the new public ideology's depiction of labor, particularly of public workers, as selfish and slothful. Further, it is most successful in times of economic growth. With the decline of the New Deal coalition's politics of accommodation, and the emergence of the zero-sum politics of budgetary conservatism (for every winner there must be a loser, and the loser will be the less powerful), business unionism is less able to deliver the results it promises, and it exposes unions to attacks from the Right.

With fiscal crisis, a typical strategy for public sector unions is straightforward defense of existing state programs. This makes sense as an approach to job protection but has severe limitations as a *union* perspective. Specifically, this has meant union defense of management programs, programs that the unions and their members may, in fact, hope to change. Program defense works in the very short run, but for the longer term the unions need their own, alternative visions of successful public programs. (For an example, see United University Professions, 1990; see also Shostak, 1991, Chapter 11).

A third approach evolves from public sector union emulation of private sector unions. The strike is often identified as a key response to attacks on jobs. But strikes are problematic today, in both the public and the private sector. The number of major work stoppages for 1994 was up somewhat from the previous year, which had seen the fewest strikes since the Bureau of Labor Statistics (BLS) began counting forty-six years ago (Bureau of Labor Statistics, 1995a). Given weakening of the private sector labor law structure, strikes are often followed by permanent replacement of workers and often of the union itself. U.S. Senate defeat of attempts to pass antistriker replacement legislation reinforced the use of the tactic. Thus, private sector unions have become very cautious in using the strike tactic. In the public sector, strikes play into the hands of the opponents of public workers. Elected officials whose programs are scuttled by a strike are in a position to "demonstrate" how strikes are really an assault on the popularly arrived at "common good." After all, politicians, not civil servants, are elected to office. Service disruption will cause pain to some segment of society. Once this happens, strikers are branded as selfish advocates of a narrow special interest, and politicians can label public workers as enemies of the public.

Strikes *will* retain an important place in the labor movement. But the special circumstances of the public sector require new practices as well.

An Alternative Approach

Public sector unions must take better advantage of the special characteristics of the public sector. Public workers operate within a unique set of laws and with a responsibility to provide public goods. They produce the direct results of democracy that citizens expect. They provide services for all segments of society. This occurs within an ideological context that, as we have argued has shifted toward blaming the public for most social ills. Thus, the first priority must be to proceed with the ideological struggle for the state. In this new era, the relationship between state and economy must, and will, be restructured. It is necessary to seek "an alternative to the arbitrary exercise of governmental power on the one hand and regulatory paralysis on the other" (Block, 1987, 30). In Fred Block's terms, this requires "debureaucratization" of the state: decentralizing power; pursuing substantive, rather than procedural, regulation; and greater reliance on citizen participation (32). The unions must develop their own vision of the public and pursue it in a campaign at least as powerful as that conducted by antistate forces in the late 1970s.

As central aspects of this endeavor, unions must (1) strengthen alliances; (2) improve the quality and performance of government; and (3) build internal strength.

Alliances

A first and obvious place to start is to build links to clients. Clients know about services, and they may be in a position to influence political decision makers. Union–clientele partnerships increase the ability of public sector workers to shift the public debate from wages to the *quality and necessity* of public goods produced. They highlight the benefits of government rather than simply its costs. Thus, public sector struggles may emphasize better services, not simply job and benefit protection.

Building effective and stable alliances between government workers and their clients is extremely difficult. They often meet in unpleasant settings, and their relationships are bound by relatively restrictive bureaucratic rules. In the case of public assistance, the clients are desperate, the workers overworked, and the money never enough. These two often see each other as adversaries not potential allies. This happens as well with police (who may be seen as occupiers, not protectors), teachers, tax collectors, environmental protection agents, and others. Victims may, in fact, blame the state for their troubles and thus blame state workers. But positive relationships are possible, in the right circumstances (Withorn, 1984, 183–188).

One key element in building relations to clients could be voter registration. The bulk of America's 50 million plus nonvoters come from the socially and economically disadvantaged. They have a clear and direct interest in high-quality public products. While incumbents in both political parties are likely to resist massive voter registration, unions can pursue this activity on their own. One result might be to bring the Democratic Party back toward labor. Another might be to strengthen the movement toward a labor party.

Public sector unions will also increase their political effectiveness through greater participation in union–community coalitions (Brecher and Costello, 1990; Flood, 1991; Fitzgerald, 1991; Herod, 1991, 1994). These coalitions, organized around such issues as plant closings, welfare rights, and political corruption, provide additional ways for the unions to demonstrate their solidarity with clients. They increase the likelihood of community protection of the public sector when it is threatened.

Two other coalitional efforts are important: among the various public unions and between public and private sector unions.

In the public sphere, politicians and managers often play one union against the other. Cutbacks may lead to "cannibalism" as unions point to each other's members as the appropriate source of cuts. This obviously creates distrust and divides and weakens public workers. The principle of solidarity, often difficult to practice, is essential. The experience of New York's four statewide public unions is a good starting point. Not only did the four organizations hold a series of joint rallies to protest cuts, but they also created an ideological and research arm to counteract the rhetoric of the new public ideology. Their Fiscal Policy Institute attempts to change the public agenda from shrinkage of the public sphere to the need for a fair and progressive tax structure. The rhetoric of "the rich not paying their fair share," backed by fact-filled studies released to the media, met with some limited success when the New York State legislature passed a bill increasing the personal income tax on incomes above $150,000. Important examples of cooperation are found in other states as well. In California, for example, the American Federation of Teachers (AFT), the National Education Association (NEA), and the American Association of University Women (AAUP) came together in an "unprecedented show of unity" concerning attacks on state higher education ("Unions Wage Budget Battles," 1992).

New York also saw coalition building between public and private sector unions. A broad-based public/private labor coalition, working within central labor bodies across the state and with the New York State AFL–CIO, joined with the Fiscal Policy Institute to promote a more progressive tax system. This coalition is in its infancy, but it plans to remain active. There are other examples of effective coalitions, such as Jobs with Justice and the Federation for Industrial Retention and Renewal, national organizations that bring together local coalitions of unions and community groups (Early and Wilson, 1992; Federation for Industrial Retention and Renewal, 1994).

Better Public Services

Unions can, and must, contribute to the improvement of public services. Coalitions with clients and support from citizens will improve as perceptions of public services change. As Brendan Martin argues, "[M]any citizens experienced some public sector institutions as controlling rather than enabling, as limiting options rather than expanding them, as wasting rather than making the best use of resources" (B. Martin, 1994, 3). While such problems are not simply the responsibility of public employees, the workers must be part of the solutions.

The Canadian National Union of Public and General Employees (NUPGE) published a valuable document promoting improved services entitled "More for Your Money: How to Improve the Delivery of Public Programs and Services" (Centre for Research on Work and Society, 1993). After presenting a proclamation of the *rights* of citizens to public services, it focuses on four needs: a better theoretical basis for action, emphasis on both government worker and customer, and consideration of broad issues.

Additionally, public unions must continue to promote citizen power and equitable distribution in public service provision. The public character of government services requires that they relate to the needs of the people, as the people understand those needs, and be evaluated by criteria other than ability to pay.

A key strategy here will be to enlarge the struggle for more control over the workplace. A remarkable body of literature and experience demonstrates the value, for quality and efficiency, of replacing Taylorism with worker participation and control. Experiments in "new labor–management relations" are being conducted throughout the private sector and in some government agencies. While worker participation is appropriately controversial (Klare, 1988; Weiler, 1990; Parker and Slaughter, 1988), many workers do want it. A significant level of participation will be essential to the reinventing government efforts. A clear benefit can be higher-quality goods and services for the public. In the words of the AFL–CIO Public Sector Department, "{R}estructuring government programs to improve public services can succeed. But only if those who know the programs best—the front-line workers and the unions that represent them—are involved right from the beginning" (AFL–CIO Public Employee Department, 1991a, 1).

Expanded worker involvement in public service decision making without co-optation will require a major commitment by the unions. It is happening, as indicated in the case studies presented in *Making Government Work* (AFL–CIO Public Employee Department, 1991a) and *Excellence in Public Service* (AFL–CIO Public Employee Department, 1994a).

Rank-and-File Support

Finally, unless the unions find ways to increase rank-and-file participation, the preceding approaches will simply fail. Critics point to unresponsive leaders, divorced from the realities of the membership, whose primary concern appears to be the maintenance of power. But, as leaders have learned by bitter experience, unions are only as strong as their memberships. An active, informed, militant rank and file makes for a strong and powerful organization. Union leaders have a responsibility to support rank-and-file efforts to democratize the organizations and to devise ways to empower the membership. Open and direct elections of leaders, the free flow of communication, and adequate financial independence for locals are essential to development of trust and involvement of the membership ("An Organizing Model," 1991).

Pubic union efforts to build alliances and strengthen internal support will benefit from more extensive use of the new communications technologies. As Marc Belanger of the Canadian Union of Public Employees (CUPE) makes clear, "A labor union is a communications system" (Belanger, 1994). Computer networking provides a vast new resource for communication. Electronic mail and document transfer are excellent organizing tools, and conferencing allows unionists around the world to "talk" with each about common concerns. PUBLABOR, a list-serve moderated by Katie Buller at the University of Wisconsin–Madison, is an example of a "place" for debate, analysis, and sharing among public unionists. The AFL–CIO Public Employee Department is also on-line, through LaborNet in Compuserve. The American Federation of Teachers currently works through America On-Line, but there is pressure for it to establish its own network. Public unions should become leaders in the use of the new technologies, to reach members, allies, and the community at large.

Public sector unions must continue to pursue a strong and clear political-legislative agenda. On that agenda are resistance to privatization; *critical* participation in reinventing government efforts; expansion of bargaining rights protections to all public employees (Schneider, 1993a); continued attention to negative impacts of so-called free trade on state and local taxes and prerogatives (Sawicky, 1993); principled resistance to wholesale tax and benefit giveaways by states and localities attempting to attract business (Federation for Industrial Retention and Renewal, 1993; Schweke, Rist, and Dabson, 1994).

There are, of course, further threats. Unions remain under attack, privatization continues, "free trade and open markets" continue to have ideological appeal. Public sector layoffs and cutbacks continue. Total union membership remains at below 16 percent of employed wage and salary workers (Bureau of Labor Statistics, 1995b). The current Supreme Court is not promising.

The coming decade will see a continuing struggle over the powers of the state and the relationship of state to market. This presents public unions with the clichéd "threat and opportunity." By themselves, the unions will not prevail. But with strong alliances and commitment to the ideological contest, those seeking a positive (and improved) role for government can succeed. In Stephen Bronnor's phrase, "[I]t is not merely the specific degree of mix between a free market and traditional forms of state planning which is at issue in the present debate, it is also the future of democracy itself" (Bronner, 1992, 132–33).

The Role of Law and Union Organizing: Thoughts on the United States and Canada

James B. Atleson

In 1984, a joint committee of the U.S. House of Representatives held hearings on the state of the National Labor Relations Act (NLRA) and ultimately concluded in forceful terms that the promises of the Act had not been fulfilled (U.S. Congress, 1984). Union witnesses had strongly criticized what they viewed as a hostile administration and National Labor Relations Board (NLRB), an especially serious perception since unions had come to rely on the state for protection and support. Many union witnesses stressed that the dire situation could not be altered by mere statutory tinkering. As Richard Trumka, president of United Mine Workers (UMW) and a lawyer, later wrote: "[The NLRB's] bias on the merits is fatal to virtually any claim of workers' rights. Even if the Board does grant an occasional victory to workers or their unions, its administrative processes are so impossibly drawn out that the victory is pyrrhic" (Trumka, 1987).

Although a focus on state support is not surprising, given the power of their business opponents, many unions had seemingly come to believe that most of their power derived from federal protection. Thus, many believed that the marked reduction in union strength was directly related to increasingly restrictive interpretations of the National Labor Relations Act by the NLRB and the courts (Weiler, 1983, 1990). Yet, the criticism of individuals, institutions, and particular legal rulings tended to mask some of the problems of labor regulation in the United States. NLRB and Supreme Court decisions during the Reagan and Bush years did reflect hostility to union aims, resulting often in reversals of even recent precedent, but criticism may be directed more to the effects than the causes of union weakness. The current rules of law, in other words, may not simply be the *cause* of union weakness, for the rules and doctrines may also be seen as the *result* of a perception that unions are weak. A recognition of this fact must inform any discussion of the possibilities for judicial or legislative labor law reform. The prospect for more sympathetic rulings or helpful legislative amendments may be unlikely unless unions are viewed as a vibrant, or at least a troublesome, force.

Despite the call for repeal or the circumvention of the NLRA, few would question that the statute has granted employees and unions a significant zone of protection. Nevertheless, many of the promises of the Wagner Act of 1935 have obviously not been delivered, and certain of the clearly expressed goals of the act have simply been ignored. The courts generally stress the statute's professed goal of industrial peace, for instance, but other goals, such as equality of bargaining power and industrial democracy, have routinely been ignored (Atleson, 1983; Klare, 1978). A "Clinton" Board will no doubt be more sympathetic to the aims of the statute, but it, like other Democratic boards before it, will operate within a system of values and assumptions created over many years.

Decisions by the National Labor Relations Board and the Supreme Court in the 1980s, restricting the scope of mandatory bargaining in cases of partial closings or work transfers or weakening the stability of working conditions during the life of a collective agreement, call into question both the viability of collective bargaining and the concept that the collective agreement provides both sides with stability and predictability during its term. The Reagan board routinely based its reversals of prior holdings on earlier NLRB decisions. True, earlier boards could legitimately be characterized as unsympathetic to the goals of the act, although one would have to go back to the 1950s to find one even approaching the level of unconcern of the Reagan board. Bush appointees generally hewed a more moderate course, but two observations can be made. First, any modest upturn in union legal fortunes from a newly constituted NLRB is unlikely to be matched by rulings of the federal courts in the near future. Even so, these decisions will not likely stem the slide of labor's fortunes. Second, even if we consider the highly restrictive rulings of the Reagan board, the difference will be one of degree, since the judiciary, usually the appellate courts and often the Supreme Court, have historically restricted the potential scope of the act by infusing it with their own set of values.

THE HISTORICAL CONTINUITY OF JUDICIAL VALUES

Many important labor decisions are understandable in light of a set of values that would be both familiar and congenial to a nineteenth-century judge. Indeed, the values reflected in the decisions of modern courts are not new, having been employed to reach restrictive rulings for over 150 years. Whether the question in the past focused on the extent to which the common law should regulate unions, the possible application of antitrust laws, or the scope of the National Labor Relations Act, courts have applied their own ideas and values throughout American history (Atleson, 1983, 1–16). The decisions have been based on a set of cultural verities, and courts have seemingly been oblivious to the existence of other, conflicting values and sentiments.

Although it was generally believed that the National Labor Relations Act would restrict the policymaking role of the judiciary, statutory interests can be, and have been, limited in a variety of ways. For instance, the applicable right granted by the statute can be read narrowly. Rights to engage in collective action for "mutual aid" and statutory protection against "interference" or "discrimination" are sufficiently open-textured to permit a decision-maker to arrive at a variety of results depending on the values held. Exclusions or limitations may be found to be "implicit" despite any support in statutory language or in the formal legislative history. Most revealingly, express statutory rights or interests can be outweighed by often vaguely phrased and overlapping employer interests, such as property, management rights, or managerial prerogatives. The problem is not simply one of bias but that each decision maker focuses problems through a personal lens that refracts light in different ways.

A small number of assumptions seem to underlie a substantial portion of existing legal doctrine, and I have commented upon them in greater detail elsewhere (Atleson, 1983.) These judicially created assumptions can be phrased as follows:

1. Continuity of production must be maintained, limited only when statutory language *clearly* protects employee interference.
2. Employees, unless controlled, will act irresponsibly.
3. Employees possess only limited status in the workplace, and, correspondingly, they owe a substantial measure of respect and deference to their employers.
4. The enterprise is under management's control, and great stress is placed upon the employer's property rights in directing the workplace.
5. Despite the participatory goals of the NLRA, employees cannot be full partners in the enterprise because such an arrangement would interfere with inherent and exclusive managerial rights.

These values or assumptions stated above do not exhaust the list, for one could trace other views throughout American legal history. Courts have, for instance, frequently viewed workers and unions as inherently violent (Avery, 1988–89), and they have often treated unions as outsiders to the "employment relationship," seen as encompassing only the employer and individual employees. This view, however, overlooks the actual employee–union relationship, ignoring the fact that unions *are* the employees, but the "outsider" focus obviously taps into long-held themes in American individualism. Such a perception merges with the traditional American aversion to "outsiders," a commonly voiced concern by employers in organizing campaigns.

One of the historic struggles affected by the Wagner Act's passage in 1935 involved whether bargaining over terms and conditions of employment was to be done individually or collectively. In the first half of the nineteenth century, for instance, many usual types of union collective action were treated as criminal conspiracies (Atleson, 1983, 1–18; Holt, 1984). Yet, it was not unlawful for an individual employee to refuse to work with employees who were willing to work for less, to boycott products from a particular employer, or to seek higher wages or better benefits. Yet, when all these individual rights to contract were combined into a collective effort, a common law crime was somehow created (Gregory and Katz, 1979, 13–30). The union—the collectivity—was different from individual members.

In these early cases, many ideas appear that will run through American judicial opinions for the next 150 years. For instance, courts adopted the notion that there is no battle, or no allowable battle, over the apportionment of profits. In addition, courts stressed that increases in wages necessarily resulted in increased prices, thereby weakening the competitive position of employers in any particular community. This is also the judicial origin of the notion that employers, not employees, tend to represent the community's interest.[1]

Common law courts also expressed great concern and consideration for employees, then called "scabs" or "blacklegs," who were willing to work at less than the craft scale. Why courts professing the values of laissez faire would seek to protect one group of employees over another is not clear, except perhaps on the theory that unions were arbitrary agents affecting the right to contract; that is, unions interfered with the rights of any particular employee and an employer to contract. That is what the courts said. Unions were "artificial"; that is, they interfered with the individual's "freedom to contract" as well as the invisible forces of supply and demand. It was irrelevant that individual bargaining was inherently unequal and that there was no freedom not to work or that employers themselves routinely combined to set wage rates (Wallace, 1978, 18–22, 48–55; Kulik, 1978).

Another and closely related notion is revealed in the following quotation from an 1836 decision *People v. Faulkner* (Commons et al., 1910, 330–31): "Every American knows, or ought to know, that he has no better friend than the laws, and that he needs no artificial combination for his protection. . . . They [the societies of journeymen] are of foreign origin, and I am led to believe they are mainly upheld by foreigners." The language illustrates the longevity of the notion that unions are somehow undemocratic and of foreign origin, for this quotation, it should be unnecessary to add, is made only fifty years after the creation of the American republic.

Criminal prosecutions for conspiracy became infrequent by the late nineteenth century, not because of changes in substantive law but because employers had discovered a much more effective remedy—the injunction (Witte, 1926). In a small number of states like New York, there was no vice in collective action—groups could lawfully engage in any activity that could be lawful undertaken by a single individual. New York, however, was a minority jurisdiction, and most states regulated labor under an "unlawful means—unlawful ends" test that provided courts considerable freedom to apply their own social and economic values. There was no rational way to explain the decisions in most states barring, for instance, secondary or consumer boycotts, for at the same time employers could combine and act in their own self-interest, despite causing economic harm to rival firms and competitors or to the public by monopolizing the market.

The eighteenth- and nineteenth-century common law decisions could be explained by simple hostility to unions, but certainly part of the explanation is that, in light of the courts' view of individualism, unions were seen as arbitrary interferences with a labor market that was necessarily based on dealings between individual employees and their employer. A conflict was perceived to exist between American individualism and collective attempts to secure goals such as uniform wage rates or influence over working conditions.

These views of unions have not been limited to the past. For instance, in the 1947 House of Representatives Report on the Taft–Hartley Act, the Republican majority stated the following concerning whether supervisory employees could form unions under the NLRA: "It seems wrong, and it is wrong, to subject people of this kind, who have demonstrated their initiative, their ambition and their ability to get ahead, to the leveling processes of seniority, uniformity and standardization that the Supreme Court recognizes as being fundamental principles of unions" (H.R. Rep. No. 245, 80th Cong., 1st Sess., 16–17 [1947]). This argument was one of the primary explanations for excluding from the act those rugged individualists called foremen. The occasion for the exclusion and for the concern for the liberties of foremen was the fact that foremen were organizing and joining unions during World War II. No one forced foremen to join unions, and, indeed, they were joining for many of the same reasons that motivated rank-and-file employees in the mass production industries (Lichtenstein, 1982, 117–18; Lichtenstein, 1989; Seitz, 1984).

It seems clear that economic and social values and assumptions stemming from as early as the nineteenth century mediate legal decision making. Common law notions, for instance, of inherent work obligations, operate and often limit the seeming implications of federal labor law. No doctrine more readily reveals this conclusion than *MacKay Radio & Telegraph* (304 U.S. 333 [1938]) which noted that workers engaging in a legally protected strike could nevertheless be *permanently* replaced. The doctrine, stemming from dicta in the 1938 decision, mocks the protection of the right to strike mentioned twice in the act, but it does continue the earlier common law notion that workers have no property interest in their job. Efforts to overturn this doctrine in Congress failed in 1994, despite optimistic forecasts. (see Gramm, 1992). Relatedly, the employee's right to bargain over job content or critical investment decisions is limited by notions of inherent managerial prerogatives. Modern labor decisions, just like their nineteenth-century contract predecessors, are infused with the older master–servant doctrines. These decisions demonstrate that the values read into the act are as important, or more important, than the goals and rights expressly set out in the statute (Atleson, 1983).

The post-1935 history of the NLRA, paralleling early legal history, suggests that any legislative reform of the National Labor Relations Act that is sympathetic to employee organization risks serious limitation by the courts. Such risk is reduced by careful drafting, and the Norris–LaGuardia Act is one notable example, but one can expect that courts will tend to introduce their own values, which will, to some extent, frustrate the hopes of the drafters. The long continuity of such perceptions caution against overly optimistic hopes for more judicial responsiveness to unions.

COLLECTIVE ACTION AND LEGISLATION

It is depressing to focus only upon courts, and it is a serious mistake to view American values and culture only through the lens of judicial decisions. Throughout American history, employees and unions have often presented a set of values radically different from those traditionally enunciated by courts. Moreover, we should remember that legislatures often reflected sentiments that were sympathetic to collective action, reacting supportively to organizational campaigns and to union militance, whether in the area of safety, injunctions, or collective bargaining itself. The alleged exceptionalism of the United States is substantially based upon judicial activism in the late nineteenth and early twentieth centuries that invalidated many state and federal statutes (Forbath, 1989). But not all statutes were struck down, and, most important, in every case where courts invalidated a statute, there *was* at least a statute (Urofsky, 1985; McCurdy, 1984). Therefore, one must be careful to avoid the all too common tendency to assume that the labor views of certain judges reflect the predominant statement of American values and culture. Employees and unions and, sometimes, legislatures expressed a quite different set of values that recognized the need for employee protection and for collective action to counteract the powerlessness of individual workers.

The recent federal legislation dealing with plant closings and polygraphs reveals continued legislative willingness to intervene in the employment relationship. Indeed, the experience of the last twenty-five years suggests the continued possibility of federal and state legislation to protect important aspects of the employment relationship. The tolerance among legislators for labor bills is clearly limited, however, since the political costs of union support are considered high. Although Congress has been willing to intervene in areas of occupational health and safety, plant closing, discrimination, and pensions, prospects for reform of the National Labor Relations Act may be slight, even given a Democratic administration.

In general, special circumstances have been necessary to pass any legislation dealing with unionization and collective bargaining, beginning with the Erdman Act, passed as a response to massive railway disputes such as the Pullman boycott of 1894. It is difficult to believe that the Wagner Act would have been passed, for instance, and perhaps even declared constitutional, but for the widespread collective action of committed and courageous workers between 1932 and 1935. The Taft–Hartley Act of 1947, on the other hand, is generally thought to be a response to the wave of postwar strikes. The statute, however, reflected hostility to unions and the NLRA, which had surfaced as early as 1937 and 1938, and passage also was a result of wartime strikes, primarily those of the United Mine Workers, which had weakened labor's political support. Practically, of course, Taft–Hartley was a response to the Republican capture of both houses of the Congress. Finally, the passage of the Landrum–Griffin Act of 1959 (the Labor–Management Reporting and Disclosure Act) stemmed, in large part, from the televised revelations of Senator McClellan's hearings on union corruption. The prospect for legislation reform may well be hopeful in certain areas, but it may be overly optimistic to expect substantial amendment to, or reform of, the National Labor Relations Act.

THE LAW AND THE PERCEPTION OF UNION POWER

If there is any hope for legislative reform of the National Labor Relations Act or for more sympathetic interpretation from the courts and the National Labor Relations Board, something will be required in addition to continued and increased lobbying for legislative reform. Initially, there must be an improvement in the public perception of unions, since the sympathetic light in which unions were viewed in the 1930s no longer exists. In 1981, for instance, the approval/disapproval rating of labor unions (55 percent/35 percent) stood at the lowest point since the Gallup poll first asked that question in 1936. In ratings of the ethical and moral practices of various occupational groups in the early 1980s, labor leaders stood at the bottom. Such concerns may partly be due to a perception that unions are less than democratic, which makes it imperative for unions to respond much more vigorously than they have to protect democratic rights within their organizations (Summers, 1951, 1960). In addition, it is commonly believed that unions are part of the problem of America's economic problems rather than part of the solution to them. Moreover—and this returns to an earlier point—the labor movement is not perceived as being the same as the working class. In a 1976 poll, for example, 82 percent expressed positive feelings toward workers, while only 32 percent expressed such feelings toward unions. Consistently, opinion polls register concern over the power of the labor unions, based perhaps on the notion that unions support inefficient work practices (Brody, 1989).

Yet, it would be a mistake to overstress "public opinion," as if it were the only valid starting point or an independent variable for determining strategy. Public perceptions, after all, are also *formed*, especially by the media, which have historically been less than sympathetic to unions. Indeed, the treatment of unions by the media is part of a larger problem involving the increasing concentration of control over the channels of communication. Television and the press are the prime means of communication, but these avenues are accessible only to those groups able to reach into deep pockets. Moreover, the media tend to be controlled by a handful of persons or corporations that have similar viewpoints, and, increasingly, it is a smaller handful (Atleson, 1985).

The media are a prime force in constricting the range of discourse in the United States. The narrowing is nowhere clearer than in discussions of investment decisions and control of capital. Both the media and the courts tend to agree that capital must be able to move freely, unhampered by the employee community or the needs of the general community at large. Should the United States take over U.S. Steel? It already has the right name—or at least it used to. In the United States, however, such possibilities are not even discussed. Whether other kinds of arrangements are feasible or workable may be debatable, but my point is that discussion of different economic arrangements or structures, even though they may exist in other capitalistic countries, tends to be outside the range of permissible political discourse in the United States. When the media focus on unions, attention is generally drawn to the "problems" they cause and, more recently, their serious reduction in both size and power (Puette, 1992). These perceptions are important because they affect the likelihood that Congress *or* the courts will respond affirmatively to employee concerns.

The weakness of relying on the public approval rating of unions as an explanation of their success in organization or in the courts is demonstrated by the situation in Canada. There has been a growing interest in Canada's labor policy, especially as union density rates between the two countries are seen as disparate. Today, for instance, approximately 38 percent of Canada's nonagricultural workforce is unionized, compared to less than 16 percent in the United States.

Canada, with a similar workforce and similar industrial base, has not experienced the same rapid decline in union organization as the United States. For instance, the AFL–CIO Committee on the Evolution of Work stated that with "roughly the same kind of economy, . . . many similar employers [and comparable changes affecting the labor market], the percentage of the civilian labor force that is organized [in Canada] increased in the period 1963–1983 from roughly 30% to 40%, at the same time that the percentage of organized workers declined in the United States from 30% to 20%" (Huxley, Keller, and Struthers 1986). In addition, some studies discount the notion that the differences in the two countries can be explained by the type of industries present in each country. Noah Meltz argues that "if Canada were more like the United States in its employment distribution there would be a greater difference in the overall rates of organization" (Meltz, 1985, 322).

Nor can one focus on variations in occupational groups. It is true that there is more extensive unionization of the public sector in Canada, and this may account for much of the seeming difference in union rates in the two countries. Nevertheless, Meltz reports that "all broad occupational sectors were more highly unionized in Canada than in the United States (319)." Indeed, studies in both countries reveal a similar relative decline in the manufacturing sector and a growth of government and service-related sectors. But even so, the patterns of unionization in the two countries reveal a sharp contrast.

A number of authors have concluded that the differences in union density between Canada and the United States are primarily due to legal and administrative policies concerning the enforcement of unfair labor practices or the certification of unions as bargaining agents. This assumes that the law is more favorable to union organization in other countries, especially so in Canada. It is true that Canadian federal and provincial labor statutes are more sympathetic in encouraging union organization. Moreover, Canadian statutes seem to have more effective remedies, especially since they often certify unions without the need for an election campaign, which many believe is the heart of the problem. Canadian legislation generally gives public agencies greater power to regulate and enforce unfair labor practices and provides stronger mandates to foster union growth. Thus, Peter Bruce of the Massachusetts Institute of Technology (MIT) Political Science Department notes that

Canadian labor boards have the authority to: (a) certify unions without formal union representation elections; (b) make quick and final decisions in unfair labor practice cases with little intervention with the courts; and (c) impose first contracts when employers refuse to bargain with newly certified unions. Compared to the U.S., Canadian labor laws also have given public sector workers more rights to strike, to compulsory arbitration, and to bargaining over wages. Numerous studies show that these institutions have curbed employer ULPs more effectively and have given workers in Canada more incentives to unionize. (Bruce, 1989, 122)

In Ontario, for instance, the most industrialized and populated province in Canada since 1930, containing 35 percent of Canada's unionized workers, the Ontario Labor Board limits judicial review and is empowered to certify unions without elections, and the law places the burden of proof on management in discrimination cases, something that would be considered extremely radical in the United States. A 1992 statute passed by the New Democratic Party government provides even greater protection for union organizing (Chapter 21, Statutes of Ontario, 1992). Most noteworthy to an American audience are provisions that prohibit management from using managerial employees from any site to perform the work of strikers. Employers may use temporary replacement workers in strike situations in only a narrow range of situations, and strikers cannot be permanently replaced.

If Canada's laws are more effective, more pro-organization, we have to ask how this situation arose. Granting a more sympathetic statutory scheme in Canada, can we assume, as many recent writers have, that union density rates are higher in Canada *because* of legal policies? Alternatively, may these policies be accurately viewed as a societal response to militant unions? One thing seems clear—it is not because of national differences in public opinion. Public approval rating of unions is no better in Canada. Bruce notes that Canada's proportion of favorable attitudes to unions has generally been 5 percent or more below that in the United States. In sum, he states that as far as pro-union sentiments are concerned, "Canadians have consistently been less favorable than people in the United States" (Bruce, 1989, 119).

Thus, Canadian unions seem to have been relatively more successful and seem to operate under more favorable legislation, even though their public approval rating is no higher than in the United States. One must, therefore, obviously look elsewhere for an explanation. Even if it were otherwise, experience suggests that there is not always a clear connection between public opinion and legislative or judicial and administrative responses.

Many American unions do seem to be less aggressive and socially conscious than unions in other Western societies, but they have certainly been very militant. Nowhere in the Western world has there been as much labor-related violence as in the United States, and the U.S. strike rates have often been higher than in Western Europe. Nevertheless, a good deal of this violence has been due to the opposition of employers and the intervention of the state. The state has often intervened in repressive fashion, in ways that would be anathema in Europe. It is almost a cliché to add that American employers are more strongly resistant to unions than employers elsewhere, and American unions operate in a system far more hostile than in any other Western democracy. American employers have historically been overtly hostile to union organization, often acting in ways that shock European observers. Moreover, with the exception of the Wagner Act in 1935, the state, both federal and state governments, has often been hostile to union organization, acting through militia, the army, and the courts.

It is relevant to add, however, that in the 1950s, at the time when the union decline began, unions began to reduce their expenditures on union organization. In this period union organizing efforts decreased substantially (Wallace, 1989). Thus, Freeman and Medoff conclude that "possibly as much as a third of the decline of union success through NLRB elections is linked to reduced organizing activity" (Freeman and Medoff, 1984, 228–230). It was also in the 1950s that many union activists, often possessing a far broader social vision than union leaders, were removed from the workforce either directly by McCarthyism or as a defensive measure by unions.

From 1961 on, on the other hand, "Canada experienced a cycle of union growth in militancy . . . beyond any level of unrest in the United States" (Huxley, Kettler, and Struthers, 1986, 125). Large and long strikes during the 1960s and early 1970s ended the use of the ex parte injunction as provincial governments tended to adopt more conciliatory approaches. Thus, Huxley concludes that "the most striking differences between the Canadian and American unions during the past two decades is the increasing importance of more adversarial and political unionism in Canada, marked above all by the interdependence and effective mutual aid between key unions and the New Democratic Party in English Canada, and analogous developments in Quebec "(Huxley, 1986, 131). During this period in the United States, union concerns were only intermittently of interest to the Democratic Party. Indeed, labor has recently been characterized by some Democratic leaders as one of the dreaded "special interests" necessitating that a cool distance be maintained to avoid the perceived political costs of an overly affectionate embrace.

In the United States, Congress and the courts seem to respond affirmatively to unions only when they are seen as troublesome. Admittedly, legislative action in American history has often been restrictive of unions rather than supportive, the most noteworthy exception being the Wagner Act of 1935. Even this statute, however, was not passed solely to protect the interests of employees, for one of the primary concerns was the felt need to decrease the incidence of strikes by promoting collective bargaining and by resolving representation disputes by peaceful, administrative means. Yet, recent studies have argued that increases in unionization may indeed lead to more strikes, but, importantly, unionization is also a *consequence* of strikes (Wallace, 1989; Wallace, Rubin, and Smith, 1988). That is, unions tend to grow and expand when they are seen as active protectors and militant representatives of employees.[2] Critically, at these times, the law responds to expression of collective vigor.

Even judges appear to react, for many judicial decisions seem to be based, at least in part, on perceptions of union power. In the 1944 *Hearst* (322 U.S.

111 [1944]) decision, for instance, the Supreme Court upheld a broad definition of "employee" so as to include within the act all those who *needed* the protection of the Wagner Act, no matter whether they would be treated as employees or independent contractors under traditional common law rules originally created for locating responsibility in civil cases. The Supreme Court stressed that the NLRA should be read broadly so that it could "bring industrial peace by substituting . . . the rights of workers to self organization and collective bargaining for the industrial strife which prevails where these rights are not effectively established." The stress on "industrial peace" and "interruption of commerce" clearly reflected the Court's understanding that the NLRA, passed in the midst of the turbulent depression, could not fulfill its goals without a liberal, inclusive interpretation.

More recently, however, in *Bell Aerospace, Division of Textron* (416 U.S. 267 [1974]) and *Yeshiva University* (444 U.S. 672 [1980]), the Court has, without any supporting legislative history, *excluded* from the statute perhaps hundreds of thousands of employees deemed to be "managerial employees." This judicial policymaking has profound effects, especially given the changing nature of the workplace and increased concern with decentralizing "managerial" decision making (Piore and Sabel, 1984). Not a word will be found in these recent opinions about industrial strife or the need to institutionalize labor conflict within the beneficial embrace of the statute. Perhaps the Court does not perceive a need to read the NLRA broadly because it no longer fears the "industrial strife which prevails where these rights are not effectively established."

The same pattern can be seen in other areas. The Court in the 1960s, for instance, held that the subcontracting of bargaining unit work was within the mandatory scope of bargaining because "one of the primary purposes of the act is to promote a peaceful settlement of industrial disputes by subjecting labor-management controversies to the mediatory influence of negotiation. The act was framed with an awareness that refusals to confer and negotiate had been one of the most prolific causes of industrial strife" (*Fibreboard Paper Products Corp. v. NLRB*, 379 U.S. 203 [1964]). It is true that the Court continually refers to industrial strife as if that was the only policy of the act, ignoring other policies such as industrial democracy and equality of bargaining. Nevertheless, "industrial peace" was often employed up to the 1970s to justify a fairly liberal interpretation of the NLRA. As late as 1979, for instance, the Court upheld a NLRB ruling holding that the prices of Ford Motor Company's in-plant food service were a subject of mandatory bargaining. The employees had boycotted the food service, and the Court referred to that action as an example of the kind of "labor strife" that might occur if the scope of bargaining was not read in a broad fashion. Yet, in *First National Maintenance* (452 U.S. 666 [1981]), the Court held only two years later that a partial closing of the enterprise, obviously much more important to employees than cafeteria food prices, was *not* within the scope of mandatory bargaining.

The *Bell, Yeshiva,* and *First National Maintenance* cases are consistent with the view that courts no longer feel a need to read the act broadly so as to institutionalize labor conflict and reduce strikes. Thus, it is reasonable to assume that the likely responses of both the Court and Congress are related to the perception of weakened union power. Courts as well as Congress, therefore, are affected by what is happening in bargaining rooms, the workplace, and the streets.[3] Not only do current decisions of the courts embody certain values that resonate throughout American legal history, but the state of the law also reflects the perceived relative strength of unions just as much as the hostility or indifference of any federal administration.[4]

Obviously, union power is adversely affected by restrictive NLRB and Supreme Court decisions. But the point I wish to stress is that the law, whether we look at legislative possibilities or court decisions, also reflects the current perception of union strength. This perception has been affected by the failure of the Labor Reform and Situs Picketing bills in the 1970s, Reagan's behavior, especially in regard to the air controllers, and the strong managerial attack of the last decade. Yet, as was the case with the passage of the Wagner Act, only when unions are perceived to be a force to be reckoned with does the legal system respond in favorable ways.[5] Although the legal system sometimes acts repressively, there will be no possibility of a positive response, perhaps unfortunately, unless unions are perceived to be vital and potentially disruptive economic actors. It is, thus, quite possible to view the current legal situation as the *result* of the perception of union weakness and not simply a *cause* of that weakness.

Union organizational and bargaining efforts not only may lead to more advantageous legal rulings but obviously have value of their own. Importantly, unions have focused so much of their efforts on law and governmental regulation that they may tend to forget that the system favors the strong and the troublesome.

NOTES

1. This view is perhaps most clearly expressed in *Commonwealth v. Pullis* (the Philadelphia Cordwainer's case), the first major American labor law case. See Commons, et al., 1910. Also see Atleson, 1983, 8–10.

2. There was a marked decrease in union election activity in the 1980s. The American Federation of Labor and Congress of Industrial Organizations (AFL-CIO) reacted with its Report on the Evolution of Work in 1985 and the creation of an Organizing Institute in 1989. The number of representation elections continued to decline, however, and evidence suggests that organizing is of secondary importance to servicing current members. See Jarky, Delaney, and Fiorito et al., 1992.

3. The argument presented here parallels the finding by Francis Fox Piven and Richard Cloward that rapid growth of expenditures for relief and welfare is typically a political response to civil disorder (Piven and Cloward, 1971).

This is not to suggest that the Supreme Court, for instance, never interprets the statute to favor unions. As Professor St. Antoine has noted, "The Supreme Court's labor philosophy is a crazy quilt. It often downplays cherished union values, like collective action, and modes of expression, like picketing. At the same time it embraces other union priorities, such as work preservation and dispute settlement through binding arbitration" (St. Antoine, 1992).

4. Public opinion shifts, and the public is not immune to the impact on labor of the events of the past decade. A Roper Poll released in February 1990, prepared for the AFL–CIO Executive Council, indicated that 50 percent of Americans had a "high" or "fairly good" opinion of labor leaders compared with 37 percent in 1982. Stockbrokers and politicians ranked below labor leaders. An increasing number felt that unions "need to do a great deal more to improve the quality of life for workers." The number who felt excessive union demands make the cost of living rise too much fell from 60 percent in 1981 to 40 percent. In addition, 33 percent, as compared with 28 percent in 1977, said they instinctively side with unions when they learn of a strike. This is the highest level of support for unions received since Roper began asking this question over twelve years ago (Bureau of National Affairs, 1990, 273).

Recent scandals in the political and financial arena may account for some of these results, combined with the lack of any newsworthy labor corruption stories. But it cannot be a coincidence that those years involved a resurgence of labor militance at, for instance, Pittston, International Paper, Hormel, and Eastern Airlines.

5. Lawrence Rothstein has contrasted the quite different responses of steelworkers facing plant shutdowns in Youngstown, Ohio, and Longwy, France. The French workers' struggle involved militant, collective action whereas Youngstown steelworkers, at least initially, ceded responsibility to an organization of area clergy and, except for two occupations of U.S. Steel offices, primarily opted for a litigation-based strategy.

The "forms and militancy of labor struggles depend on institutional supports and belief systems," and Rothstein notes that the Longwy workers received substantial and early support from nation union organizations as well as certain elected officials, political parties, and the public (Rothstein, 1986, Chapter 4, 1988).

Bibliography

Abraham, Katherine G. 1988. "Restructuring the Employment Relationship: The Growth of Market-Mediated Work Arrangements." Washington, DC: Brookings Institution.

Adams, Roy J. 1992. "The Role of the State in Industrial Relations." In D. Lewin, et al., *Research Frontiers in Industrial Relations and Human Resources*. Madison, WI: Industrial Relations Research Association.

Adler, Glen, and Doris Suarez. 1993. *Union Voices: Labor's Responses to Crisis*. Albany, NY: SUNY Press.

AFL–CIO. 1987. "Guidelines Help Unions Assess ESOPs." *AFL–CIO News*, August 27.

———. 1989. "Pension Terminators: Workers' Pension Plans Stripped of $20 Billion." *AFL–CIO News*, June 10, 6–7.

———. 1991. "AFL–CIO Policy on Pension Investments." Washington, DC.

———. 1992. *International Trade: Where We Stand*. Washington, D.C.

AFL–CIO Committee on the Evolution of Work. 1985. *The Changing Situation of Workers and Their Unions*. Washington, DC: AFL–CIO.

AFL–CIO Executive Committee. 1987. *A Statement by the AFL–CIO Executive Committee on Corporate Takeovers*, Washington, DC.

AFL–CIO Executive Council. 1992. Statement on Public Employee Pension Funds, February 20, Bal Harbour, FL. Quoted in *Labor & Investments* 12 (2), 1992, p.5.

AFL–CIO Public Employee Department. 1991a. *Making Government Work: Employee Involvement, Union Leadership*. Washington, DC: AFL–CIO.

———. 1991b. *PED Forum* 7(4) Fall.

———. 1993. *PED Forum* 9(2), Fall.

———. 1994a. *Excellence in Public Service: Case Studies in Labor–Management Innovation*.

———. 1994b. *PED Forum* 10 (1), Summer.

———. 1994c. "Privatization Update." Summer.

Aho, Michael C. 1993. "America and the Pacific Century: Trade Conflict or Cooperation." *International Affairs* 69 (1), January, 19–38.

American Federation of State, Municipal and County Employees. n.d. "Fact versus Fiction: Debunking the American Legislative Council's Report Blaming Public Employees for Government's Fiscal Problems." Washington, DC. Photocopy.

Appelbaum, Eileen. 1987. "Restructuring Work: Temporary, Part-Time, and At-Home Employment." In Heidi I. Hartmann, ed., *Computer Chips and Paper Clips: Technology and Women's Employment, Vol. 2: Case Studies and Policy Perspectives*. Washington, DC: National Academy Press.

Appelbaum, Eileen, and Judith Gregory. 1988. "Union Responses to Contingent Work: Are Win-Win Outcomes Possible?" In Kathleen Christensen and Mary Murphree, eds., *Flexible Workstyles: A Look at Contingent Labor*. Conference Summary, U.S. Department of Labor Women's Bureau. Washington, DC: U.S. Government Printing Office.

Aronowitz, Stanley, and William DiFazio. 1994. *The Jobless Future: Sci Tech and the Dogma of Work*. Minneapolis: University of Minnesota Press.

Aschauer, David. 1990. *Public Investment and Private Sector Growth*. Washington, DC: Economic Policy Institute.

Atleson, James B. 1983. *Values and Assumptions in American Labor Law*. Amherst: University of Massachusetts Press.

———. 1985. "Reflection on Labor, Power and Society." *Maryland Law Review* 44, 856–71.

Atleson, James B., Robert J. Rabin, George Schatzki, Herbert Sherman, and Eileen Silverstein. 1984. *Collective Bargaining in Private Employment*. St. Paul, MN: West.

Auerbach, Alan J., ed. 1988. *Corporate Takeovers: Causes and Consequences*. Chicago: University of Chicago Press.

Avery, Dianne. 1988–89. "Images of Violence in Labor Jurisprudence: The Regulation of Picketing and Boycotts, 1894–1921." *Buffalo Law Review* 37 (1), Winter, 1–117.

Bacon, David. 1994. "Labor Law Reform: Another Sellout of the Workers." *Nation*, May 30, 748.

Baer, Werner. 1993. "U.S.–Latin America Trade Relations: Past, Present and Future." In Gerald P. O'Driscoll, Jr., ed., *Free Trade within North America*. Proceedings of 1991 Conference on the South West Economy. Dallas: Federal Reserve Board.

Baldwin, Robert E. 1992. "Are Economists' Traditional Trade Policy Views Still Valid?" *Journal of Economic Literature* 30(2), June, 804–29.

Ball, Edgar. 1987. "United Steelworkers of America: An International Union Takes Initiative." *Entrepreneurial Economy* 6(4),13.

Banks, Andrew. 1988. "Dennis Walton's Capital Wars." *Labor Research Review* 12, Fall, 39–48.

Banks, Andrew, and Jack Metzgar. 1989. "Participating in Management: Union Organizing on a New Terrain." *Labor Research Review*, 14,1–55.

Baran, Paul, and Paul Sweezy. 1966. *Monopoly Capitalism*. New York: Monthly Review Press.

Barber, Randy. 1987. "Whose Job Is It Anyway? Capital Strategies for Labor." *Labor Research Review* 6(1), 31–44.

Barber, Randy, and Jeremy Rifkin. 1978. *The North Will Rise Again*. Boston: Beacon Press.

Barnet, Richard, and Ronald Muller. 1974. *Global Reach: The Power of Multinational Corporations*. New York: Simon and Schuster.

Becker, Eugene H. 1984. "Self-Employed Workers: An Update to 1983." *Monthly Labor Review*, July, 14–18.

Belanger, Marc. 1994. "Solinet: A Computer Conferencing System Designed for Trade Unions." *CYREV*, July. (An electronic journal).

Bellace, Janice R. 1994. "Labor Law Reform for the Post Industrial Workplace." *Proceedings of the 1994 Spring Meeting*, Industrial Relations Research Association, Madison, WI, 460–465.

Belman, Dale, and John Heywood. 1993. *The Truth about Public Employees: Underpaid or Overpaid?* Washington, DC: Economic Policy Institute.

Belous, Richard S., and Rebecca S. Hartley. 1990. *The Growth of Regional Trading Blocks in the Global Economy*. Washington, DC: National Planning Association.

Bennett, Amanda. 1991. "Downsizing Doesn't Necessarily Bring an Upswing in Corporate Profitability." *Wall Street Journal*, June 6, B1.

Berle, Adolph, and Gardener Means. 1932. *The Modern Corporation and Private Property*. New York: Macmillan.

Bernard, Elaine. 1993. "What a Labor Party Would Do for the American Labor Movement." *Labor Notes*, 168, March, 11.

Bernstein, Aaron. 1990. "Soon, LBOs May Be Union-Made," *Business Week*, February 26, 91.

———. 1991. "What Happened to the American Dream?" *Business Week*, August 16, 104–5.

———. 1993. "Now, Labor Can Be Part of the Solution." *Business Week*, March 1, 35.

Bernstein, Harry. 1988. "Sheet Metal Pension Fund Sets Example for Innovation." *Los Angeles Times*, March 8, Business section, 1.

Bernstein, Nina. 1985. "Changing Workforce: Boom in Temporary Employees Hits Hardest in the Midwest." *Milwaukee Journal*, October 25, 1985.

Bhagwati, Jagdish. 1991. *The World Trading System at Risk*. Princeton, NJ: Princeton University Press.

———. 1994. "Which Way? Free Trade or Protection?" *Challenge* 27(1), January–February, 17–24.

Blasi, Joseph. 1988. *Employee Ownership: Revolution or Rip-Off?*, Cambridge, MA: Ballinger.

Blinder, Alan. 1991. *Growing Together: An Alternative Economic Strategy for the 1990s*. N.p.: Whittle Direct Books.

Block, Fred. 1987. *Revising State Theory*. Philadelphia: Temple University Press.

Block, Richard N. 1992. "The Legal and Institutional Framework for Employment Security in the United States: An Overview." In Kazutoshi Koshiro, ed., *Employment Security and Labor Market Flexibility: An International Perspective*. Detroit: Wayne State University Press, 127–49.

"Blotting Out the Red Ink." 1994. *Governing*, August, 37–39.

Bluestone, Barry. 1989. "Goodbye to the Management Rights Clause." *Labor Research Review* 14, 66–72.

Bluestone, Barry, and Irving Bluestone. 1992. *Negotiating the Future: A Labor Perspective on American Business.* New York: Basic Books.

Bluestone, Barry, and Bennett Harrision. 1982. *The Deindustrialization of America: Plant Closings, Community Abandonment, and the Dismantling of Basic Industry.* New York: Basic Books.

Boal, Ellis. 1994. "The Dunlop Commission Report: Analysis and Comment." Available from *Labor Notes.*

Bowles, Samuel, David Gordon, and Thomas Weisskopf. 1983. *Beyond the Wasteland.* Garden City, NY: Anchor Books.

Bozeman, Barry. 1987. *All Organizations Are Public: Bridging Public and Private Organizational Theories.* San Francisco: Jossey-Bass.

———. 1988. "Exploring the Limits of Public and Private Sectors: Sector Boundaries and Maginot Line." *Public Administration Review*, March–April, 674–75.

Braverman, Harry. 1974. *Labor and Monopoly Capitalism.* New York: Monthly Review Press.

Brecher, Jeremy, and Tim Costello. 1990. *Building Bridges: The Emerging Grassroots Coalition of Labor and Community.* New York: Monthly Review Press.

Brill, Steven. 1978. *The Teamsters.* New York: Simon and Schuster.

Brody, David. 1989. "Barriers of Individualism in the Path of American Unions." *Dissent*, Winter, 71–77.

Bronfenbrenner, Kate. 1988a. "Bargaining for Part-time and Temporary Workers." *Labor Notes*, August, 11–12.

———. 1988b. "Organizing the Contingent Workforce." New York State School of Industrial and Labor Relations, Cornell University. Prepared for presentation to the AFL–CIO Organizing Department, September 14.

Bronner, Stephen. 1992. *Moments of Decision: Political History and the Crises of Radicalism.* New York: Routledge.

Brown, Earl V. 1988. "Deja Vu to a Discredited Past: Civil RICO in Labor Disputes." *RICO Law Reporter*, 8(2), 202.

Bruce, Peter. 1989. "Political Parties and Labor Legislation in Canada and the U.S." *Industrial Relations* 28, Spring, 115–141.

Bryant, Adam. 1993. "United Air Buyout Plan Is Confirmed." *New York Times*, August 27, D 3.

———. 1994. "After Seven Years, Employees Win United Airlines." *New York Times*, July 13, A1.

Buffalo Financial Plan Commission. 1993. "Five Year Finanacial and Management Plan for the City of Buffalo." Buffalo, NY. Photocopy.

Bureau of Labor Statistics. 1988. *Industry Wage Survey: Temporary Help Supply Industry 1987.* Washington, DC: U.S. Government Printing Office.

———. 1989. "Multiple Jobholding Reached Record High in May 1989." *Bureau of Labor Statistics News*, November 6.

———. 1991a. "The Employment Situation: September 1991," *Bureau of Labor Statistics News*, October 4.

———. 1991b. "Multiple Jobholding Unchanged in May 1991." *Bureau of Labor Statistics News*, October 28.

———. 1992. "Workers on Flexible and Shift Schedules." *Bureau of Labor Statistics News*, August 14.

———. 1993. *News*, February 8.

———. 1994. "Union Members in 1993." USDL: 94–58, February 9.

———. 1995a. "Major Work Stoppages, 1994." USDL: 95–25, January 27.

———. 1995b. "Union Members in 1994." USDL: 95–40, February 8.

Bureau of National Affairs. *Labor Relations Reporter* 135, March.

——— . 1986. *The Changing Workplace: New Directions in Staffing and Scheduling.* Special Report. Washington, DC: BNA.

———. 1990. *Labor Relations Reporter* 133, March.

Burroughs, Eugene. 1985. "Donovan v. Walton Opinion Provides Guidelines for Fiduciaries." *Pension World*, October, 58.

Business Research Publications. 1994. "Labor Law D.O.A." *Labor Trends*, November 12.

Callaghan, Polly, and Heidi Hartman. 1991. *Contingent Work: A Chart Book on Part-Time and Temporary Employment.* Washington, DC: Economic Policy Institute.

Canadian Center for Policy Alternatives. 1992. *Which Way for the Americas: Analysis of NAFTA and the Impact on Canada.* Ottowa, Ontario.

Capece, Matthew. 1991. "Contract Workers in the Construction Industry." Presentated at Economic Policy Institute Conference on New Policies for Part-Time and Contingent Workers, Washington, DC, March 26.

Carey, Max L., and Kim L. Hazelbaker. 1986. "Employment Growth in the Temporary Help Industry." *Monthly Labor Review*, April, 29–36.

Carr, Shirley. 1988. "Why Canadian Labor Opposes the Free Trade Agreement." *Canadian Speeches* 1, February, 4–6.

Carré, Françoise. 1994. "Temporary, Short-term and Part-Time Employment in French Banks and Insurance Companies During the 1980s: An Institutionalist Approach." Ph.D. dissertation, Department of Urban Studies and Planning, Massachusetts Institute of Technology, Cambridge, MA.

———. 1992. "Temporary Employment in the Eighties." In Virginia L. duRivage, ed., *New Policies for Part-Time and Contingent Workers.* Armonk, NY: M. E. Sharpe.

Carré, Françoise J., Virginia duRivage, and Chris Tilly. 1994. "Representing the Part-Time and Contingent Workforce: Challenges for Unions and Public Policy." In S. Friedman, R. Hurd, R. Oswald, and R. Seeber, eds., *Restoring the Promise of American Labor Law.* Ithaca, NY: Industrial and Labor Relations Press, Cornell University.

Cavanagh, John, Lance Compa, Alan Ebert, Bill Gould, Kathy Selvaggio, and Tim Shorrock. 1988. *Trade's Hidden Cost: Worker Rights in a Changing World Economy.* Washington, DC: International Labor Rights Education and Research Fund.

Cavanagh, John, Robin Broad, and Peter Weiss. 1994. "World Economy: Forging a Global New Deal." In Richard Caplan and John Feffer, eds., *State of the Union 1994.* Boulder, CO: Westview Press, 29–45.

Centre for Research on Work and Society. 1993. "Working Paper Series Number 4." York University, Toronto.

"The Changing Product Mix: Labor—Growing Pains." 1986. *Progressive Grocer*, October, 62–64.

Chernoff, Joel. 1985. "Door Ajar for Union Job Tie," *Pensions & Investment Age*, June 10, 1, 61.

———. 1990. "Unions' Investments Spark DOL Lawsuit." *Pensions and Investment Age*, August 6, 1, 27.

———. 1991. "Ego Leads to Dennis Walton's Downfall." *Pensions and Investment Age*, July 8, 1, 38.

Claiborne, William. 1993. "States' Fiscal Crises Force Cuts in Programs for Poor." *Washington Post*, February 10, A2.

Cobble, Dorothy Sue. 1990. "Union Strategies for Organizing and Representing the New Service Workforce." Paper presented at the 43rd Annual Conference of the Industrial Relations Research Association, December 28, Washington, DC.

———. 1991. "Organizing the Postindustrial Workforce: Lessons from the History of Waitress Unionism." *Industrial and Labor Relations Review*, April, 419–436.

———, ed. 1993. *Women and Unions: Forging a Partnership*. Ithaca, NY: ILR Press.

Colatosti, Camille. 1990. "Department Store Clerks Organize Against Sales Quotas; Vote UAW." *Labor Notes* June, 4, 10.

Commission on the Future of Worker–Management Relations. 1994. *Fact Finding Report*. Washington, DC: U.S. Department of Labor and U.S. Department of Commerce.

———. 1995. *Final Report*. Washington, DC: U.S. Department of Labor and U.S. Department of Commerce.

Commission of Inquiry into Part-Time Work. 1983. *Part-Time Work in Canada*. Ottawa, Ontario: Ministry of Labour.

Commons, John, Ulrich Phillips, Eugene Gilmore, Helen Summer, and John Andrews. 1910. *A Documentary History of American Industrial Society*, Vol. 3. Cleveland: Arthur H. Clark.

Compa, Lance. 1992. "The Dangers of Worker Control." In L. Krimerman and F. Lindenfeld, eds., *When Workers Decide: Workplace Democracy Takes Root in North America*. Philadelphia: New Society, 157–61.

Congressional Research Service. 1988. *Health Insurance and the Uninsured: Background Data and Analysis*. Washington, DC: Congressional Research Service.

Cook, Christopher. 1994. "Temps—The Forgotten Workers." *Nation*, January 31, 124–128.

Cooperative Home Care Associates. 1992. "Good Jobs and Good Service: Status Report." Bronx, NY.

Costello, Cynthia B. 1989. "The Clerical Homework at the Wisconsin Physicians Service Insurance Corporation." In Eileen Boris and Cynthia R. Daniels, eds., *Homework: Historical and Contemporary Perspectives on Paid Labor at Home*. Champaign–Urbana, IL: University of Illinois Press.

Council of Economic Advisers. 1994. *Economic Report of the President*. Washington, DC: U.S. Government Printing Office.

Cowling, Keith. 1994. "A More Creative Role for Industrial Policy." *Journal of the Economics of Business* 1(1), 15–17.

Cowling, Keith, and Roger Sugden. 1987. *Transnational Monopoly Capitalism*. Brighton, Ontario: Wheatsheaf.

Cox, Wendell, and Samuel Brunelli. 1992. "America's Protected Class: Why Excess Public Employee Compensation Is Bankrupting the States." *State Factor* 18(3), February, American Legislative Exchange Council.

Coyle, S. 1993. "National Partnerships for Community Investment." Unpublished paper on file with the author.

Craypo, Charles. 1975. "Collective Bargaining in the Conglomerate, Multinational Firm: Litton's Shutdown of Royal Typewriter." *Industrial and Labor Relations Review* 29(1),3–25.

———. 1990. "The Decline of Union Bargaining Power." In Bruce Nissen, ed., *U.S. Labor Relations 1945–1989: Accommodation and Conflict*. New York: Garland.

Croft, Tom. 1992. "Achieving City Pride." *Labor Research Review 19*, 11(1), Fall, 1.

Dantico, Marilyn. 1987. "The Impact of Contracting Out on Women and Minorities." In AFSCME Research Department, *When Public Services Go Private*. Washington, DC.

Davidson, T. S. 1990. "Multiemployer Housing Assistance." *IF National Opinion Panel*. Brookfield, WI: International Foundation of Employee Benefit Plans.

Davis, Mike. 1986. *Prisoners of the American Dream*. London: Verso Press.

Dawson, Steven. 1987. "First Class Employee Ownership." *Entrepreneurial Economy* 6(4), 2.

Deardorff, Alan, and Robert M. Stern. 1987. "Current Issues in Trade Policy." In Robert M. Stern, ed., *U.S. Trade Policies in a Changing World Economy*. Cambridge: MIT Press.

Deppe, Frank. 1992. "The Future of the European Community." *International Journal of Political Economy* 22(1), Spring, 63–81.

Dillon, Rodger L. 1987. *The Changing Labor Market: Contingent Workers and the Self-Employed in California*. Washington, D.C.: Senate Office of Research.

Donovan v. Walton. 1985. *Donovan v. Walton*, 609 F. Supp. 1221, SD Fla 1985,(aff'd sub nom. Brock v. Walton, 794 F.2d 586. 11th Cir. 1986).

Drucker, Peter. 1976. *The Unseen Revolution: How Pension Fund Socialism Came to America*. New York: Harper and Row.

duRivage, Virginia L. 1992. "Social Policy and the Contingent Workforce." In V. duRivage, ed., *New Policies for Part-Time and Contingent Workers*. Armonk, NY: M. E. Sharpe.

duRivage, Virginia, and David Jacobs. 1989. "Home-Based Work: Labor's Choices." In Eileen Boris and Cynthia R. Daniels, eds., *Homework: Historical and Comparative Perspectives on Paid Labor at Home*. Champaign–Urbana: University of Illinois Press.

Early, Steve, and Rand Wilson. 1992. "Jobs with Justice: Health Care Reform from the Bottom Up." *New Politics* 3(4) (New Series), Winter, 109–114.

Edwards, Richard. 1993. "Reshaping Employee Protection for a Global Economy." *Challenge* 27(1), January–February, 34–39.

Ellerman, David. 1986. *The Legitimate Opposition at Work*. Somerville, MA: Industrial Cooperative Association.

Ellerman, David, and Peter Pitegoff. 1983. "The Democratic Corporation." *New York University Review of Law & Social Change* 11(3), 441–72.

Employee Benefits Research Institute. 1988. *Uninsured in the United States: The Non-Elderly Population without Health Insurance, 1986*. Washington, DC: Employee Benefits Research Institute.

Erfani, Julie A. 1992. "NAFTA's Ties to Potential Authoritarianism in Mexico." *Labor Law Journal* 43, 8, August, 530–534.

"ESOPs: Are They Good for You?" *Business Week*, May 15, 1989, 116723.

Federation for Industrial Retention and Renewal. 1993. "The Great American Giveway." *News* 5(2), Winter, 1–19.

———. 1994. "Where Was the Invisible Hand During the Crash?" *News* 6 (1), Spring.

Feekin, Lynn, and Burce Nissen. 1991. "Early Warnings against Plant Closings: Issues and Prospects." *Labor Studies Journal* 16(4), Winter, 20–33.

Feuille, Peter. 1991. "Unionism in the Public Sector: The Joy of Protected Markets." *Journal of Labor Research* 12(4), Fall, 351–33.

Fiorito, Jack, and Wallace E. Hendricks. 1987. "Union Characteristics and Bargaining Outcomes." *Industrial and Labor Relations Review* 40(4), July, 569–584.

Fitzgerald, J. 1991. "Class as Community: The New Dynamics of Social Change." *Environment and Planning D: Society and Space* 9, 117–128.

Flood, Lawrence G. 1987. "Part-Time Faculty and Staff: A Union Perspective." Paper presented at the 41st Annual Conference of the New York Political Science Association, April 3–4.

———. 1991. "Union–Community Relations in Buffalo: A Preliminary Assessment." *Buffalo Law Review* 39(2), 445–71.

Forbath, William. 1989. "The Shaping of the American Labor Movement." *Harvard Law Review* 102, 1109–1257.

Fox, Kenneth. ca. 1981. *Crisis in the Public Sector: A Reader*. New York: Monthly Review Press.

Fox, Neil. 1985. "PATCO and the Courts: Public Sector Labor Law as Ideology." *University of Illinois Law Review* 2, 245–312.

Freeman, Chris, and Luc Soete. 1994. *Work for All or Mass Unemployment*. New York: Pinter.

Freeman, Richard. 1986. "Unionism Comes to the Public Sector." *Journal of Economic Literature* 24 (March), 41–86.

Freeman, Richard, and Casey Ichniowski. 1988. "The Public Sector Look of American Unionism." In R. Freeman and C. Ichniowski, *When Public Workers Unionize*. Chicago: University of Chicago Press, 1–15.

Freeman, Richard, and James Medoff. 1984. *What Do Unions Do?* New York: Basic Books.

Fried, Rona. 1989. "Cooperative Home Care Associates: A Healthy Situation." *Workplace Democracy* 63, Winter, 7.

Fromstein, Mitchell. 1988. "Rising Use of Part-Time and Temporary Workers: Who Benefits and Who Loses?" Testimony before Subcommittee on Housing and Employment Opportunity of the Committee on Government Operations, U.S. House of Representatives. May 19.

Fukuyama, Francis. 1989. "The End of History." *The National Interest*, summer, 3–18.

Garcia v. San Antonio Metropolitan Transit Authority. 1985. 469 U.S. 528.

Gaynor, Pamela. 1989. "South Side Venture Advances." *Pittsburgh Post Gazette*, February 13.

Geoghegan, Thomas. 1991. *Which Side Are You On: Trying to Be for Labor When It's Flat on Its Back*. New York: Farrar, Straus, and Giroux.

Ghilarducci, Teresa. 1992. *Labor's Capital: The Economics and Politics of Private Pensions*. Cambridge: MIT Press.

Glyde, Gerald P. 1986. "Labor in a Changing Industrial Relations Environment." In Gerald P. Glyde and Donald Kennedy, eds. *Contemporary Labor Issues*. Dubuque, IA: Kendall/Hunt.

———. 1993. "Canadian Labor and the Free Trade Agreement." *Labor Studies Journal* 17 (4), Winter, 3–23.

Goldberg, Michael. 1985. "The Duty of Fair Representation: What the Courts Do In Fact." *Buffalo Law Review* 34, Winter, 89–171.

Golden, Lonnie, and Eileen Appelbaum. 1992. "What Is Driving the Boom in Temporary Employment?" *American Journal of Economics and Sociology* 51 (4), October, 473–492.

Golden, Miriam, and Jonas Pontusson, eds. 1992. *Bargaining for Change: Union Politics in North America and Europe*. Ithaca, NY: Cornell University Press.

Goldfield, Michael. 1987. *The Decline of Organized Labor in the United States*. Chicago: University of Chicago Press.

Goldman, Debbie, comp. 1992. *Reinvigorating the Public Service: Union Innovations to Improve Government*. Washington, DC: AFL–CIO Public Employee Department.

Gordon, Michael, ed. 1994. "Issues for the Future of Labor/Management Relations." *Workplace Topics* 4(1), June.

Gore, Al. 1993. *Creating a Government That Works Better and Costs Less: Report of the National Performance Review*. New York: Times Books.

Gramm, Cynthia. 1992. "Labor's Legislative Initiatives to Restrict Permanently Replacing Strikers." Paper presented at Industrial Relations Research Association's 44th Annual Meeting.

Grant, David. 1983. *Celebrating the First Sixty Years*. New York: Amalgamated Bank of New York. Brochure.

Greaney, Thomas. 1991. "Any Merger Used to Be Worth a Try." *Cleveland Plain Dealer*, March 6, B1.

Green, Roy E. 1993. *The Enterprise for the Americas Initiative*. Westport, CT: Praeger.

Greenberg, Edward. 1986. *Workplace Democracy: The Political Effects of Participation*. Ithaca, NY: Cornell University Press.

Gregory, Charles. 1946. *Labor and the Law*. New York: Norton.

Gregory, Charles, and Harold Katz. 1979. *Labor and the Law*. New York: Norton.

Greider, William. 1981. "The Education of David Stockman." *Atlantic* 248, December, 52.

Grenier, Guillermo. 1988. *Quality Circles and Anti-Unionism in American Industry*. Philadelphia: Temple University Press.

Grob, Gerald. 1961. "Knights of Labor." In *Workers and Utopia*. Evanston, IL: Northwestern University Press, Chapter 3.

Grossman, Jonathan P. 1945. *William Sylvis: Pioneer of American Labor—A Study of the Labor Movement during the Era of the Civil War*. New York: Columbia University Press.

Gunn, Christopher. 1984. *Workers' Self-Management in the United States*. Ithaca, NY: Cornell University Press.

Gutchess, Jocelyn. 1992. "International Comparison of Employment Adjustment." In Kazutoshi Koshiro, ed., *Employment Security and Labor Market Flexibility: An International Perspective*. Detroit: Wayne State University Press, 196–217.

Guydon, Linda. 1989. "Council Urged to Save Bakery Jobs." *Pittsburgh Post Gazette*, May 3.

Hansmann, Henry. 1990. "When Does Worker Ownership Work? ESOPs, Law Firms, Codetermination, and Economic Democracy." *Yale Law Journal* 99(8), 1749.

Hanson, Gary, and Frank Adams. 1987. "Saving Jobs and Putting Democracy to Work." *Labor Management Cooperation Brief*, no. 11, U.S. Department of Labor.

Harrison, Bennett, and Barry Bluestone. 1988. *The Great U-Turn: Corporate Restructuring and the Polarizing of America*. New York: Basic Books.

Hartmann, Heidi, and June Lapidus. 1989. "Temporary Work." Paper prepared for the U.S. Department of Labor, Commission on Worklife Quality and Labor Market Efficiency, June.

Haugen, Steven E. 1986. "The Employment Expansion in Retail Trade: 1973–1985." *Monthly Labor Review*, August, 9–16.

Hayes, Robert H., and William J. Abernathy. 1980. "Managing Our Way to Economic Decline." *Harvard Business Review* 58(4), 67–77.

Hazeltine, T. 1988. "Canada–U.S. Free Trade? Not So Elementary, Watson." *Canadian Public Policy* 14, June, 204–13.

"Health Care Reform Means Change for Part-Timers." 1993. *Wall Street Journal*, September 28, 1.

Hearst v. NLRB. 1944. 322 U.S. 111.

Heckscher, Charles. 1988. *The New Unionism*. New York: Basic Books.

Henderson, Keith. 1993. "U.S. Co-opts Key State Taxes." *Wall Street Journal*, March 10, 8.

Herod, Andrew. 1991. "Local Political Practice in Response to a Manufacturing Plant Closure: How Geography Complicates Class Analysis." *Antipode* 23(4), 385–402.

———. 1994. "Further Reflections on Organized Labor and Deindustrialization in the United States." *Antipode* 26(1), 77–95.

Hester, Stephen. 1988. "Employee Ownership: A Union View." In S. Estreicher and D. Collins, eds., *Labor Law & Business Change: Theoretical and Transactional Perspectives*. New York: Quorum Books.

Hoerr, John. 1989. "The Payoffs from Teamwork." *Business Week*, July 10, 62.

———. 1990. "The Strange Bedfellows Backing Workplace Reform." *Business Week*, April 30, 57.

———. 1991. "What Should Unions Do?" *Harvard Business Review* 69(3), May–June, 30–45.

Holt, Wythe. 1984. "Labour Conspiracy Cases in the U.S., 1805–1842." *Osgoode Hall Law Journal* 226, 591–659.

Hornack, Joseph, and Staughton Lynd. 1987. "The Steel Valley Authority." *New York University Review of Law & Social Change* 15(1), 113.

House Republican Conference. 1994. *Contract with America*. Washington, DC.

Huxley, Christopher, David Kettler, and James Struthers. 1986. "Is Canada's Experience Especially Instructive?" In Seymore Martin Lipset, ed., *Unions in Transition: Entering the Second Century*. San Francisco: Institute for Contemporary Studies, 113–132.

Hyde, Alan. 1991. "In Defense of Employee Ownership." *Chicago–Kent Law Review* 67, 159–211.

Hyde, Alan, and Craig L. Livingston. 1989. "Employee Takeovers." *Rutgers Law Review* 41(4), 1131–95.

ICA. 1991. "Plant Closings: John Roberts, Ltd." In ICA Group, *Annual Report*. Boston: The ICA Group.

Icahn, Carl. 1989. "The Case for Takeovers." *New York Times Magazine*, January 29, 34.

Industrial Union Department. 1986. "Building Trade Interest in Establishing Union-Owned Banks and Thrifts Grow." *Labor and Investments* 6(7) September, 1, 4.

———. 1987. "Benefit Funds Purchase Thrift Bank in Boston." *Labor and Investments*, 7, March.

———. 1991. "AFL-CIO Housing Investment Trust Expands Range of Housing Investments." *Labor and Investments* 11(4), 8.

———. 1992. "Labor Cannot Afford Passive Role in Fund Management." *Labor and Investments* 12(2), 273.

Institute for Policy Innovation. n.d., ca. Spring 1993. "America's No. 1 Growth Industry Is Government." Washington, DC. Press Release.

International Labour Office. 1989. "Part-Time Work." *Conditions of Work Digest* 8(1).

Jacoby, Sanford. 1987. *Employing Bureaucracy*. New York: Columbia University Press.

Jarley, Paul, John Delaney, and Jack Fiorito. 1992. "Embracing the Committee on the Evolution of Work Report: What Have Unions Done?" In Industrial Relations Research Association, *Proceedings* of the 44th Annual Meeting, 500–511.

Jensen, Jane, and Rianne Mahon. 1993. *The Challenge of Restructuring: North American Labor Movements Respond*. Philadelphia: Temple University Press.

Jensen, Michael, and William Meckling. 1979. "Rights and Production Functions: An Application to Labor-Managed Firms and Codetermination." *Journal of Business* 52, 469 ff.

Johnson, Anna Gutierrez, and William F. Whyte. 1977. "The Mondragon System of Worker Production Cooperatives." *Industrial and Labor Relations Review* 31(1), 18–30.

Johnston, Paul. 1988. "The Politics of Public Work: A Comparative Study of Labor Relations in the Public Sector." Doctoral diss., University of California at Berkeley.

———. 1994. *Success While Others Fail: Social Movement Unionism and the Public Workplace*. Ithaca, NY: ILR Press.

Jones, Ronald W. 1994. "America's High-Tech Industries: Tyson's Policy Proposals." *Journal of the Economics of Business* 1(1), 151–157.

Josephson, Matthew. 1952. *Sidney Hillman: Statesman of American Labor*. Garden City, NY: Doubleday.

Juravich, Tom, and Kate Bronfenbrenner. 1995. "Premature to Write Labor's Obituary." *Houston Chronicle*, January 30.

Kahne, Hilda. 1985. *Reconceiving Part-Time Work*. Totowa, NJ: Rowman and Allanheld.

Kaufman, Bruce, and Morris Kleiner, eds. 1993. *Employee Representation: Alternatives and Future Directions*. Madison WI: IRRA.

Kaufman, Julie. 1989. "Democratic ESOPs." *Labor Lawyer* 5, 825–44.

Kelly, Maryellen, and Bennett Harrison. 1992. "Unions, Technology and Labor–Management Cooperation." In Lawrence Mishel and Paula Voos, eds., *Unions and Economic Competitiveness*. Armonk, NY: M. E. Sharpe, 247–286.

Kerson, R., and Greg LeRoy. 1989. *State and Local Initiatives on Development Subsidies and Plant Closings*. Chicago: Federation for Industrial Retention and Renewal.

Kettl, Donald F. 1994. *Reinventing Government? Appraising the National Performance Review*. Washington, DC: Center for Public Management, Brookings Institution.

Kilborn, Peter. 1990. "New Fund to Help Unions Buy Ailing Factories." *The New York Times*, February 20, D8.

Klare, Karl. 1978. "Judicial Deregulation of the Wagner Act and the Origins of Modern Legal Consciousness." *Minnesota Law Review* 62, 265–339.

―――. 1988. "The Labor–Management Cooperation Debate: A Workplace Democracy Perspective." *Harvard Civil Rights–Civil Liberties Law Review* 23(1), Winter, 39–84.

Kleingartner, Archie, and Alan Paul. 1992. "Member Attachment and Union Effectiveness in Arts and Entertainment." Paper presented at the 44th Annual Meeting of the Industrial Relations Research Association, January 3, New Orleans.

Kochan, Thomas, Harry Katz, and Nancy Mower. 1984. *Worker Participation and American Unions: Threat or Opportunity?* Cambridge: MIT Press.

Kochan, Thomas, Harry Katz, and Robert McKersie. 1986. *The Transformation of American Industrial Relations*. New York: Basic Books.

Kreiner, Sherman. 1987. "Worker Ownership as the Basis for an Integrated, Proactive Development Model." *New York University Review of Law & Social Change* 15(1), 227.

―――. 1992. *The Crocus Fund: Business Plan Summary*. Winnipeg, Manitoba: Crocus Investment Fund.

Krimerman, Len, and Frank Lindenfeld. 1992. *When Workers Decide: Workplace Democracy Takes Root in North America*. Philadelphia: New Society.

Krugman, Paul R. 1994. "Competitiveness: A Dangerous Obsession." *Foreign Affairs* 73 (2), March–April, 28–44.

Kulik, Gary. 1978. "Pawtucket Village and the Strike of 1824: The Origins of Class Conflict in Rhode Island." *Radical History Review* 17, 5–37.

Labor Advisory Committee for Trade Negotiations and Trade Policy. 1992. *Preliminary Report: Labor Advisory Committee on the North American Free Trade Agreement*. Washington, DC.

Labor Research Association. 1990. "Winners and Losers." *Economic Notes*, May–June, 1–3.

LaBotz, Dan. 1990. *Rank and File Rebellion*. New York: Verso.

Lake, David A. 1988. *Power, Protection and Free Trade*. Ithaca: Cornell University Press.

Lapidus, June. 1989. "The Temporary Help Industry and the Operation of the Labor Market." Ph.D. diss., University of Massachusetts–Amherst.

Laxer, James. 1987. *Decline of the Superpowers*. Toronto: Lorimer.

Leckie, Norm. 1993. "An International Review of Labour's Adjustment Policies and Practices." *Queen's Papers in Industrial Relations*. Kingston, Ontario: Queen's University, 1993–15.

Lee, R. Alton. 1990. *Eisenhower and Landrum–Griffin*. Lexington: University of Kentucky Press.

Levitan, Sar, and Elizabeth Conway. 1988. "Part-Timers: Living on Half Rations." *Challenge*, May–June, 9–16.

Levitt, Martin Jay. 1993. *Confessions of a Union Buster*. New York: Crown.

Lewin, David, Peter Feuille, Thomas Kochan, and John Delancy. 1988. "Background and Overview." In *Public Sector Labor Relations*, 3d ed. Lexington, MA: Lexington Books, 1–19.

Lichtenstein, Nelson. 1982. *Labor's War at Home: The CIO in World War II*. Cambridge, MA: Cambridge University Press.

———. 1989. "'The Man in the Middle': A Social History of Automobile Industry Foremen." In N. Lichtenstein and S. Meyer, eds., *On the Line: Essays in the History of Auto Work*. Urbana: University of Illinois Press, 153–182.

Liebeler, Susan. 1993. "The Politics of NAFTA." In Alan M. Rugman, ed., *Foreign Investment and NAFTA*. Columbia: University of South Carolina Press, 27–46.

Lueck, Thomas. 1987. "A Noble Experiment Goes Bankrupt." *New York Times*, May 3, Section 3, 1.

Lustig, Nora, Barry P. Bosworth, and Robert Z. Lawrence, ed. 1992. *North America Free Trade: Assessing the Impact*. Washington, DC: Brookings Institution.

Lynd, Staughton. 1982. *The Fight against Shutdowns: Youngstown's Steel Mill Closings*. San Pedro, CA: Singlejack Books.

Lynd, Staughton, and Alice Lynd. 1991. "Labor in the Era of Multinationalism: The Crisis in Bargained-for Fringe Benefits." *West Virginia Law Review* 93, 907.

MacDonald, Jeffrey, and Anne Bingham. 1986. *Pension Handbook for Union Negotiators*. Washington, DC: Bureau of National Affairs.

Magaziner, Ira C., and Robert B. Reich. 1982. *Minding America's Business: The Decline and Rise of the American Economy*. New York: Harcourt Brace Jovanovich.

Maher, Thomas. 1991. "At ULLICO They Know What 'In' Talk Means." *Life and Health/Financial Services Edition*, March 19, 25.

Maranto, Cheryl, and Jack Fiorito. 1987. "The Effect of Union Characteristics on the Outcome of NLRB Certification Elections." *Industrial and Labor Relations Review* 40(2), January, 225–240.

Marchak, Patricia M. 1989. "The Ideology of Free Trade: A Response to Smith." *Canadian Public Policy*, 220–225.

Martin, Brendan. 1994. "Public Service and the New World Order." *Blueprint for Social Justice* 47(7), March, 1–7.

McCarthy, Michael. 1994. "Holders of UAL Approve Bold $4.8 Billion Buyout." *Wall Street Journal*, July 13, A3.

McCurdy, Charles W. 1984. "The Roots of 'Liberty of Contract' Reconsidered: Major Premises in the Law of Employment, 1867–1937," *Supreme Court Historical Society Yearbook 1984*, 20–33.

McDermott, John. 1991. *Corporate Society: Class, Property and Contemporary Capitalism.* Boulder CO: Westview Press.

McEwan, Arthur, and William Tabb. 1989. *Instability and Change in the World Economy.* New York: Monthly Review Press.

McNulty, Paul. 1980. *The Origins and Development of Labor Economics.* Cambridge: MIT Press.

Mellor, Earl, and Steven Haugen. 1986. "Hourly Paid Workers: Who They Are and What They Earn." *Monthly Labor Review*, February, 20–26.

Meltz, Noah. 1985. "Labor Movements in Canada and the United States." In Thomas A. Kochan, ed., *Challenges and Choices Facing American Labor.* Cambridge: MIT Press.

Metzgar, Jack. 1984. "The IAM 100 'Model'—A Debate." *Labor Research Review* 5, 81–116.

"Mismanagement and What Unions Can Do about It." 1987. *Labor Research Review* 10, 17–109.

Mishel, Lawrence, and David M. Frankel. 1992. *The State of Working America: 1990–91.* Armonk, NY: M. E. Sharpe.

Mishel, Lawrence, and Jared Bernstein. 1994. *The State of Working America: 1994–95.* Armonk, NY: M. E. Sharpe.

Mishel, Lawrence, and Paula Voos, eds. 1992. *Unions and Economic Competitiveness.* Armonk, NY: M. E. Sharpe.

Moe, Ronald. 1987. "Exploring the Limits of Privatization." *Public Administration Review*, November–December, 453–60.

———. 1988. "'Law' Versus 'Performance' as Objective Standard." *Public Administration Review*, March–April, 674–675.

Moody, Kim, and Mary McGinn. 1992. *Unions and Free Trade: Solidarity and Competition.* Detroit: Labor Notes.

Moore, Patricia. 1994. "Teamsters See Chance to Gain UAL Workers." *Chicago Sun-Times*, May 18, 69.

Morris, Charles, ed. 1971. *The Developing Labor Law.* Washington, DC: Bureau of National Affairs.

National Association of Temporary Help Services. 1992. *Co-employment: A Review of Customer Liability Issues in the Staffing Services Industry.* Washington, D.C.

National Commission on Food Marketing. 1964. *Organization and Competition in Food Retailing.* Washington, DC: U.S. Government Printing Office.

National Labor Relations Board. 1992. *Annual Report for 1990.* Washington, DC: Government Printing Office.

National Performance Review. 1994a. *Creating a Government That Works Better and Costs Less: Status Report, September 1994.* Washington, DC: National Performance Review.

———. 1994b. *Reinventing Government: Six Month Status Report*. Washington, DC: National Performance Review.

National Lawyers Guild. 1992. *Rights of Employees and Union Members*.

Newman, Steven, and Michael Yoffee. 1991. "Steelworkers and Employee Owner-ship." *Journal of Employee Ownership Law and Finance* 3(2).

Nine to Five, National Association of Working Women. 1986. *Working on the Margins: The Growth of Part-Time and Temporary Workers in the United States*. Cleveland: Nine to Five.

Nissen, Bruce. 1990. "Union Battles against Plant Closings: Case Study Evidence and Policy Implications." *Policy Studies Journal* 18(2), Spring, 382–95.

Noah, Timothy. 1991. "Throttling Down: Instead of Tax Raises Michigan Tries to Cure Deficit with Cutback." *Wall Street Journal*, October 30, A1.

Noble, A. 1992. "Legal Restraints Imposed by ERISA on the Creation, Management and Organization of Labor Banks." Unpublished paper, SUNY at Buffalo Law School.

Noble, Barbara. 1994. "At the Labor Board, New Vigor." *New York Times*, Septem-ber 4, F21.

Nollen, Stanley. 1982. *New Work Schedules in Practice: Managing Time in a Changing Society*. New York: Van Nostrand, Reinhold.

Nollen, Stanley, Brenda Eddy, and Virginia Martin. 1978. *Permanent Part-Time Employment: The Manager's Perspective*. New York: Praeger.

Norwood, Janet. 1988. "Commissioner of Labor Statistics, Statement before the Subcommittee on Housing and Employment Opportunity of the Com-mittee on Government Operations, U.S. House of Representatives." May 19.

Office of the United States Trade Representative. 1991. *Foreign Trade Barriers*. Washington, DC: Government Printing Office.

Olson, Deborah Groban. 1989. "Unions and Employee Ownership." In *ESOPs: The Handbook of Employee Stock Ownership Plans*. Chicago: Probus.

Orchard, David. 1993. *The Flight for Canada*. Toronto: Stoddard.

"An Organizing Model of Unionism." 1991. *Labor Research Review* 17, 1–90.

Parker, Mike. 1993. "Industrial Relations Myth and Shop-Floor Reality: The 'Team Concept' in the Auto Industry." In Nelson Lichtenstein and Howell John Harris, *Industrial Democracy in America*. New York: Cambridge University Press.

Parker, Mike, and Jane Slaughter. 1988. *Choosing Sides*. Boston: South End Press.

Pearce, Diana. 1985. "Toil and Trouble: Women Workers and Unemployment Compensation." *Signs: Journal of Women in Culture and Society* 10(3), 439–59.

Piore, Michael, and Charles Sabel. 1984. *The Second Industrial Divide: Possibilities for Prosperity*. New York: Basic Books.

Pitegoff, Peter. 1987. *The Democratic ESOP*. Boston: Industrial Cooperative Associa-tion.

———. 1989. "Unions and Worker Ownership." *Policy Studies Journal* 18(2), 396–403.

Pitegoff, Peter, and Staughton Lynd. 1982. "Workers Can Be Choosers." *New York Times*, October 27.

Piven, Francis, and Richard Cloward. 1971. *Regulating the Poor: The Functions of Public Welfare*. New York: Vintage.

Plewes, Thomas. 1988. "Understanding the Data on Part-Time and Temporary Employment." In *Flexible Workstyles: A Look at Contingent Labor*. Washington, DC: U.S. Department of Labor, Women's Bureau.

Plotkin, Sidney, and William Scheuerman. 1994. *Private Interest, Public Spending: Balanced Budget Conservatism and the Fiscal Crisis*. Boston: South End Press.

Pope, James. 1989. "Two Faces, Two Ethics: Labor Union Lawyers and the Emerging Doctrine of Entity Ethics." *Oregon Law Review* 68, Winter, 1–55.

Presser, Harriet B., and Wendy Baldwin. 1980. "Child Care as a Constraint on Employment: Prevalence, Correlates, and Bearing on the Work and Fertility Nexus." *American Journal of Sociology* 85(5), 1202–13.

Prestowitz, Clyde V., Jr. 1992. "Beyond Laissez Faire." *Foreign Policy* 87, Summer, 67–87.

Prestowitz, Clyde V., Jr., Lester Thorn, Rudolph Scharping, Steven Cohen, Benn Steil, and Paul Kingman. 1994. "The Fight over Competitiveness." *Foreign Affairs* 73(4), July–August, 186–203.

Przeworski, Adam, and Fernando Limongi. 1993. "Political Regimes and Economic Growth." *Journal of Economic Perspectives* 7(3), Summer, 51–69.

Puette, William. 1992. *Through Jaundiced Eyes: How the Media View Organized Labor*. Ithaca, NY: ILR Press.

Rachleff, Peter. 1990. "Supporting the Hormel Strikers," In J. Brecher and T. Costello, *Building Bridges: The Emerging Grassroots Coalition of Labor and Community*. New York: Monthly Review Press, 57–69.

Rebitzer, James B. 1987. "The Demand for Part-Time Workers: Theory, Evidence and Policy Implications." Department of Economics, University of Texas at Austin, December. Mimeo.

Rebitzer, James B., and Thomas A. Kochan. 1992. "The Management of Contract Workers and the Risks of Accidents: Evidence from the Petrochemical Industry." *Industrial Relations Research Association Series*. Proceedings of the Forty-Fourth Annual Meeting, January 3–5: 325–31.

Rebitzer, James B., and Lowell J. Taylor. 1991. "Work Incentives and the Demand of Primary and Contingent Labor." MIT, National Bureau of Economic Research, and Carnegie Mellon University, January. Mimeo.

Reich, Robert B. 1983. *The Next American Frontier*. New York: Times Books.

_____ . 1991. *The Work of Nations*. New York: Knopf.

Reinhardt, Shirley. 1991. "Testimony Prepared for the Trade Staff Policy Committee." Atlanta, GA, August 29, 1991. Testimony compiled by Tennessee Industrial Renewal Network, Knoxville, TN.

Ritchie, Sarah. 1993. "State–Local Employment Continues to Grow." *State Fiscal Brief*, No. 15, November, Center for the Study of the States, Albany, NY: Rockefeller Institute.

Rose, Winfield. 1988. "Recent Developments in Public Sector Labor Relations Law." *Journal of Collective Negotiations* 17 (3), 207–19.

Rosen, Corey. 1989. "Looking Back on Nine Good Years." *Changing Work*, No. 9, 42.

_____ . 1991. "Employee Ownership: Performance, Prospects, and Promise." In Corey Rosen and Karen Young, eds., *Understanding Employee Ownership*. Ithaca, NY: Cornell University Press.

————. 1991. "Ten Years of Employee Ownership." *Employee Ownership Report* 11(3), 1.

Rosen, Corey, Kevin Klein, and Kathleen Young. 1986. *Employee Ownership in America: The Equity Solution.* Lexington, MA: Lexington Books.

Roth, Henry. 1975. *Labor: America's Two-Faced Movement.* New York: Petrocelli/Charter.

Rothstein, Lawrence. 1986. *Plant Closings: Power, Politics and Workers.* Dover, MA: Auburn House.

————. 1988. "Industrial Restructuring and Worker Militancy: Liberal Pluralism vs. Class Conflict in Youngstown and Longway." Unpublished paper.

Rugman, Alan M. 1990. *Multinationals and Canada—United States Free Trade.* Columbia: University of South Carolina Press.

Salwen, Kevin, and Laurie McGinley. 1993. "Labor Designee Reich Urges More Input by Workers to Aid Job Quality, Safety." *Wall Street Journal,* January 8.

Sansolo, Michael. 1987. "Take This Job . . . Please." *Progressive Grocer,* January.

Savas, E. S. 1987. *Privatization: The Key to Better Government.* Chatham, NJ: Chatham House.

Sawicky, Max. 1991. *The Poverty of the New Paradigm.* Washington, DC: Economic Policy Institute.

————. 1993. "Free Trade, Unfree People: The North American Free Trade Agreement and the U.S. Public Sector." Testimony submitted to the U.S. House of Representatives Committee on Government Operations, July 27.

Scheringer, Joseph. 1988. "Mergers." *Grocery Marketing* 54(8), 36–38.

Schneider, Karen. 1991. "Study Details Biggest Cuts in Decade in Aid to Poor." *Buffalo News,* October 19, A17.

Schneider, Krista, comp. 1993a. *The Human Costs of Contracting Out: A Survival Guide for Public Employees.* Washington, DC: Public Employee Department, AFL–CIO.

————. 1993b. *Public Employees Bargain for Excellence: A Compendium of State Public Sector Labor Relations Laws.* Washington, DC: Public Employee Department, AFL–CIO.

Schor, Juliet. 1992. *The Overworked American.* New York: Basic Books.

Schoven, John B., and Joel Waldfogel, eds. 1990. *Debt, Taxes, and Corporate Restructuring.* Washington, DC: Brookings Institution.

Schweke, William, Carl Rist, and Bryan Dabson. 1994. *Bidding for Business: Are Cities and States Selling Themselves Short?* Washington, DC: Corporation for Enterprise Development.

Seitz, Virginia. 1984. "Legal, Legislative and Managerial Responses to the Organization of Supervisory Employees in the 1940s." *American Journal of Legal History* 28, 218–35.

Service Employees International Union Local 660 Research Department. 1991. *The Public Cost of Private Contracting.* Los Angeles: Coalition to Stop Contracting Out.

Service Employees International Union, Research Department. 1993. *Part-Time, Temporary and Contracted Work: Coping with the Growing Contingent Workforce.* Washington, DC: SEIU.

Shostak, Arthur B. 1991. *Robust Unionism: Innovations in the Labor Movement*. Ithaca, NY: ILR Press, Cornell University.

———. 1993. "Contracting Out of Management Services: A Unique Opportunity for Labor Unions." *IRRA Series Proceedings of the Forty-fifth Annual Meeting*, January 5–7, Anaheim, CA, 367–373.

Silvers, Damon. 1992. "A Capital Idea." *Labor Research Review* 19, Fall, 3.

Slaughter, Jane. 1993. "Champion of Labor–Management Cooperation Wins Narrow Re-Election at G.M.'s Saturn." *Labor Notes* 170, May, 3.

Slott, Mike. 1985. "The Case against Worker Ownership." *Labor Research Review* 6, 83.

Snyder, David. 1992. "A Survey of Voting and Board Participation in Employee-Controlled Firms." *Journal of Employee Ownership Law and Finance* 4(3), 49.

Sparks, Samantha. 1992. "Sweden's Assault on Labor." *Multinational Monitor*, May, 26–30.

Special Task Force Report to Secretary of Health, Education and Welfare. 1973. *Work in America*. Cambridge: MIT Press.

St. Antoine, Theodore J. 1992. "Supreme Court Philosophy on Labor and Employment Issues." Industrial Relations Research Association Proceedings of the 44th Annual Meeting.

Starr, Paul. 1987. *The Limits of Privatization*. Washington, DC: Economic Policy Institute.

Statutes of Ontario. 1992. Chapter 21, S.O. 363. Toronto: Province of Ontario.

Stein, Janice Gross. 1992. "Living with Uncertainty: Canada and the Architecture of the New World Order." *International Journal* 48 (3), Summer, 614–29.

Stevenson, Richard. 1990. "Lockheed Gives in to Big Holders." *New York Times*, March 30, D1.

Stokes, Bruce. 1992–93. "Organizing to Trade." *Foreign Policy* 89, Winter 36–52.

Stone, Katherine V. W. 1988. "Labor and the Corporate Structure: Changing Conceptions and Emerging Possibilities." *University of Chicago Law Review* 55, 73.

———. 1991. "Employees as Stakeholders under State Nonshareholder Constituency Statutes." *Stetson Law Review* 21, 45.

Strauss, George, Daniel Gallagher, and Jack Fiorito. 1991. *The State of the Unions*. Madison, WI: IRRA.

Summers, Clyde. 1951. "Legal Limitations on Union Discipline." *Harvard Law Review* 64, 1049.

———. 1960. "The Law of Union Discipline: What the Courts Do in Fact." *Yale Law Journal*, 70.

Summers, Clyde, Joseph Rauh, and Herman Benson. 1986. *Union Democracy and Landrum–Griffin*. Brooklyn, NY: Association for Union Democracy.

Summers, Robert. 1980. "Public Sector Collective Bargaining Substantially Diminishes Democracy." *Government Union Review*, 1.

Surpin, Richard. 1987. "Cooperative Associates: A Status Report." Community Service Society, January. Unpublished paper on file with the author.

Survais, J. M. 1989. "The Social Clause in Trade Agreements: Wishful Thinking or an Instrument of Social Progress?" *International Labor Review* 128(4), 423–33.

Swinney, Dan. 1985. "Worker Ownership: A Tactic for Labor." *Labor Research Review* 6, 99.

———. 1991. "Employee Ownership and the Labor Movement." *Journal of Employee Ownership Law and Finance* 3(2), 147.

Swoboda, Frank. 1991. "Union Activism against Banks Appears to Pay Off for Virginia Firm." *Washington Post*, March 17, L1.

Thurow, Lester. 1992. *Head to Head: The Coming Economic Battle Among Japan, Europe and America*. New York: Morrow.

Tilles, Eric. 1989. "Union Receiverships under RICO: A Union Democracy Perspective." *University of Pennsylvania Law Review* 137, January, 929–66.

Tilly, Chris. 1989. "Half a Job: How U.S. Firms Use Part-Time Employment." Ph.D. diss., MIT Departments of Economics and Urban Studies and Planning.

———. 1991a. "Reasons for the Continuing Growth of Part-Time Employment." *Monthly Labor Review*, March, 10–18.

———. 1991b. "Testimony on Part-Time and Temporary Work." Arbitration Proceedings. U.S. Postal Service, National Association of Letter Carriers, and American Postal Workers Union, Washington, DC, May 7.

———. 1992. "Short Hours, Short Shrift: Causes and Consequences of Part-Time Work." In Virginia L. duRivage, ed., *New Policies for Part-Time and Contingent Workers*. Armonk, NY: M. E. Sharpe.

Tilly, Chris, Barry Bluestone, and Bennett Harrison. 1986. "What Is Making American Wages More Unequal?" *Proceedings of the Industrial Relations Research Association Annual Meetings*, December.

Troy, Leo. 1991. "Convergence in International Unionism et Cetera: The Case of Canada and the US." *Queen's Papers in Industrial Relations*. Kingston, Ontario: School of Industrial Relations/Industrial Relations Centre, Queen's University.

———. 1994. *The New Unionism and the New Society: Public Sector Unions in the Redistributive State*. Fairfax, VA: George Mason University Press.

Trumka, Richard. 1987. "Why Labor Law Has Failed," *West Virginia Law Review* 89, 878.

Turner, Lowell. 1991. *Democracy at Work: Changing World Markets and the Future of Labor Unions*. Ithaca, NY: Cornell University Press.

ULLICO. 1990. *ULLICO Inc. Annual Report 1990*. Washington, DC: ULLICO.

"Unions Wage Budget Battles." 1992. 11(4), *On Campus* February, 3.

United University Professions. 1990. "SUNY's Future: Expanding the Mission, Fulfilling the Promise." March.

———. 1992. "Part-Time Concerns Are a Full-Time Issue." UUP *Voice*, May, 3.

Urofsky, Melvin. 1985. "State Courts and Protective Legislation during the Progressive Era: A Reevaluation." *Journal of American History* 72, 63–91.

U.S. Congress. 1984. "Failure of Labor Law—A Betrayal of American Workers." Report of the Subcommittee on Labor–Management Relations of the House Committee on Education and Labor and the Subcommittee on Manpower and Housing of the House Government Operations Committee." 98th Congress, 2d Sess.

———. Joint Hearings of House Subcommittees on Economic Policy, Trade, and Environment, and Western Hemisphere Affairs. 1994. *NAFTA and American Jobs*. Washington, DC: U.S. Governmnet Printing Office.

U.S. Congress, House of Representatives. 1986. "Mergers and Acquisitions." Hearings before the Subcommittee on Monopolies and Commercial Law of the Committee on the Judiciary. 99th Congress, 1st and 2nd Sessions, April 3 and 25, 1985, and November 16, 1986, 219–390.

———. 1987b. "FTC Role in Mergers and Acquisitions." Hearing before the Subcommittee on Transportation, Tourism, and Hazardous Materials of the Committee on Energy and Commerce. 100th Congress, 1st Session, August 6.

———. 1987b. "Oversight Hearing on Mergers and Acquisitions." Hearing before the Subcommittee on Economic Stabilization of the Committee on Banking, Finance, and Urban Affairs. 1st Session, May 12.

———. 1989. "Impact on Workers of Takeovers, Leveraged Buyouts, Corporate Restructuring and Greenmail." Hearings before a Subcommittee of the Committee on Government Operations. 100th Congress, 1st Session, March 31, June 5, 1989, 4–7.

———, Select Committee on Children, Youths, and Families. 1989. *U.S. Children and Their Families: Current Conditions and Recent Trends, 1989*. Washington, DC: U.S. Government Printing Office.

U.S. Congress, Office of Technology Assessment. 1988. *Technology and the American Economic Transition: Choices for the Future*. Washington, DC: U.S. Government Printing Office..

U.S. Congress, Senate, Select Committee on Improper Activites in the Labor and Management Field. 1960. (The McClellan Committee) *Final Report*, S. Rep No. 1139, 86th Cong., 2 Sess.

U.S. Congress, Senate. 1978. "Mergers and Industrial Concentration." Hearings before the Subcommittee on Antitrust and Monopoly of the Committee on the Judiciary. 95th Congress, 2nd Session, May 12, July 27, 28, and September 21.

U.S. Department of Commerce. 1993. *Foreign Trade Highlights*. Washington, DC: International Trade Administration, Office of Trade and Economic Analysis.

U.S. Department of Labor. 1988. *Comparison of State Unemployment Insurance Laws*. Washington, DC: U.S. Government Printing Office. January.

U.S. General Accounting Office. 1991. *Workers at Risk*. Washington, DC: U.S. Government Printing Office.

U.S. Small Business Administration. 1988. *The State of Small Business: A Report of the President, 1987*. Washington, DC: U.S. Government Printing Office.

Valente, Judith. 1989. "Pilots and Machinists Emerge as Pivotal to Success of Any New Deal to Buy UAL." *Wall Street Journal*, October 26.

Veverka, Mark. 1993. "UAL Talks Stay on Runway, Wolf Exit Scenarios Are Flying." *Crain's Chicago Business*, September 6, 4.

Visclosky, Peter. 1989. H.R. 2664, 101st Cong., 1st Sess.

Waldstein, Louise. 1989. "Service Sector Wages, Productivity, and Job Creation in the U.S. and Other Countries." Background paper, Economic Policy Institute, Washington, DC.

Walker, Anne Noble. 1992. "Legal Restraints Imposed by ERISA on the Creation, Management and Operation of Labor Banks." SUNY–Buffalo School of Law. Unpublished paper on file with the author.

Walker, Samuel. 1990. *In Defense of American Liberties*. New York: Oxford University Press.

Wallace, Anthony. 1978. *Rochdale*. New York: Norton.

Wallace, Michael. 1989. "Aggressive Economism, Defensive Control: Contours of American Labor Militancy, 1947–81." *Economic and Industrial Democracy* 10, 7–34.

Wallace, Michael, Beth A. Rubin, and Brian T. Smith. 1988. "American Labor Law: Its Impact on Working Class Militancy, 1901–1980." *Social Science History* 12, 1–29.

Weiler, Paul. 1983. "Promises to Keep: Securing Workers' Rights to Self-Organization under the NLRA." *Harvard Law Review* 96, 1769–1927.

———. 1990. *Governing the Workplace: The Future of Labor and Employment Law*. Cambridge: Harvard University Press.

Wells, Donald. 1987. *Empty Promises*. New York: Monthly Review Press.

Wessel, Paul. 1986. "Job Creation for Union Members through Pension Fund Investment." *Buffalo Law Review* 35(1), 323–63.

Weston, Syd, Christopher Whelan, and Doreen McBarnet. 1993. "Adversary Accounting: Strategic Uses of Financial Information by Capital and Labour." *Accounting, Organizations, and Society* 18(1), 81–100.

White House. 1981. "America's New Beginning." February 18. (Congressional Information Service # US/PR.40.2:Ec7/1981/February).

Whyte, William, and Kathleen Whyte. 1988. *Making Mondragon: The Growth & Dynamics of the Worker Cooperative Complex*. Ithaca, NY: ILR Press.

Whyte, W. F., Reed Nelson, and Robert N. Stern, 1983. *Worker Participation and Ownership*. Ithaca, NY: ILR Press, Cornell University.

Wilkinson, Bruce W. 1992. "Regional Trading Blocks: Fortress Europe versus Fortress North America." In Daniel Drache and Meric S. Gertler, eds., *The New Global Competition, State Policy and Market Power*. Kingston, Ontario: University Press.

Wilkus, Malon. 1991. "Employee Buyouts." *Journal of Employee Ownership Law and Finance* 3(2), 121.

Williams, Randall. 1988. *Hard Labor: A Report on Day Labor Pools and Temporary Employment*. Atlanta, GA: Southern Regional Council.

Wise, Mark, and Richard Gibb. 1993. *Single Market to Social Europe*. New York: Wiley.

Withorn, Ann. 1984. *Serving the People: Social Services and Social Change*. New York: Columbia University Press.

Witte, Edwin. 1926. "Early American Labor Cases." *Yale Law Journal* 35, 825–37.

Womack, James, Daniel T. Jones, and Daniel Roos, 1990. *The Machine That Changed the World*. New York: Rawson Associates.

Woodbury, Stephen A. 1989. "Current Economic Issues in Employee Benefits." Paper prepared for the U.S. Department of Labor Commission on Workforce Quality and Labor Market Efficiency, September.

Woodruff, David. 1992. "Saturn." *Business Week*, August 17, 86.

Yochelson, John N., ed. 1985. *The United States and the World Economy: Policy Alternatives for New Realities*. Boulder, CO: Westview Press.

Yount, Linda, and Susan Williams. 1990. "Temporary in Tennessee: CATS for Stable Jobs." *Labor Research Review*, Spring, 73–80.

Zanglein, Jayne. 1991. "Pensions, Proxies and Power: Recent Developments in the Use of Proxy Voting to Influence Corporate Governance." *Labor Lawyer* 7, 771.

——. 1992. *Solely in Our Interest: Creating Maximum Benefits for Workers through Prudent Pension Investments.* Washington, DC: AFL–CIO Lawyer Coordinating Committee.

Zemke, Ron, and Dick Schaaf. 1989. *101 Companies That Profit from Customer Care.* New York: NAL Penguin.

Zieger, Robert. 1986. *American Workers, American Unions, 1920–1965.* Baltimore: Johns Hopkins University Press.

Index

About the Contributors

JAMES B. ATLESON is Professor of Law at the State University of New York at Buffalo. He is the author of *Values and Assumptions in American Labor Law* and has written numerous articles and chapters in books.

FRANÇOISE J. CARRÉ is Research Program Director at the Public Policy Institute at Radcliffe College and has completed a number of studies of employment transformation and its implications for workers.

VIRGINIA L. DURIVAGE is an Educational Specialist with the Communications Workers of America in Washington, D.C.

LAWRENCE G. FLOOD is Professor of Political Science at Buffalo State College. He is the author of several works on unions and is an active member of United University Professions.

GERALD GLYDE is Professor of Labor Studies at the Pennsylvania State University.

SUSAN JENNIK is counsel to Teamsters Local 966. She is the former Director of the Association for Union Democracy.

STAN LUGER is Assistant Professor of Political Science at the University of Northern Colorado.

BRUCE NISSEN is Associate Professor of Labor Studies at Indiana University Northwest in Gary, Indiana. He is the author of *Fighting for Jobs: Case*

Studies of Labor-Community Coalitions Confronting Plant Closings (1995) and is now working on a book on strategic directions for organized labor.

PETER PITEGOFF is Associate Professor of Law at SUNY–Buffalo. Formerly he was general counsel to the Industrial Cooperative Association, a consulting firm that assists in efforts at worker ownership and control.

SIDNEY PLOTKIN is Professor of Political Science at Vassar College. He is the co-author of *Private Interest, Public Spending*.

JOHN RUSSO is Director of the Labor Studies Program at Youngstown State University.

WILLIAM SCHEUERMAN is Professor of Political Science at SUNY–Oswego. He is the President of United University Professions and is co-author of *Private Interests, Public Spending*.

CHRIS TILLY is a labor economist and Associate Professor of Policy and Planning at the University of Massachusetts at Lowell. His book *Half a Job: Bad and Good Part-Time Jobs in a Changing Labor Market* is forthcoming in 1996.

Policy Studies Organization publications issued with
Greenwood Press/Quorum Books

International Agricultural Trade and Market Development in the 1990s
John W. Helmuth and Don F. Hadwiger, editors

Comparative Studies of Local Economic Development: Problems in Policy
Implementation
Peter B. Meyer, editor

Ownership, Control, and the Future of Housing Policy
R. Allen Hays, editor

Public Administration in China
Miriam K. Mills and Stuart S. Nagel, editors

Public Policy in China
Stuart S. Nagel and Miriam K. Mills, editors

Minority Group Influence: Agenda Setting, Formulation, and Public Policy
Paula D. McClain, editor

Problems and Prospects for Nuclear Waste Disposal Policy
Eric B. Herzik and Alvin H. Mushkatel, editors

American Indian Policy
Lyman H. Legters and Fremont J. Lyden, editors

Presidential Leadership and Civil Rights Policy
James W. Riddlesperger, Jr., and Donald W. Jackson, editors

Social Security Programs: A Cross-Cultural Comparative Perspective
John Dixon and Robert P. Scheurell, editors

International Organizations and Environmental Policy
Robert V. Bartlett, Priva A. Kurian, and Madhu Malik